Whistle-blowing in Organizations

LEA'S ORGANIZATION AND MANAGEMENT SERIES

Series Editors

Arthur P. Brief
University of Utah

James P. Walsh
University of Michigan

Associate Series Editor

Sara L. Rynes
University of Iowa

Ashforth (Au.): *Role Transitions in Organizational Life: An Identity-Based Perspective.*

Bartel/Blader/Wrzesniewski (Eds.): *Identity and the Modern Organization.*

Bartunek (Au): *Organizational and Educational Change: The Life and Role of a Change Agent Group.*

Beach (Ed.): *Image Theory: Theoretical and Empirical Foundations.*

Brett/Drasgow (Eds.): *The Psychology of Work: Theoretically Based Empirical Research.*

Chhokar/Brodbeck/House (Eds.): *Culture and Leadership Across the World: The GLOBE Book of In-Depth Studies of 25 Societies.*

Darley/Messick/Tyler (Eds.): *Social Influences on Ethical Behavior in Organizations.*

Denison (Ed.): *Managing Organizational Change in Transition Economies.*

Dutton/Ragins (Eds.): *Exploring Positive Relationships at Work: Building a Theoretical and Research Foundation*

Elsbach (Au): *Organizational Perception Management.*

Earley/Gibson (Aus.): *Multinational Work Teams: A New Perspective.*

Garud/Karnoe (Eds.): *Path Dependence and Creation.*

Harris (Ed.): *Handbook of Research in International Human Resource Management*

Jacoby (Au.): *Employing Bureaucracy: Managers, Unions, and the Transformation of Work in the 20th Century, Revised Edition.*

Kossek/Lambert (Eds.): *Work and Life Integration: Organizational, Cultural and* Individual Perspectives.

Lampel/Shamsie/Lant (Eds.): *The Business of Culture: Strategic Perspectives on Entertainment and Media.*

Lant/Shapira (Eds.): *Organizational Cognition: Computation and Interpretation.*

Lord/Brown (Aus.): *Leadership Processes and Follower Self-Identity.*

Margolis/Walsh (Aus.): *People and Profits? The Search Between a Company's Social and* Financial Performance

__Miceli/Near/Dworkin__ (Aus): Whistle-blowing in Organizations.

Messick/Kramer (Eds.): *The Psychology of Leadership: Some New Approaches.*

Pearce (Au.): *Organization and Management in the Embrace of the Government.*

Peterson/Mannix (Eds.): *Leading and Managing People in the Dynamic Organization.*

Rafaeli/Pratt (Eds.): *Artifacts and Organizations: Beyond Mere Symbolism.*

Riggio/Murphy/Pirozzolo (Eds.): *Multiple Intelligences and Leadership.*

Schneider/Smith (Eds.): *Personality and Organizations.*

Smith (Ed.): *The People Make The Place: Dynamic Linkages Between Individuals and Organizations.*

Thompson/Choi (Eds.): *Creativity and Innovation in Organizational Teams.*

Thompson/Levine/Messick (Eds.): *Shared Cognition in Organizations: The Management of Knowledge.*

Whistle-blowing in Organizations

I Marcia P. Miceli I Janet P. Near I Terry Morehead Dworkin

Routledge
Taylor & Francis Group
New York   London

Routledge
Taylor & Francis Group
270 Madison Avenue
New York, NY 10016

Routledge
Taylor & Francis Group
2 Park Square
Milton Park, Abingdon
Oxon OX14 4RN

Printed in the United States of America on acid-free paper
10 9 8 7 6 5 4 3 2 1

International Standard Book Number-13: 978-0-8058-5989-8 (Softcover) 978-0-8058-5988-1 (Hardcover)

Library of Congress Cataloging-in-Publication Data

Whistle-blowing in organizations / author/editor(s), Marcia P. Miceli, Janet Pollex Near, and Terry Morehead Dworkin.
    p. cm. -- (LEA's organization and management series) Rev. ed. of: Blowing the whistle / Marcia P. Miceli, Janet P. Near. Toronto : Maxwell Macmillan Canada ; New York : Maxwell Macmillan International, c1992.
    "The purpose of this book is to summarize existing research in the intervening years, particularly in the management and legal literature, and to describe the implications of this work for future research and practice"--P. .
Includes bibliographical references and index.
ISBN 978-0-8058-5989-8
    1. Whistle blowing. 2. Whistle blowing--Law and legislation--United States. I. Miceli, Marcia P. II. Dworkin, Terry Morehead. III. Near, Janet P. IV. Miceli, Marcia P. Blowing the whistle. V. Title. VI. Series.

HD60.M54 2008
302.3'5--dc22   2007044866

Visit the Taylor & Francis Web site at
http://www.taylorandfrancis.com

and the Psychology Press Web site at
http://www.psypress.com

Contents

Series Foreword

This is a very important book. Whistle-blowing can certainly impact all of our lives. Wrongdoing in the organizational world is often discovered only if someone on the inside stands up and speaks out. Miceli, Near, and Dworkin do an excellent job of telling us what the social science and legal communities have to say about whistle-blowing and then offer us their guidance as to the critical research questions that remain to be addressed and how they might be tackled. Without the knowledge these experts offer us, whistleblowing likely will remain too rare of an event and society will suffer for it. We are very proud they have chosen to share their insights through our series.

Arthur P. Brief
James P. Walsh

Preface

In 1992, our previous book about whistle-blowing was published. The purpose of this book is to summarize existing research in the intervening years, particularly in the management and legal literature, and to describe the implications of this work for future research and practice. This focus excludes other worthy goals that may be pursued by other authors, such as to provide an in-depth analysis of one important case, to describe or categorize all of the cases that have appeared in the media, or to undertake a normative discussion or to debate the moral or ethical justifications of whistle-blowing.

Our intended audience includes anyone interested in the scholarly study of whistle-blowing, whether they be scholars and teachers, or graduate students, in management, ethics, sociology, psychology, law or any related academic field, or people outside academia. We believe it may be time saving for readers to have a summary, with references included for readers who want to find and read the original studies. Through the years, we have heard from people outside academia, including whistle-blowers, managers, journalists, ethics officers, internal auditors, compliance specialists, trainers, counselors, and practicing attorneys. We hope our book will be of value to them. We have tried to make the book accessible and interesting to a wide variety of prospective readers, and to avoid unnecessary jargon, while including detailed references for anyone interested in reading more.

On a personal note, we have been university faculty and administrators for nearly 90 years in total. During that time, we have ourselves engaged in dissent when our organizations moved in directions we considered wrongheaded; as administrators, we also listened to colleagues' dissenting voices and found that whistle-blowing in real life can be as uncomfortable as it is necessary. We laud the whistle-blowers of the world when their cause is just: they can make life difficult for organizations but often improve organizational functioning dramatically as well as help others. Yet this book is not aimed directly at them, but rather at future researchers who we hope will devote more attention to this important topic. Too much misinformation has proven the basis for the conventional wisdom about whistle-blowers that we see promulgated in the media, in legislatures, and elsewhere. Whistle-blowing can be a force for constructive organizational and societal change, but only if we learn more about why it happens and how to best deal with its impact. This book represents our best effort to summarize what is known, based on empirical results, and to launch a plea for future research to resolve what we do not yet know about whistle-blowing.

The Authors

Marcia P. Miceli, D. B. A., is professor of Management at the McDonough School of Business at Georgetown University. She earned her doctorate in business administration at Indiana University. Her research focuses on whistle-blowing in organizations and on organizational compensation systems.

Janet P. Near, Ph. D., holds the Coleman Chair of Management at the Kelley School of Business at Indiana University. She earned her Ph.D. in sociology at the State University of New York at Buffalo. Her research program examines whistle-blowing in organizations and the relationship between life satisfaction and job satisfaction.

Terry Morehead Dworkin, J. D., is the Jack R. Wentworth Em. Professor of Business Law at the Kelley School of Business at Indiana University and an adjunct professor at the Seattle University School of Law. Her research focuses on laws pertaining to whistle-blowing and to employment.

Acknowledgments

Support for this work was provided in part by the Dean's Leadership Fund of the McDonough School of Business, Mr. Carlos M. de la Cruz for the de la Cruz Family Fellowship, and the Graduate School of Arts and Sciences, at Georgetown University; by the Coleman Chair in the Kelley School of Business at Indiana University; and by the Wentworth Chair in the Kelley School of Business at Indiana University. We would like to thank Douglas McCabe, who shared articles with us, and anonymous reviewers of the proposal and of previous drafts. Any errors or omissions, of course, are our responsibility alone.

We thank the copyright holders for their permission to use material from the following: Miceli, M. P., & Near, J. P. (2005a). Standing up or standing by: What predicts blowing the whistle on organizational wrongdoing? In J. Martocchio (Ed.), *Research in personnel and human resources management* (Vol. 24, pp. 95–136). Greenwich, CT: JAI/Elsevier Press; Miceli, M. P., & Near, J. P. (2005b). Whistle-blowing and positive psychology. In R. Giacalone, C. L. Jurkiewicz & C. Dunn (Eds.), *Positive psychology in business ethics and corporate responsibility* (Vol. 1, pp. 85–102). Greenwich, CT: Information Age Publishing; Miceli, M. P., & Near, J. P. (2006). How can one person make a difference? Understanding whistle-blowing effectiveness. In M. J. Epstein & K. O. Hanson (Eds.), *The Accountable Corporation* (Vol. 4, pp. 201–221). Westport, CT: Praeger Publishers; Miceli, M. P., & Near, J. P. (2007). Stopping organizational wrongdoing: What price do whistle-blowers pay? In S. W. Gilliland, D. D. Steiner, & D. P. Skarlicki (Eds.), *Managing social and ethical issues in organizations* (Vol. 5, pp. 295–324). Greenwich, CT: Information Age Publishing.

1

Introduction

The dim, grainy photograph is not the best he has ever taken with a president, Joseph C. Wilson IV said, glancing at a picture of himself with President George H. W. Bush, taken in January 1991, two days before the start of the Persian Gulf War. But it is the most memorable. "It gives me no pleasure whatsoever," he said of the current controversy, in an interview at his office on Friday. "It gives me great pain, in fact, because of that particular relationship, which I value, with the president's father."

Mr. Wilson has rocked the administration of President (George W.) Bush, the son, not once but twice. First he challenged the administration's claim, put forth by the president in the State of the Union address, that Saddam Hussein sought uranium ore from Niger to build nuclear weapons. Then Mr. Wilson accused a senior member of the Bush administration of leaking the identity of his wife, Valerie Plame, a CIA officer, to the press in retaliation for his dissent.

As a result Mr. Wilson finds himself enmeshed in a web of discord. His actions have drawn attention to growing public skepticism surrounding the Iraq war and its aftermath and have refocused attention on ideological clashes between the CIA and the Pentagon (Clemetson, 2003, p. 1).

Employees blowing the whistle on perceived organizational wrongdoing frequently make news (Frey, 2002). Between 1989 and 1995, 30 major newspapers published over 1,000 articles on the uncovering of wrongdoing (Brewer, 1996). Many more articles have been published since that time, involving Enron, WorldCom, Global Crossing, Tyco, and the FBI (e.g., Drawbaugh, 2005; Pearlstein, 2005; Pressler, 2003), Boeing (Graves & Goo, 2006), Merck and the U.S. Food and Drug Administration (FDA) (e.g., Nesmith, 2004; *USA Today*, 2006), Halliburton (Quinn, 2006), and many other organizations. Other highly publicized incidents suggesting substantial and continuing public concern over perceived organizational wrongdoing include the Wilson incident described previously, the indictment on bribery charges of U.S. Representative Randy "Duke"

1

Cunningham (e.g., Romano, 2005), and alleged torture and abuse by the U.S. military at the Abu Ghraib prison (e.g., Hersh, 2004).

Many of the news stories have identified substantial negative consequences of organizational wrongdoing for victims, such as employees, customers, and society at large. In the U.S. alone, the financial costs of organizational wrongdoing have been estimated to include $5 billion in employee theft, $350 billion attributable to antitrust violations, $300 billion in tax fraud, and $100 billion in health care fraud (Miethe, 1999). Around the world, annual costs of corruption have been estimated at $1 trillion (World Bank, 2004).

Aside from the tangible costs, wrongdoing also jeopardizes the safety, health, and well-being of organization members, customers, and societies at large. For example, corruption interferes with reduction of poverty (World Bank, 2004). Often the wrongdoing directly harms the health of customers and societies, as dramatized in the movie *The Insider*, when Dr. Jeffrey Wigand revealed that tobacco industry executives suppressed evidence that ingredients increasing addictive properties were added to cigarettes, which are known to cause cancer (e.g., Armenakis, 2004).

At a time when modern organizations have become so complex that outsiders are unlikely to become aware of organizational actions—without learning inside information from current or former employees—the role of whistle-blowers such as Wigand has become critical to the identification of organizational wrongdoing (Miethe, 1999). Without whistle-blowers, we might never have learned of these organizational problems, and we depend on them to alert us to future problems as well. If organizational "insiders" are essential, then societies must find better mechanisms for encouraging appropriate whistle-blowing. After more than 25 years of empirical research about whistle-blowing, researchers have learned quite a lot, much of it counterintuitive to the common wisdom propagated in the popular press, and some of it very "commonsensical" or fitting with prior expectations. In both cases, we think it is important to dispel the mythology that has grown up around whistle-blowing and to cite what has actually been examined in empirical studies. Further, the legal environment for whistle-blowing has changed dramatically in recent years, especially since the passage of the Sarbanes-Oxley Act (SOX) (Sarbanes-Oxley Act, 2002), and these changes could influence the nature of whistle-blowing activities in myriad ways in the future.

Therefore, our focus is not normative, but descriptive; we attempt to summarize what is known based on social science research and to describe the direction of legal initiatives pertinent to whistle-blowing. Much of this is research we have completed; happily, more research is being conducted by other scholars entering the field as well. However, it is still true that, too frequently, we must conclude that more research is needed before we can know the full answer to some particular question about whistle-blowing.

Thus, two key purposes of this book are to describe research findings and to suggest new directions for future research in order to address the critical questions still remaining concerning whistle-blowing. We will devote a chapter each to the personal predictors of whistle-blowing (Chapter 2) and the situational predictors of whistle-blowing (Chapter 3), the predictors of retaliation against whistle-blowers (Chapter 4), and the predictors of overall effectiveness of whistle-blowers in getting wrongdoing stopped (Chapter 5). In each chapter, we identify questions that require further research. We then describe the current legal status of whistle-blowing in the United States (Chapter 6). Finally, we discuss the implications of legal developments and the research findings for managerial practice and for legislators and policy makers (Chapter 7).

In this book, we focus primarily on the United States, for several reasons. First, much of the research has been conducted in North American settings. But societal cultures and organizational environments that may influence whistle-blowing differ, and research conducted in North American settings may not generalize to other cultures, not even to all North American cultures. Second, laws relevant to whistle-blowing vary substantially across countries, a point to which we will return in Chapter 6. Third, the body of empirical literature concerning whistle-blowing outside of North American settings is in its infancy, so we do not know to what extent the findings might be representative. However, we do include international studies, where they are available, in the chapters that follow.

Finally, we wish to alert readers that we do not consider in detail normative issues involving ethics, morality, or philosophy with regard to whistle-blowing, for example, the conditions under which (a) it may be morally justifiable, or deemed more desirable to societies, or (b) individuals are morally obliged to act. Some books on business ethics address these issues (e.g., Bowie, 1982; DeGeorge, 1986). Further, more general issues of ethical decision making and behavioral ethics in organizations have been reviewed comprehensively elsewhere (e.g., Treviño, Weaver, & Reynolds, 2006); here, our focus is more narrow, though we attempt to integrate some relevant ideas from this literature. We hope that the empirical findings and theory we present regarding whistle-blowing, and our analysis of the legal environment surrounding whistle-blowers, will prove of interest to readers with more general interests in ethics, philosophy, or behavioral ethics in organizations.

To provide a foundation for these chapters, we hope to accomplish three purposes in this introductory chapter. First, we define wrongdoing, whistle-blowing, and other terms that will be used throughout the book. We provide both a conceptual definition and an operational definition for each term. Second, we describe evidence of the extensiveness of (a) the wrongdoing whistle-blowers say they have witnessed; (b) whistle-blowing; (c) the retaliation whistle-blowers believe they experience; and (d) the effectiveness of whistle-blowing. Third, we provide an overview of the types of empirical studies of whistle-blowing that have been conducted, and the methodological issues raised in those studies. As with many areas of social science research, the "devil is in the details" with regard to studies of whistle-blowing; conflicting results produced by different researchers are often a function of differences in research methodology, at least in part. Readers need to be aware of the diversity of methods and the trade-offs involved in their use, in order to appropriately assess the credibility of the results.

Definitions

Wrongdoing

Conceptual Definition   Research on wrongdoing in organizations has focused on activities as diverse as white-collar crime (e.g., Sutherland, 1949), corporate criminal behaviors (e.g., Clinard, 1979), and illegal corporate behavior (e.g., Baucus & Baucus, 1997; Baucus & Near, 1991). In the definition of whistle-blowing that we will provide, wrongdoing is defined broadly, as "illegal, immoral, or illegitimate practices" (activities and omissions). This definition thus does not limit wrongdoing to illegal behavior, as some seem to have interpreted it (e.g., Warren, 2003). For example, an employee may consider acts such as managers firing employees arbitrarily, bullying employees, or grossly misallocating resources (e.g., spending millions of dollars on replacement parts for obsolete machinery) to be immoral or illegitimate in the Weberian sense (Weber, 1947). These actions are typically not illegal in the United States, but they can be considered triggering events for whistle-blowing.

Operational Definition   Questionnaire-based research about whistle-blowing has typically asked respondents to read a checklist of possible wrongdoings and note those they have observed within a given time period, such as the previous year. This is a technique the U.S. Merit Systems Protection Board (MSPB) developed and used in three surveys of federal employees, administered in 1980, 1983, and 1992. To generate a list of specific types of wrongdoing (e.g., fraud, employee theft) employees might witness, the MSPB drew upon definitions from the Merit Systems Protection Act, talked with employees, and pretested the surveys.

In the three resulting MSPB surveys, respondents were asked to check all wrongdoing events they had witnessed during the last 12 months. The limited time period was intended to increase the accuracy of their recall of events. Respondents could choose from the original list, which included a dozen types of wrongdoing, or from a longer list provided in the later MSPB studies and in studies by other researchers (e.g., Miceli, Near, & Schwenk, 1991; Rothschild & Miethe, 1999).

To reduce the complexity that would result from asking a respondent who observed many different types of activities to answer more detailed questions about each of them, respondents who had observed any of these forms of wrongdoing were asked to select the wrongdoing that they thought was most important or that affected them most directly and answer subsequent questions about that wrongdoing; we refer to this as the "focal wrongdoing." Thus, results reported in this book generally refer to the respondents' characterization of their response to the focal activity, that wrongdoing that they thought was most important or affected them most directly from the checklist of wrongdoings they may have observed.

Whistle-Blowing and Whistle-Blowers

Conceptual Definition   Whistle-blowing is discussed by researchers in a variety of fields, including psychology, sociology, ethics, law, and public policy. Therefore, it is important to clarify what we mean by whistle-blowing. Whistle-blowing is "the disclosure by organization members (former or current) of illegal, immoral, or illegitimate practices under the control of their employers, to persons or organizations that may be able to effect action" (Near & Miceli, 1985, p. 4).

This definition has been used in studies of persons in a variety of occupations and professions, including nurses (King, 1997), internal auditors in for-profit, not-for-profit, and governmental organizations (Miceli & Near, 1994b; Miceli, Near, & Schwenk, 1991), and managers (e.g., Keenan, 2002b). It has been used in investigations using diverse samples from various industries (e.g., Rothschild & Miethe, 1999), including federal employees (e.g., Miceli, Rehg, Near, & Ryan, 1999), and employees of for-profit organizations (e.g., Miethe, 1999). It has been used in studies conducted in a variety of countries (e.g., Keenan, 2002a; Tavakoli, Keenan, & Crnjak-Karanovic, 2003). As such, this definition appears to be the most widely used definition in empirical research about whistle-blowing (King, 1997).

Related Concepts.   We should also be clear about what behaviors are not covered by this definition. Whistle-blowers disclose organization practices or omissions that they consider to represent wrongdoing. If the individual does not consider the action to be wrong, but only misguided or stupid, it is not whistle-blowing but may be some other organization behavior, such as "issue selling," as when an employee tries to persuade top management to change behavior on some issue of concern to them (Dutton & Ashford, 1993; Dutton, Ashford, O'Neill, Hayes, & Wierba, 1997; Dutton, Ashford, O'Neill, & Lawrence, 2001) or "taking charge," when an employee engages in "discretionary behavior intended to effect organizationally functional change" (Morrison & Phelps, 1999). Research is needed to clarify relationships and boundaries among all of these constructs. But, for the time being, we feel that it is important to distinguish whistle-blowing from other employee actions aimed at creating organizational change in the workplace.

Similarly, this definition differs from those used by other researchers in that it is not concerned with whistle-blowers' motivations; often they may be "principled" (Graham, 1986), or altruistic (Miceli & Near, 2005b), or positive (Van Dyne, Cummings, & McLean Parks, 1995) but under other conditions they may be antisocial (Miceli & Near, 1997). The definition includes all of these cases, not limiting whistle-blowing to situations where particular motivations are evident. In reality, research findings suggest that whistle-blowers often have multiple motivations that may not be easily identified or disentangled (Miceli & Near, 1992); perhaps these influence how the whistle-blowing process plays out, but this is an empirical question that cannot be examined unless cases of whistle-blowers with varied motivations are considered.

Finally, potential whistle-blowers who decide not to reveal the wrongdoing may differ from others who keep silent in the workplace. Persons who have observed wrongdoing but do not disclose it have been termed "inactive observers" (Miceli & Near, 1988) or "silent observers" (Rothschild & Miethe, 1999). Inactive observation may be similar to "organizational silence" in which employees keep quiet about concerns that they have about actions of other employees in the workplace because of two shared beliefs: (a) that speaking up about problems in the organization is not worth the effort, and (b) that voicing one's opinions and concerns is dangerous (Morrison & Milliken, 2000, 2003). Organizational silence is a broader concept, however, encompassing situations where employees have observed incidents of concern that do not necessarily constitute illegal, immoral, or illegitimate practices (Morrison & Milliken, 2000). The interactive "spiral of silence" that occurs when individuals curb their public views due to fear of isolation from the group begins when they perceive their opinions as being in disagreement with those of the majority—and then self-censor their opinions, in turn causing others to overestimate the amount of actual support for the "majority" opinion (Noelle-Neumann, 1974, 1991, 1993). Noelle-Neumann's concept of the spiral of silence or Morrison's and Milliken's concept of organizational silence refer to any situation in which an individual may feel group pressure to keep quiet; in the whistle-blowing process, additional variables may buy the employee's silence (e.g., fear of retaliation) that may not apply in quite the same way when the individual is silent about a proposed organizational change or public opinion issue.

Channels.   This definition includes whistle-blowers who use internal channels (e.g., to an ombudsperson) or external channels (e.g., to the media) to blow the whistle, because empirical studies have shown few substantial differences in antecedents or outcomes of whistle-blowing as a function of type of channel used (Miceli & Near, 2005a). Whether internal whistle-blowing constitutes "true" whistle-blowing has been a matter of speculation by authors of conceptual works for some time (Farrell & Petersen, 1989; Johnson, 2002; Jubb, 1999) but differences between internal and external whistle-blowers should be investigated empirically—and this cannot occur if one or the other is excluded from study.

Recently, both *Time* magazine (Lacayo & Ripley, 2002) and the Academy of Management—the primary professional association for professors and others interested in the study of management—honored Sherron Watkins of Enron as a whistle-blower. Watkins initially wrote a letter to the CEO and, eventually, her letter became known outside the organization (and its advisers) only after investigations of Enron by the federal government were underway and she testified before Congress. We thus consider her an "internal" whistle-blower who subsequently became an "external" whistle-blower. We believe that the reasons and evidence for considering internal and external whistle-blowing to be two types of one broad class of behavior comprise a more compelling argument than the argument that they are two essentially unrelated behaviors. Some of these reasons have been detailed elsewhere (Miceli & Near, 1992); we will summarize them here.

Some ethicists have offered definitions of whistle-blowing or whistle-blowers that appear to require that "the public" be informed, that is, that at least one channel external to the organization be used. For example, drawing on work by Bok (1980), Bowie (1982) defined a whistle-blower to be: "an employee or officer of any institution, profit or non-profit, private or public, who believes either that he/she has been ordered to perform some act or he/she has obtained knowledge that the institution is engaged in activities which a) are believed to cause unnecessary harm to third parties; b) are in violation of human rights; or c) run counter to the defined purpose of the institution and *who inform the public of this fact*" (Bowie, 1982, p. 142) (our emphasis). But research indicates that nearly every observer of perceived wrongdoing who reports it to someone outside the organization reports it to at least one party within the organization (Miceli & Near, 1992), and subsequent research has shown that internal reports typically precede external reports, rather than the reverse (e.g., Rehg, Miceli, Near, & Van Scotter, in press; Rehg, Near, Miceli, & Van Scotter, 2004). This suggests that, from the standpoint of the whistle-blower, external whistle-blowing is continuing a process— perhaps because internal efforts to get wrongdoing corrected have failed—rather than doing something radically different.

Further, internal whistle-blowers who fail to continue their crusade externally are sometimes criticized as being "selfish," or not being sufficiently ethical or courageous. For example, Watkins—who asked Ken Lay to investigate questionable accounting deals within Enron—"is getting heat for not taking her concerns about accounting and insider deals to regulators, the press, or even the company's board" (e.g., Zellner, 2002, p. 110), who might have been able to save the pensions of thousands of Enron employees and the investments of others who were defrauded. This calls into question both the treatment of internal challenges as "not really whistle-blowing" and the view of external whistle-blowing as unethical in every case.

Second, as will be discussed in Chapter 6, the question of whether internal reports can constitute whistle-blowing is important legally. Some state and federal statutes protect whistle-blowers from retaliation only when they use internal channels and others only when external channels (e.g., a report to an official body designated to receive complaints, such as the police or the Occupational Safety and Health Administration) are used, although bringing wrongful firing suits is also possible (Near, Dworkin, & Miceli, 1993). The Sarbanes-Oxley Act (SOX) specifically protects reports through internal channels (Sarbanes-Oxley Act, 2002). Therefore, using the term "whistle-blower" when referring to internal complaints and to external complaints is consistent with legal usage, and distinguishing the two categories is important because legal protections may vary, at least in part, according to channels used.

Third, an inclusive definition permits empirical examination of differences among types of whistle-blowers; omitting internal whistle-blowers like the three *Time* "Persons of the Year" from study would lead us to ignore information that might be helpful in understanding the process. Does research show that internal and external reporters are extremely dissimilar, having different characteristics, encountering different situations, and experiencing different reactions from their organizations? Or are external reporters, for various reasons, simply extending a process that began with an internal report (and hence largely similar to internal reporters)? If so, this would be one factor suggesting that both should be considered whistle-blowers.

The evidence more strongly supports the latter view. Many studies have shown that nearly all whistle-blowers who use external channels do so after first using internal channels; they may go outside because the wrongdoing was not corrected after the internal report, because they experienced retaliation, or because the nature of the wrongdoing required it (e.g., some types of wrongdoing such as fraud or workplace violence must be reported to authorities) (Miceli & Near, 1992). Results of extensive research concerning potential differences between internal and external whistle-blowers have suggested that their characteristics are generally similar (e.g., Dworkin & Baucus, 1998).

Research also shows that the two groups of whistle-blowers differ much more from other groups of organizational members, such as persons who believe they have not observed wrongdoing, or those who have but have chosen not to report it ("inactive observers") (e.g., Miceli & Near, 1992; Miceli, Van Scotter, Near, & Rehg, 2001a; Near & Miceli, 1996). Following are three examples. Whistle-blowers tend to be moderately committed to the organization, whereas inactive observers tend to be either uncommitted or highly committed, as in the "organization man" stereotype (Somers & Casal, 1994). Both internal and external whistle-blowers perceive wrongdoing that tends to be more serious than that perceived by inactive observers (e.g., Miceli & Near, 1985). Both internal and external whistle-blowers (along with inactive observers) tend to believe their organizations are less supportive, with less effective channels for whistle-blowing, than do nonobservers (e.g., Miceli, Van Scotter, Near, & Rehg, 2001b).

Operational Definition   Typically, survey research has followed the lead of the MSPB studies that began in 1980. Respondents are asked whether they reported the focal activity to any party. They may be cautioned that discussing something casually with friends or family does not constitute a report. Respondents are then given a list of potential complaint recipients, such as their supervisor, someone above their supervisor, the media, etc.

In scenario studies, participants are typically presented with a scenario describing questionable activity in his or her work setting, such as a nurse's providing the wrong medication to, or threatening, a patient (King, 2001). Then, participants are usually asked either whether they would report the wrongdoing or whether they believe that the "employee" in the scenario should do so. For example, in one study (King, 2001, p. 8), "respondents (registered nurses) were asked to read each hypothetical wrongdoing that could occur by a registered nurse. Afterwards, indicate on a scale of one to five (one = definitely report, five = definitely not report) whether or not the wrongdoing should be reported to a member of upper management." This design can be problematic, because what one says she or he might do in a given situation may be very different from what she or he would do if actually faced with it. For example, some research suggests that decision makers are not as good or as ethical as they think they are (Banaji, Bazerman, & Chugh, 2003). Further, other research suggests that unethical behavior can occur without the actor's conscious awareness (Bazerman & Banaji, 2004). These are points to which we will return when discussing methodology later.

Retaliation against Whistle-Blowers

Conceptual Definition   Following a definition we and our coauthors proposed earlier (Rehg, Miceli et al., in press; Rehg, Near et al., 2004), we define retaliation against whistle-blowers to be undesirable action taken against a whistle-blower—and in direct response to the whistle-blowing. Consistent with other researchers (e.g., Keenan, 2002a), we consider undesirable action to include both adverse actions taken against the whistle-blower (e.g., demotion) and positive actions that were not taken, but otherwise would have been taken had the employee not blown the whistle (e.g., promotion).

In our definition, we include current employees and former employees, both of whom could be whistle-blowers according to our definition of whistle-blowing given above. While it may require more imagination for an organization to retaliate against a former employee than against a current employee, it is certainly not impossible for an organization to do so. For example, an organization can falsely accuse the individual in the press or in recommendations sought by prospective employers, as in claiming that the whistle-blower had embezzled the organization or committed other wrongdoing against the organization. Unfortunately, most studies have considered retaliation against current employees only, because former employees have typically not participated in the surveys. This may have the effect of underestimating the proportion of whistle-blowers who suffer reprisal by firing and therefore do not participate in studies conducted in the workplace.

We remind readers that the whistle-blower may be reporting wrongdoing that is not illegal or even covered by the whistle-blowing statutes of the pertinent state government or federal government. Nonetheless, if the action constitutes whistle-blowing, as defined above, then proving the validity of the accusation of wrongdoing is not necessary for establishing that retaliation has taken place. For example, in a growing number of court cases alleging sexual harassment or other unfair discrimination, employers were found to have retaliated illegally against whistle-blowers who had not proved the original discrimination to the court's satisfaction (e.g., Karr, 1998a; Lane, 2006a).

Related Concepts.   The rationale for developing the conceptual definition of retaliation arose from an examination of the extant literature on revenge and on retaliation against whistle-blowers. Retaliation against whistle-blowers is similar to acts of revenge, as investigated by justice researchers, and power variables predict both revenge (Aquino, Tripp, & Bies, 2001; Kim, Smith, & Brigham, 1998) and retaliation against whistle-blowers (Near & Miceli, 1996).

Revenge is "an action in response to some perceived harm or wrongdoing by another party that is intended to inflict damage, injury, discomfort, or punishment on the party judged responsible" (Aquino et al., 2001, p. 53). Revenge involves an organization member who intentionally harms a second organization member, who in turn exacts revenge (Skarlicki & Folger, 1997), often in order to restore a sense of justice to a situation judged unjust by the second member. For example, an employee who was denied a promotion because another employee lied to the boss that he had a drinking problem may find ways to "get even" with the liar, perhaps by spreading rumors about her. Skarlicki and Folger (1997) also defined "organizational retaliation behavior" (ORB) as "the behavioral responses of disgruntled employees to perceived unfair treatment" (Skarlicki, Folger, & Tesluk, 1999). The target of this ORB is frequently the organization; for example, in one empirical study, the ORB measure included a coworker's assessment of whether an employee "on purpose damage(s) equipment or work process" or "take(s) supplies home without permission" (Skarlicki et al., 1999).

However, we cannot use these definitions of revenge and ORB for investigating retaliation against whistle-blowers. They deal with fundamentally different processes and behaviors, and the constructs differ in at least three important ways from our concept of retaliation against whistle-blowers, requiring a separate definition. As will be discussed later, there is empirical evidence (e.g., Cortina & Magley, 2003) supporting these conceptual distinctions.

First, in whistle-blowing, the retaliatory actor(s) are often the organization itself, or agents who believe they are acting on its behalf may be the retaliators, and the retaliatory target is by definition the whistle-blower(s), usually an individual or group of individuals. In ORB, the roles are generally reversed.

Second, ORB is triggered by perceived harm or wrongdoing, but not all whistle-blowers are perceived to cause "harm or wrongdoing," at least not intentionally. For example, the Enron whistle-blower, Watkins, did not clearly intend harm to the firm or any persons. Believing that the CEO was unaware of the wrongdoing, Watkins informed him of financial mismanagement by upper executives (Swartz, 2003).

Third, in whistle-blowing, many retaliators intend not to "inflict damage, injury, discomfort, or punishment" out of anger or a sense of injustice (as required by ORB), but rather, to discourage further reporting of the wrongdoing, so that the status quo will not be changed (Weinstein, 1979). For example, the whistle-blower described in the case opening this chapter, Joseph Wilson, filed a civil suit, in which he and his wife, Valerie Plame Wilson, alleged that top U.S. government officials attempted to "discredit, punish and seek revenge against the plaintiffs that included, among other things, disclosing to members of the press Plaintiff Valerie Plame Wilson's classified CIA (Central Intelligence Agency) employment" (Weiss & Lane, 2006, p. A03). Further, they alleged that "White House officials 'embarked on an anonymous 'whispering campaign' designed to discredit and injure the plaintiffs and deter other critics from speaking out'" (Weiss & Lane, 2006, p. A03). At the time of this writing, the civil suit had been dismissed by a U.S. district judge (Leonnig, 2007), and the Wilsons have filed an appeal (Sloan, 2007).

The separation of the terms "discredit, punish, and seek revenge" and "discredit, injure, and deter" is important, because within each of the two phrases, they imply three different possible motives and consequences. The primary motivation (and effect) may have been to control employees of the federal government (and others), that is, to show would-be whistle-blowers and critics that they would pay a considerable price for speaking out and thus discourage them from doing so. It is not clear that the exclusive or even primary motivation of the alleged retaliators was to restore justice as they defined it, although this may have been part of their motivation, and it is not clear that others would generally agree that Wilson's report created injustice in the first place.

For these three reasons, we distinguish the construct of retaliation against whistle-blowers from the construct of revenge against an employee for committing some perceived harm. We thus use the terms "reprisal" (but not revenge) and "retaliation" interchangeably. In developing the definition of retaliation, we turned to previous research on defining retaliation against whistle-blowers.

One early definition (Rehg, 1998, p. 17) stated that "retaliation against whistle-blowers represents an outcome of a conflict between an organization and its employee, in which members of the organization attempt to control the employee by threatening to take, or actually taking, an action that is detrimental to the well-being of the employee, in response to the employee's reporting, through internal or external channels, a perceived wrongful action." A similar definition (Keenan, 2002a, p. 82) viewed retaliation as "taking an undesirable action against an employee or not taking a desirable action because that employee disclosed information about a serious problem."

Some authors have proposed that retaliation is multidimensional. In his model integrating models of retaliation processes proposed by earlier theorists, Rehg argued that formal control processes exerted by management could be executed only through use of formal procedures of retaliation; informal reprisal could take other forms, including informal sanctions from coworkers (Rehg, 1998). A whistle-blower could be exposed to formal retaliation from management but none from coworkers, or vice versa. He defined formal retaliation to include actions involving written documentation and governed by procedures for implementation, whereas informal retaliation involved actions that did not require approval from supervisors or initiation of paperwork. Because, by definition, different dimensions have different predictors, he developed a separate model to predict each. However, as discussed in Chapter 4, most previous research has not separated these dimensions.

Similarly, Cortina and Magley (2003) separated work-related retaliation—"adverse work-related actions that are often tangible, formal, and documented in employment records"—from social retaliation, which comprises "antisocial behaviors, both verbal and nonverbal, that often go undocumented" (Cortina & Magley, 2003, p. 248). Work-related retaliation includes "discharge, involuntary transfer, demotion, poor performance appraisal, and deprivation of perquisites or overtime opportunities," whereas examples of social retaliation include "harassment, name-calling, ostracism, blame, threats, or the 'silent treatment'" (Cortina & Magley, 2003, p. 248). Consistent with the conceptual distinctions described previously, the authors argued convincingly that both work-related retaliation and social retaliation differ from ORB. Cortina and Magley argued that "work-related retaliation" represented more formal and tangible retaliatory behaviors than did "social retaliation."

There is evidence that, of those whistle-blowers who suffered retaliation, informal, social retaliation is common. Cortina and Magley found that 30% of whistle-blowers experienced social retaliation and 36% experienced both work-related and social retaliation (Cortina & Magley, 2003). Rehg found that 87% of whistle-blowers who suffered retaliation had experienced informal retaliation (Rehg, 1998).

Operational Definition Given the complexity of defining retaliation, the question arises as to how it should best be measured empirically. Retaliation should not be viewed as a dichotomous (i.e., experienced retaliation vs. did not experience retaliation) variable. The situations of (a) a whistle-blower who experiences a little "cold shoulder" treatment from one coworker and (b) a whistle-blower who believes nothing negative happened, may be far more similar than either situation is to that of (c) a whistle-blower who receives a highly negative performance appraisal after years of stellar ratings, whose office is moved to a remote location, who is given inconsequential work to do, and who is deliberately excluded from important meetings. How researchers quantify degrees of retaliation is important: losing one's job is clearly serious, but how can a researcher judge whether a low performance rating is more serious than being denied access to training? The former may be more serious for a senior employee and the latter for a junior employee.

In the first known study of organizational retaliation (Parmerlee, Near, & Jensen, 1982) and in many subsequent studies (e.g., Lee, Heilmann, & Near, 2004), it was measured as number of types of retaliation suffered or threatened, or "comprehensiveness." This approach is consistent with the "composite" approach used in revenge research, which is desirable because "studying clusters of behavior provides more reliable and valid measures of the underlying constructs than does studying individual behaviors" (Skarlicki et al., 1999, p. 105, citing previous research).

Cortina and Magley (2003) found that a two-factor structural equation modeling (SEM) of retaliation was strongest, with social retaliation and work-related retaliation loading on two separate but related ($r = .65$) factors. Seven types of retaliation loaded on each of the two factors, suggesting that retaliatory behaviors tend to occur in groups (e.g., poor performance appraisal and demotion), rather than singly (e.g., demotion alone).

For most whistle-blowers who suffer retaliation, there seems to be a pattern of repeated incidences of retaliation, often from different sources. For these reasons, we believe that the severity of retaliation against a whistle-blower is best assessed on the basis of how many types of reprisal the whistle-blower has suffered or been threatened with.

Effectiveness of Whistle-Blowing

The popular press tends to focus on why whistle-blowers act and what happened to them. An equally important question is whether whistle-blowers are effective in getting the wrongdoing corrected. For example, as we appraise the results achieved by the whistle-blowers at Enron, the FBI, and WorldCom, we would have to conclude that their relative effectiveness varied—and that our appraisal itself would have varied depending on when it was made in the history of their whistle-blowing efforts.

Conceptual Definition   The effectiveness of whistle-blowing is defined as "the extent to which the questionable or wrongful practice (or omission) is terminated at least partly because of whistle-blowing and within a reasonable time frame" (Near & Miceli, 1995, p. 681). This definition was derived from one of the earliest empirical findings on this question: that surveyed whistle-blowers perceived the process to have been effective if they were successful in changing management's views about the wrongdoing (Near & Jensen, 1983). Our definition goes a step further; it requires corrective action on the wrongdoing itself.

Our definition of effectiveness differs in at least two ways from Perry's definition of the related construct of "resolution" (Perry, 1992). Resolution "involves whether the controversy reaches closure," which may occur "when an authoritative source inside or outside the organization vindicates the whistleblower's position and punishes wrongdoers. A variety of other scenarios are possible as well, among them that the controversy continues and the issue dissipates without any formal resolution" (Perry, 1992, p. 311). Thus, one difference between *resolution* and *effectiveness* is that *resolution* could be said to occur if the whistle-blower agrees to stop complaining, for example, out of weariness or to receive a cash settlement, even if the wrongdoing is not corrected at all. However, we would consider this whistle-blowing to be ineffective. Another difference between *resolution* and *effectiveness* is that a whistle-blower can be completely effective even if the wrongdoers are not punished.

Operational Definition   In a recent study, we measured effectiveness with multiple, Likert-type items (Van Scotter, Miceli, Near, & Rehg, 2005). Because many whistle-blowers reported wrongdoing to more than one complaint channel, they were asked to describe, for each channel used, "the way things turned out *after* you acted." The five-point response scales ranged from 1 = "the problem worsened" to 5 = "the problem was completely resolved." Because respondents were asked this question for each channel they used and at each step of the process, the response that represented the most favorable outcome was used as the dependent variable. For example, if they first blew the whistle to their supervisor and "the problem continued" but then blew the whistle to the media and "the problem was completely resolved," we coded this variable with the highest response (i.e., 5). This coding follows past studies (Miceli & Near, 2002) and allows for maximal variance across a wide array of responses (e.g., distinguishing a worsened problem from a continuing problem, which may differ).

There are also obvious methodological problems with this approach. First, time matters when assessing effectiveness. A whistle-blower who appeared ineffective at first may have had huge impact on the organization when viewed several years hence. Second, whenever self-reported data are used, questions can be raised. Do whistle-blowers believe they have been *more* effective than outsiders might perceive, because they cannot bear the cognitive dissonance created by the fact that they have gone through tremendous perils only to be ineffective—so they report that they have succeeded in changing the organization? Or, do whistle-blowers believe they have been *less* effective than outsiders might perceive, because they know better than outsiders just how dysfunctional the organization is and therefore have higher ethical standards for cessation of wrongdoing? Of course, the validity of outsiders' views or other standards of effectiveness can also be questioned.

Embedded in these questions is yet a third issue: when we ask whether whistle-blowing was effective, we must also ask the question, "effective for whom?" Was whistle-blowing effective at Enron because it protected future shareholders who would have unwittingly invested in a firm about to go under? Or ineffective because it did not protect those shareholders who had already invested and therefore lost their nest eggs? In many ways, this is the most difficult variable to measure, of all the variables concerned with whistle-blowing. We may reach a relatively objective and accurate assessment of whether an individual observed wrongdoing, blew the whistle, and suffered retaliation. It is much more difficult to make a valid and reliable estimate of whether the whistle-blowing process was effective in leading to the termination of wrongdoing. A satisfactory resolution to these definitional questions awaits future research. We now turn our attention to empirical evidence about the incidence of wrongdoing, whistle-blowing, and retaliation.

How Widespread Are Wrongdoing and Whistle-Blowing, and What Does the Typical Whistle-Blower Experience?

Incidence of Wrongdoing

Organizational members engage in wrongdoing for many reasons, including environmental pressures or need for wrongdoing (e.g., opportunity or resource scarcity), "rational choices" to engage in wrongdoing in the face of low probability of being caught (e.g., when regulators are not vigilant) or suffering stiff penalties, and "predisposition" of the organization (e.g., past history) or its managers toward wrongdoing (e.g., Baucus, 1994). There may be pressure from leaders, through role modeling and authorization of corruption (e.g., Brief, Buttram, & Dukerich, 2001), or from changes (e.g., a merger), "when chains of command are disrupted and established business patterns are left in disarray" (Grimsley, 2000, p. E02). An exploration of all types of wrongdoing, and all causes of them, is beyond our scope. Clearly, if wrongdoing was rare or inexpensive, we would not be concerned with it. This raises the question: is organizational wrongdoing really occurring in the epidemic proportions alleged by the popular press? Empirical studies show wide variation in the amount of wrongdoing observed in different types of organizations at different times.

Using the operational measure of wrongdoing described previously, observation of wrongdoing was found to vary from 80% of all internal auditors in one study (Miceli, Near, & Schwenk, 1991) to 45% in the first MSPB study to 37% among military and civilian employees of a large base (Near, Van Scotter, Rehg, & Miceli, 2004) to 33% in nonrandom samples of employees from various organizations (Rothschild & Miethe, 1999) to 18% in the second MSPB study and 14% in the last MSPB study (Miceli et al., 1999). Two other surveys of public and private sector employees were conducted by the consulting firm KPMG and by the nonprofit Ethics Resource Center. Nearly 75% of 3,075 workers surveyed by KPMG said they had seen violations of the law or company standards within the previous six months (Grimsley, 2000). Approximately 33% of 1,500 public and private sector workers surveyed by the Ethics Resource Center said they had witnessed misconduct within the past year.

Why Do the Percentages Vary So Much?   Although research is needed to identify all factors accounting for this range in figures, we can offer some comments on them. First, all of these numbers are self-reported perceptions; wrongdoing is obviously to some extent in the eye of the beholder—a point to which we will return shortly—and not all observers of questionable activity will agree.

Second, the methods varied. More comprehensive lists of wrongdoing or instructions restricting the definition to "serious" events will produce different results; for example, less serious wrongdoing such as misuse of sick leave is included along with more serious wrongdoing in some but not all studies. Not all studies used the same time periods; for example, if all other conditions were held constant, the use of a two-year versus six-month observation period would produce higher percentages of employees who said they have observed wrongdoing.

Third, by far the highest percentage was reported in the study of internal auditors; auditors are required by their jobs to look for certain types of wrongdoing and employees report such wrongdoing to them. So, if during the course of the year an internal auditor said she or he was unaware of *any* wrongdoing, one might wonder if she or he was doing his or her job. Other occupations and professions vary in the extent to which observing wrongdoing is part of the job, and job settings may vary as well.

Fourth, there are likely to be very real differences across organizations and industries in their success at defining and preventing wrongdoing. These factors were not constant across all of the studies. Thus, one conclusion is that wrongdoing is quite frequently observed, especially by individuals holding jobs where they are likely to be privy to information about wrongdoing (e.g., internal auditors), and in all kinds of organizations, including both public and private sector employees. But the "why" behind this conclusion is less clear.

Types of Wrongdoing   Some types of wrongdoing were observed more than others. For example, a recent survey (Near et al., 2004) indicated that the types of wrongdoing observed in one large organization fell into seven broad groups:

1. Stealing (10% of all wrongdoing), including stealing of federal funds or federal property, accepting bribes/kickbacks, use of position for personal benefit; unfair advantage to contractor; and employee abuse of office.
2. Waste (44%), including waste by ineligible people receiving benefits or a badly managed program or waste of organizational assets.
3. Mismanagement (11%), including management's cover-up of poor performance or false projections of performance.
4. Safety problems (8%), including unsafe or noncompliant products or working conditions.
5. Sexual harassment (8%).
6. Illegal discrimination (13%).
7. Other violation of law (7%). Some refer to illegal behavior, others to behavior that merely constitutes wrongdoing; most observers would agree that all these behaviors are wrong, but determining whether a given event falls into a category is sometimes difficult (e.g., when is a product unsafe?).

The "Eye of the Beholder Problem"   The validity of the complaint is one of the most difficult to assess of all the characteristics of the whistle-blowing process—yet it is one of the most important in that it is likely to affect the overall effectiveness of the whistle-blower in creating change (Miceli & Near, 2002; Near & Miceli, 1995; Perry, 1991) and may also affect the likelihood of retaliation against the whistle-blower (Miceli & Near, 1992). One difficult issue is determining whether wrongdoing has actually occurred. This is a problem when an employee is trying to assess whether wrongdoing has occurred, because different people may have different views of the situation. If wrongdoing is overlooked, then—obviously—appropriate corrective action cannot be taken. It is also a problem if the employee judges an incident to be wrongful and reports it but complaint recipients do not agree that wrongdoing has taken place.

Research on incidents that have been reported thus may be of interest. One indication of validity is the extent to which the complaint recipient is convinced of a problem. There is little controlled research on the proportion of whistle-blowing complaints that are judged by authorities to be valid, and estimates from anecdotal sources reveal wide variations in estimates. In one study (Tavakoli et al., 2003, p. 62), the authors reported, "a survey (Figg, 2000) of more than 125 chief internal auditors concluded that 76% of employee whistle-blowing complaints were found to be true."

Studies of complaints filed with federal agencies reveal much lower percentages.

> New federal and state legislation, such as the Truth in Lending laws, the Fair Credit Reporting Act, and the Environmental Protection Act, protected the public from illegal or unethical business practices. Many of these laws also contained provisions against reprisal for reporting violations. Although these laws appear to protect whistleblowers, a 1976 study of OSHA showed only 20% of the complaints filed that year were considered valid. About half of these claims were settled out of court, and of the 60 claims taken to court, only one was won. (Ravishankar, 2004)

In the late 1990s, the U.S. Equal Employment Opportunity Commission (EEOC) dismissed 90% of employees' charges (Karr, 1998b). More recently, in fiscal year 2006, "reasonable cause" was found in only 5.3% of the more than 75,000 charges of discrimination filed with the EEOC (Society for Human Resource Management, 2007).

Such numbers are far out of line with the perceptions of employees in general, when surveyed anonymously, as described previously. Employee perceptions may sometimes be in error, but presumably most employees have no incentive consciously to distort their perceptions on an anonymous questionnaire. Taken together, these findings suggest that the validity estimates offered by some official complaint recipients (e.g., the Office of the Inspector General in a federal agency or an ombudsperson in a firm) are too low.

Some factors that could produce this effect are understaffing or inadequate budget in the complaint recipient's office, and a wish to appear effective at preventing wrongdoing. Complaint recipients may find it difficult to get independent evidence on some sensitive complaints and thereby conclude that there simply is no evidence of wrongdoing. Other factors could include: (a) management's unwillingness to take complaints seriously; (b) management's inability to understand what is wrong (i.e., using a "window dressing" approach rather than vigorous policies); or (c) management's wish to continue to engage in wrongdoing. Complaint recipients may also feel it is best to pursue only certain types of complaints and consider the rest to be unfounded. But even with these factors operating, each situation will differ, and it is entirely possible that in some situations, employees simply misperceive or exaggerate what they are seeing.

Therefore, it is true that wrongdoing is to some extent difficult to define unambiguously. But it is also true that, for civilized societies to function effectively, there must be consensus on some level as to what constitutes wrongdoing and what evidence is needed to say reasonably that it did or did not occur; otherwise, judges and juries could never draw any conclusions. Obviously, more research is needed to sort out these issues.

Incidence of Whistle-Blowing

Although the popular press may convey the impression that whistle-blowers are everywhere, research results suggest that only about half of all employees who observe wrongdoing blow the whistle about it. When observers of wrongdoing are asked whether they reported it, there is great variation in the incidence with which they did so. In 1992, the most recent systematic survey of federal employees, approximately 48% of observers blew the whistle (Miceli et al., 1999). In a subsequent survey of federal employees, 1,280 reported being the victim of sexual harassment, but only 67 (about 4%) blew the whistle (Lee et al., 2004). In 1997, only 26% of the observers of wrongdoing at a large military base blew the whistle; this sample was composed of about half military and half civilian employees (Near et al., 2004). Among directors of internal auditing—whose job it is to ferret out and report financial wrongdoing internally in their organizations— about 90% of those who observed wrongdoing reported it (Miceli, Near, & Schwenk, 1991).

These figures suggest that typical employees, who do not see whistle-blowing as part of their jobs, are not inclined to act when they see wrongdoing. In contrast, employees whose jobs legitimate and even require whistle-blowing are willing to report wrongdoing. Of course, there are other differences too among these employees, but the basic question remains the same: why do so many employees who observe wrongdoing *not* blow the whistle? And what variables separate those who do from those who do not? These issues are explored further in Chapters 2 and 3.

Incidence of Retaliation

Whistle-blowing may have positive consequences for the whistle-blower, such as financial reward or personal gratification (Miethe, 1999), but existing research (e.g., Rothschild & Miethe, 1999), although incomplete, suggests that the percentage of whistle-blowers who receive such rewards is probably low. As noted previously, we know of no private sector organizations that offer financial rewards for employees' whistle-blowing, other than as part of the normal performance of certain jobs such as internal auditors. Certainly few qualify for awards under the False Claims Act, which are available only for whistle-blowers whose actions enable the federal government to recover funds lost to fraud (e.g., Zingales, 2004).

Accounts of whistle-blowing in the press seem more often to focus on the downside, including retaliation and its long-term effect on the personal life of the whistle-blower. In fiscal 1998, more than 17,000 charges of retaliation were filed with the EEOC (Karr, 1998a). Since 1992, retaliation charges have more than doubled and now account for a record 30% of charges filed (Lublin, 2006). But formal complaints external to the organization may represent only a tiny fraction of perceived retaliation incidents.

Estimates of the incidence of retaliation against whistle-blowers have varied dramatically. Data collected from nonrandom samples of whistle-blowers indicated that huge majorities of the samples suffered retaliation, leading some to conclude that most whistle-blowers in the population suffer retaliation (e.g., Glazer & Glazer, 1989; Perry, 1992; Rothschild & Miethe, 1999). Data collected from random samples of federal employees, in contrast, indicated that the percentage of identified whistle-blowers who suffered retaliation varied from a low of 17% in 1980 to a high of 38% in 1992 (Miceli et al., 1999)—despite the fact that legal sanctions against retaliation were passed into law in 1978, effective in 1980. A later study showed that civilian and military employees of a large military base reported a retaliation rate of 37% (Near et al., 2004). Further, a recent survey of Food and Drug Administration scientists indicated that 40% of the respondents feared retaliation if they were to blow the whistle externally (Union of Concerned Scientists, 2006).

Thus, we might have expected retaliation to decline during this time period, as knowledge of the law became more widespread, but it did not. Many factors might account for the increase, many of which are discussed in this book, such as the difficulty of maintaining cultures to prevent all cases of wrongdoing and retaliation, and legal enforcement issues. For example, the law itself does not apply to all federal employees; FBI employees, such as Colleen Rowley, who blew the whistle on poor performance following the 9/11 terrorist attack, are not protected from firing if they blow the whistle (Rowley, 2004). A bill to extend protections to federal employees in intelligence agencies has been proposed (Barr, 2007); this bill also would change some provisions of current law for other federal whistle-blowers, which whistle-blower advocates have said "makes it almost impossible for federal employees to defend themselves from reprisals when speaking out on waste, fraud and abuse" (p. D4).

On the other hand, an important fact is that these percentages show that retaliation as perceived by the whistle-blower occurs in less than half of all cases, by some estimates, far less than half. Thus, its occurrence is not an inevitable consequence for federal whistle-blowers. But what is not clear is the extent to which the findings extend to other types of organizations.

When we consider employees of nongovernmental organizations (i.e., for-profits and not-for-profits), the incidence of retaliation is more difficult to assess. To date, the only known random sample of employees from private employers involved directors of internal auditing, of whom only 6% suffered retaliation (Miceli, Near, & Schwenk, 1991). Several nonrandom samples of employees from various occupations and industries have also been surveyed, and they reported higher levels of retaliation (Rothschild & Miethe, 1999). About half of whistle-blowers surveyed by the National Whistleblower Center said they were fired, and most of the rest said they experienced other retaliation (Hananel, 2002). However, the survey was described as "unscientific" and was based on a random sample of 200 cases reported to the Center (Hananel, 2002). A 1998 survey reported that 23% of 448 emergency physicians who complained about an issue reported having been fired or threatened with termination (Zingales, 2004); sampling techniques were not described.

The nonrandom samples may have yielded biased estimates of the incidence of retaliation. On the other hand, directors of internal auditing (in the only known random sample that included private sector employees) benefit from much stronger protections from retaliation by virtue of their position and support from their professional association, the Institute of Internal Auditors, when compared to other employees. At this point, then, we cannot ascertain whether sample variance in rates of retaliation resulted from factors differing in populations or situations, such as legal or professional protections from retaliation, informal norms, or organizational support for some types of whistle-blowing versus others. Differences in findings may instead have resulted from methodological factors, including the use of nonrandom samples.

Incidence of Effectiveness

In one study (Van Scotter et al., 2005), of the respondents who blew the whistle, 11.1% said, "The problem worsened"; 53.7% noted that "The problem continued"; 9.5% said, "The case is pending" or "I don't know what happened"; 16.3% believed that "The problem was partially resolved"; and 9.5% stated that "The problem was completely resolved." These respondents were drawn from the population of a large U.S. military base; whistle-blowing effectiveness would obviously vary greatly depending on the organizational setting and other factors.

As noted above, we see substantial variation across organizations in the incidence figures for employees who blow the whistle, suffer retaliation, or have an effect on the wrongdoing. In part these differences reflect real differences in the organizations and their employees, but in part the differences may be attributable to differences in

research methods used to collect the data. We elaborate on some of
the differences and issues below because we believe that readers need
to be aware of the diversity of methods and the trade-offs involved in
their use, in order to appropriately assess the validity and reliability
of the results generated through each of these methods.

Methodological Issues

A variety of research designs can be considered, but each of these
has serious limitations for studying the predictors and consequences
of whistle-blowing, retaliation, and effectiveness. Causal designs
are very desirable, but are rare in field organizational research for
many reasons (Scandura & Williams, 2000). Such designs are virtually impossible to conceive and execute when exploring the sensitive
nature of organizational wrongdoing and the risks in reporting it.
Subjecting people to wrongdoing important enough to warrant
action, and to reprisal that matters (e.g., docking students' grades
if they blow the whistle), raises ethical issues. The types and nature
of wrongdoing and retaliation that would pass ethical or university
research committee standards would likely not result in a design
realistic enough or powerful enough to evoke meaningful variance
across conditions. Further, it may be impossible to simulate the
complex and ongoing relationships an employee would encounter.
These and other threats to internal validity (e.g., Campbell & Stanley,
1966) are serious problems.

Consequently, very few field experimental or true laboratory
studies have been completed (e.g., Everton, 1996; Miceli, Dozier,
& Near, 1991). In the Miceli et al. study, students were exposed to
a confederate wrongdoer who appeared to be a research assistant
asking students to "fudge" the results in order to confirm the
experimenter's hypothesis. They were given the opportunity to blow
the whistle when a student presenting himself as a representative of
the university committee on research asked participants to complete
a short questionnaire at the end of the session. Although not conducted in a business organization, this study can be considered a
field experimental study primarily because students were members
of the organization that also employed the "wrongdoers" (the experimenter and the research assistant). All students were debriefed
immediately after the sessions. In the Everton study, a similar design

was followed, but in it, the experimenter "punished" or "rewarded" a confederate "participant" for his or her "whistle-blowing," avoiding the ethical problem of applying these consequences directly to the study participants. Participants were asked how acceptable, ethical, and likable were the research assistant and his or her actions, and participants' own whistle-blowing was not among the dependent variables. Perhaps because of the need to weaken the conditions, many hypotheses in both of these studies were not confirmed.

Alternative quasi-experiments include scenario studies, in which, for example, subjects are presented with stories describing wrong-doing and conditions varied by the researchers, and are asked how they would respond to the wrongdoing. Scenario studies are commonly used (e.g., Ferguson & Near, 1987, 1989; Keenan, 2002a, 2002b; King, 1997; Sims & Keenan, 1998; Starkey, 1998; Wise, 1995). These offer the advantages of enabling anonymity of response and focus on the conditions of greatest interest to the researcher, allowing tests of theory. Between-subject scenario designs can avoid same source problems, because the experimenter can manipulate the independent variable. But would people responding to hypothetical situations know how they would act if actually faced with the wrongdoing described in the scenarios? And would they accurately report their behavior to the researcher, or would they fall victim to social desirability bias (e.g., Smith & Ellingson, 2002), in which they report what they believe most others would want to see happen rather than what would actually happen? Or would they be susceptible to experimenter demand bias, in which they give the researcher the responses they believe would support the researcher's hypotheses, or what the researcher would approve, rather than their "real" feelings or observations?

A recent meta-analysis showed the best predictors of actual (self-reported) whistle-blowing are generally not the same as the best predictors of the actions respondents said they would take in hypothetical wrongdoing situations, that is, whistle-blowing intent (Mesmer-Magnus & Viswesvaran, 2005). Further, the relationships between predictors and intent were generally stronger than were those between predictors and actual (self-reported) whistle-blowing in field studies (Mesmer-Magnus & Viswesvaran, 2005). For readers unfamiliar with meta-analysis, it is a "study of studies." Essentially, it provides a statistical means of examining existing studies to determine if a given variable consistently has a relationship with another variable across multiple study settings; multiple relationships (involving multiple variables) can be examined. However, all meta-analyses are limited by the research available and included in the meta-analyses; the "garbage in-garbage out" principle applies, to some extent. For example, if few studies have examined a variable, or if there are similar design flaws across multiple studies, results may be weak or misleading. And, researchers must also make judgment calls (e.g., Ostroff & Harrison, 1999). Readers seeking more information are encouraged to consult the original source reporting the meta-analysis to which we will frequently refer (Mesmer-Magnus & Viswesvaran, 2005).

The Randomized Response Technique has been used to assess the incidence of wrongdoing in survey data (e.g., Burton & Near, 1995). But it does not allow researchers to examine predictors of respondents' behaviors, because individual respondents cannot be separated from the aggregated data.

In-depth case studies (e.g., Alford, 2001) often provide rich and complex qualitative data that are helpful in building theory and identifying possible causal influences. These studies have relied on whistle-blowers' descriptions of the situation or of retaliation suffered, mostly in an unstructured question format for collecting information. In some cases, the sample of interviewees was selected from news articles and other sources where the whistle-blower's actions were made public in part because the whistle-blower had already suffered retaliation (Perry, 1991). But this nonrandom selection process raises questions of the extent to which the case is representative of the population, and unless non-whistle-blowers are included, it is difficult to make comparisons and draw conclusions. For example, whistle-blowers whose cases are presented in the media may involve much more serious or unusual retaliation than is typically experienced, and the researcher cannot examine how their demographic characteristics, personalities, or wrongdoing witnessed differ from those of observers who do not blow the whistle. Nowhere is this problem better illustrated than in current research on retaliation, where research results based on nonrandom samples suggest that a large majority of whistle-blowers suffer retaliation, whereas research findings based on random samples indicate just the opposite, as will be described later in this book.

Further, in-depth case studies are quite costly, in terms of researchers' time, to conduct. In order to study whistle-blowers over time, or to investigate their families' views of the process, researchers developed long-term and even close relationships with whistle-blowers who would trust the researchers sufficiently to consent to this type of invasive study. Obviously, these study subjects could not remain anonymous. Even more importantly, they would need to fully trust the researchers to treat their information as confidential—which in itself might preclude validation of the information by data collections from other employees involved in the whistle-blowing.

Legal case studies have also been used as a way to collate data from records of lawsuits (Dworkin & Baucus, 1998; Dworkin & Near, 1987). This method has the advantage of using data from public and external sources, not subject to the self-report bias of the whistle-blower. Samples of whistle-blowers who have filed lawsuits also suggest that at least an attorney agrees that the case may have merit, but these then are limited to whistle-blowers reporting illegal behavior, as opposed to other forms of legal wrongdoing. The disadvantages—and they are large—include that not all whistle-blowing cases involve lawsuits, that is, the nonrandom sampling problem identified with other case studies. When lawsuits are filed, they often concern retaliation subsequent to the original whistle-blowing and to additional events, rather than immediately after the whistle-blowing. Another important disadvantage is that data are available for only a few variables, and not necessarily those variables that the researcher wishes to study.

Longitudinal nonexperimental field surveys may suggest possible cause and effect, and often can reduce same source method problems (e.g., where measures include participants' perceptions of a situation and their reactions to it) to some degree, simply by having measures separated in time. Unfortunately, such data are extremely hard to obtain (Mesmer-Magnus & Viswesvaran, 2005) for many reasons, and the external and internal validity of such studies may be questionable. For example, few organizations and their employees will cooperate with designs that require identification of participants to enable pairing of information with follow-up or supplementary data collection, and these may not be representative of organizations in general (e.g., would wrongdoers permit such studies?). Also, respondents who have already suffered or fear future retaliation are unlikely to participate in samples where their identity is known, for obvious reasons. Thus, promises of confidentiality are unlikely to be sufficiently believable to attract respondents. Offering anonymity precludes any collection of longitudinal data from the same respondents. Elaborate methods to link anonymous respondents' questionnaires to later questionnaires or to other respondents who can verify the respondents' views also are unlikely to work effectively. For example, participants must be willing to be identified or to trust in researchers' techniques, for example, that if they are asked to choose a number or symbol to remember and use in subsequent administrations, these will not be somehow connected with their names or revealed by the researchers. Because respondents can forget these numbers or leave their jobs, some loss of data may occur as well, a particular problem in whistle-blowing research where the base rate of actual whistle-blowing is extremely low and where leaving may result from retaliation.

Cross-sectional questionnaires combined with other sources of data (e.g., asking coworkers for their perception of the wrongdoing to "validate" the respondent's perception) enable researchers to avoid some potential same-source problems. But these designs are not only difficult to employ for whistle-blowing; they have many of the same problems as longitudinal designs (e.g., Miceli & Near, 1992), such as difficulties in identifying respondents in order to "validate" the data obtained by cross-checking with other observers of the whistle-blowing. Further, it is not at all clear that objective measures or "hard" data exist for important whistle-blowing variables, for example, in defining wrongdoing, individual ethical standards necessarily come into play. Nor is it clear that the perceptions of managers or coworkers are more valid than those of whistle-blowers, because others may simply not know of or have paid as much attention to evidence of wrongdoing as has the would-be whistle-blower, and because motivations to distort (such as fear of getting caught) are often present.

For these reasons, it is probably no accident that most field research investigating whistle-blowing has surveyed employees or managers in organizations about actual experiences in their organizations, without connecting these data with other sources of data, because anonymity was assured. Because of all of the methodological challenges we have highlighted, it is not surprising that many important research questions remain unanswered and that rigorous published studies are few. On the other hand, because of the importance of the topic, we cannot afford to sit back and rely on journalistic accounts of the process.

We believe that the solution is twofold. First, researchers must make careful trade-offs to address methodological dilemmas that we have identified, and adhere to the highest methodological standards. When submitting the paper for review, they must articulate clearly (a) what these trade-offs and their likely consequences were, and (b) the limitations of their studies. Second, editors and reviewers should become more familiar with the dilemmas in whistle-blowing research, and be supportive of researchers who have taken appropriate care, rather than presuming, as one example, that researchers are uninformed, negligent, or lazy, in relying on a single source. Editors and reviewers should impose consistent standards; it should be impossible to find—in the recent issues of the same journals—studies with the same design features to which they object in a whistle-blowing study, especially not studies on other topics where trade-offs are far less challenging. Conveying a consistent message as to how trade-offs "should" be made will also help send a clear signal to authors in early stages of their work. And, where reviewers object to the trade-off decisions of authors, to be fair to authors and to encourage whistle-blowing research, editors should insist that reviewers offer real and workable solutions that are in fact superior to those decisions made by the authors, that take into account problems created as well as those apparently solved; editors should not deem adequate a simplistic, standard reply. It is our belief that, once reviewers are put in this position, most of the time they may better understand that they may not be able to offer a superior design, which is helpful not only for authors but also a useful learning process. Certainly, this challenge would increase the likelihood that someday, perhaps as methodological advances (or legal developments) occur, ingenious, realistic designs for future study will be developed.

It is often said that there is a trade-off in research between relevance and rigor. Nowhere is this truer than in research on whistle-blowing. We believe that research in this area is sorely needed and has never been more relevant. If large, complex organizations have unprecedented opportunity to commit wrongdoing, at a time in history when oversight is nearly impossible because of increasing organizational complexity and size (e.g., Miethe, 1999), and when members who decide to blow the whistle may be the best hope for identifying their organization's wrongdoing, then understanding the whistle-blowing process has never been more important. Unfortunately, collecting data from representative samples of whistle-blowers requires holding in abeyance some of the field's most stringent requirements for careful research design. In this instance, we believe that relevance justifies research, with appropriate rigor to the extent feasible.

Summary

The general purpose of this chapter was to provide a foundation for what is to come. We defined key terms and addressed some controversies concerning definitions. We described evidence of the extensiveness of (a) the wrongdoing whistle-blowers say they have witnessed, (b) whistle-blowing, (c) the retaliation whistle-blowers believe they experience, and (d) the effectiveness of whistle-blowing. We provided an overview of the types of empirical studies of whistle-blowing that have been conducted. Finally, we discussed some critical methodological challenges faced by those who conduct research concerning whistle-blowing. In the next chapter, we will describe theoretical development concerning the prediction of whistle-blowing, and we will describe in more depth the empirical research that focuses on one general category of predictors of whistle-blowing—that dealing with individual differences.

2

Who Blows the Whistle? The Prosocial Organizational Behavior Model and Personal Predictors of Whistle-Blowing

> When she woke up on Monday morning, Jan. 14 (2002), Sherron Watkins was just one of the legions of high-powered executive moms, the kind of woman who drove an SUV, who liked to take her 2½-year-old daughter to preschool on the way to the office, who caught up with her sister by cell phone during her morning commute.
>
> At age 42, Watkins had climbed to the rank of vice president at Enron, she owned a lovely home in an upper-class Houston neighborhood, and she finally had the family she'd so long desired.
>
> Twenty-four hours later, she was the so-called "whistle-blower" in one of the biggest corporate scandals in modern memory, the woman who had warned Enron's now-former chairman, Kenneth Lay, of major irregularities in the company's accounting practices months before the corporation collapsed, embroiled in a major Securities and Exchange Commission investigation. (Frey, 2002, p. C1)

Sherron Watkins may be one of the best-known whistle-blowers in the United States. But is she a "typical" whistle-blower? Are there personal characteristics that cause some employees to be more likely to blow the whistle than others when they observe wrongdoing? Most importantly, from the standpoint of executives, can we predict in advance which employees are "whistle-blower types"?

We believe that many, if not most, incidents of whistle-blowing—which attempts to prevent the substantial negative consequences of wrongdoing for employees, customers, stockholders, communities, and societies—are positive behaviors, though certain incidents of whistle-blowing can be antisocial (Miceli & Near, 1997). Unfortunately, many organizational leaders do not see whistle-blowing as positive. According to a recent article in an influential international

33

publication, "sadly, few firms are yet persuaded that such procedures (to encourage internal whistle-blowing) are in their own best
interests. In America at least, it is almost always thought cheaper to
fire whistleblowers than to listen to them, despite years of legislation
designed to achieve the opposite. 'No matter how many protections
whistleblower laws have created over the years,' says Kris Kolesnik,
director of the National Whistleblower Centre in Washington, D.C.,
'the system always seems to defeat them'" (Anonymous, 2002, p. 56).

Obviously, it can be argued that even if avoiding and stopping
wrongdoing benefits society but not the organization, it is still a
positive behavior, and managers of that organization are ethically,
and sometimes legally, obliged to put the interests of society first. In
other words, we would argue that it is the managers' social responsibility to balance their roles as agents of their organizations and as
citizens of the broader community.

But less obviously, whistle-blowing can help the organization;
often the same action that benefits constituents such as employees
and community members also directly benefits the organization.
For example, the very existence of Enron, Arthur Andersen, and
Bridgestone/Firestone has been shaken by wrongdoing (Anonymous,
2002), which might have been avoided had top management
responded appropriately to internal whistle-blowers. In addition to
anecdotes, there is also preliminary controlled evidence of benefits
to organizations of stopping wrongdoing (e.g., Glomb, Richman,
Hulin, Drasgow, Schneider, & Fitzgerald, 1997; Miceli et al., 2001b).
Management that responds appropriately to whistle-blowers reduces
exposure to lawsuits and potential punitive damages (e.g., Dworkin
& Callahan, 2002). Further, offering the opportunity for employees
to voice their concerns creates an alternative to the organization's
losing excellent employees, who would otherwise choose to leave
rather than work for an organization that tolerates wrongdoing and
squelches dissent (e.g., Farrell & Rusbult, 1990; Hirschman, 1970).
Enlightened managers acting in their organizations' self-interest
certainly would prefer to reduce dysfunctional turnover.

Because whistle-blowing is generally a positive response to
negative circumstances, it should be more strongly encouraged by
organizations and by society. Even better would be creating organizational structures and climates that discourage wrongdoing in
the first place, so that employees understand fully what constitutes
wrongdoing and recognize that it is not to be condoned. Either

reacting well to whistle-blowers or responding proactively to potential whistle-blowing by reducing wrongdoing would help managers to create more effective organizations. However, published advice as to how this can be achieved is not always informed by existing scientific literature on the topic. Accordingly, the purpose of this chapter is to describe existing theoretical and empirical literature relevant to the question of "who blows the whistle?" with the focus on (a) personal variables that may be associated with whistle-blowing, and (b) research since the last comprehensive review of this question (Near & Miceli, 1996). We begin, in this chapter, by describing an evolving model of whistle-blowing, and then review empirical research. In Chapter 3, we cover additional variables that predict when employees who observe wrongdoing will blow the whistle, with a focus on variables that do not pertain to the individual whistle-blower's characteristics. Thus, this chapter and the next are best viewed as an integrated whole.

Whistle-Blowing as Prosocial Organizational Behavior: The POB Model

Development of the POB Model

For more than 20 years, researchers have viewed whistle-blowing as a prosocial behavior, that is, behavior intended to benefit other persons (Staub, 1978), such as bystander intervention in crime and emergencies, altruism, or other types of helping. Prosocial behavior was first studied by social psychologists; for example, the theory of bystander intervention (e.g., Latané & Darley, 1968, 1970) ultimately formed the basis of social impact theory (e.g., Latané, 1981).

To illustrate one element of this theory, Latané, Darley, and their colleagues identified a "diffusion of responsibility" effect explaining why none of the more than 40 witnesses who heard a victim screaming while being brutally attacked in New York City called the police. Each witness knew that others must have heard, and consequently felt less personally responsible for reporting the act than if he or she were the only witness. Each thought someone else was going to report it, and thus the responsibility was "diffused" across multiple persons. Essentially, the bystander intervention model proposed that observers of an emergency or wrongdoing ask themselves a series of questions, including: "Do I believe an emergency or wrongdoing is occurring? Is action warranted? Am I responsible for acting? Is there something that I could do that might stop the wrongdoing? Will the benefits of a considered action outweigh the costs?" Affirmative answers to all the questions increase the probability of intervention.

Later, organizational researchers extended the bystander intervention model into organizational contexts, for example, to prosocial organizational behavior, including whistle-blowing (Brief & Motowidlo, 1986) or intervention by observers of sexual harassment against targets other than the self (Bowes-Sperry & O'Leary-Kelly, 2005). Research suggests that many acts of whistle-blowing are prosocial organizational behaviors (Dozier & Miceli, 1985; Miceli et al., 2001a). Prosocial organizational behavior has been defined as behavior that is "(a) performed by a member of an organization; (b) directed toward an individual, group, or organization with whom he or she interacts while carrying out his or her organizational role; and (c) performed with the intention of promoting the welfare of the individual, group, or organization toward which it is directed" (Brief & Motowidlo, 1986, p. 711).

Behavior does not have to be altruistic to be considered prosocial (Dozier & Miceli, 1985); whistle-blowers can have mixed motives at the time of deciding to act (and it is often difficult empirically to ascertain motives). After the fact, they can experience some personal gain while behaving prosocially. For instance, whistle-blowers who complain about unsafe working conditions benefit personally—along with coworkers—if those unsafe conditions are remedied.

Likewise, whistle-blowers who receive cash awards are still whistle-blowers; they are acting to stop wrongdoing and often take on huge career risks like other whistle-blowers. For example, Douglas Durand, the pharmaceutical sales representative, certainly benefited handsomely from blowing the whistle on physicians' overcharges of government medical programs for the prostate cancer drug Lupron; he received 14% of the $875 million fine imposed on manufacturers, because he saved the federal government far more (Haddad & Barrett, 2002). Yet, at the time Durand reported the problems he had no guarantee of a payoff, and knew the process would likely be long and arduous. Although the number of such cases has grown quickly since the inception of legal processes for providing cash awards to whistle-blowers, the effects of cash awards need more empirical attention (e.g., Callahan & Dworkin, 1992).

Therefore, although research suggests that whistle-blowers feel more morally compelled to act than do inactive observers (Miceli, Near, & Schwenk, 1991), researchers generally agree that requiring that whistle-blowing be purely altruistic in order to be morally acceptable imposes an unrealistically high standard (Dozier & Miceli, 1985; Perry, 1991). If "purely altruistic" means that there is absolutely no benefit to the actor, there would be virtually no whistle-blowing. Whistle-blowers almost always benefit from the cessation of wrongdoing, at least psychologically, if not more tangibly as in the case of cash rewards. For example, research shows that employees are less satisfied when sexual harassment occurs in the workplace, regardless of whether they personally are directly targeted by the harasser (Glomb et al., 1997); therefore, even a male whistle-blower who took on the risks and costs of fighting harassment directed at a female coworker would not be purely altruistic.

The POB Model: General Description

Drawing from this theoretical tradition, we developed a model predicting who will blow the whistle, based on earlier models that have been refined by empirical results reported over the years (Dozier & Miceli, 1985; Miceli et al., 2001a). In Chapter 3, we will discuss other theory relevant to whistle-blowing and its relationship to this model, but we will begin here with a basic description of this model alone.

As shown in Figure 2.1, the prosocial organizational behavior (POB) model of whistle-blowing proposes that, when questionable activity occurs, organizational members experience up to three general phases of decision-making or affective reactions, which influence their actions. Variables and processes that affect any of these phases will thus determine whether whistle-blowing occurs, a point to which we will return after describing the three phases.

Decisions to Be Made by the Organization Member

Phase 1   In Phase 1, organization members assess whether the focal activity, such as the preparation of false financial reports, is wrongful. We use the term "focal activity" because the observer may believe there is other wrongdoing in the organization. For example,

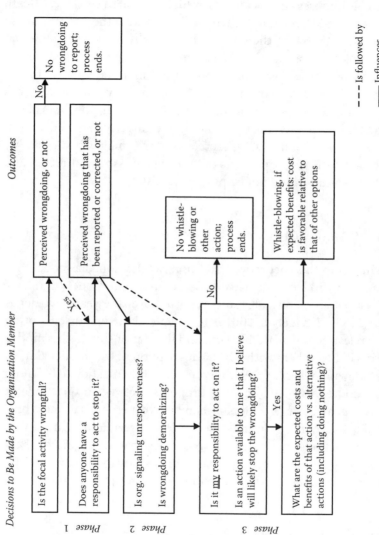

Figure 2.1   Phases in the POB model of whistle-blowing.

an employee who believes she has been sexually harassed may also believe women are illegally denied promotion opportunities or equal pay based on gender. Because we are trying to predict how the observer will act in response to the sexual harassment, we want to clarify which wrongdoing is our primary focus—for example, in this case, sexual harassment rather than gender discrimination with regard to promotion or pay.

The first outcome in Phase 1 is perceived wrongdoing versus no perceived wrongdoing. Some nonobservers do not believe they have witnessed wrongdoing because, by any standard, none has actually occurred. But evaluating wrongdoing often involves subjectivity. Some employees do not perceive wrongdoing even when most others believe it does exist, and some employees define certain events as wrongful that others may not. If the employee believes no wrongdoing has occurred, then there is nothing to report, and the whistle-blowing process ends.

If the employee believes wrongdoing has occurred, the next decision is whether anyone has a responsibility to act to stop it. If the observer believes that the organization is in the process of correcting it, or that someone has already reported it, then no one—including the observer—has a responsibility to act, and the process ends because there is nothing to report. However, if the observer believes someone does have a responsibility to act (e.g., because powerful authorities do not know wrongdoing is occurring) then the wrongdoing is perceived to be unreported or uncorrected—a second outcome of Phase 1—and the process continues to the next phase.

Phase 2 The POB model proposes that, in Phase 2, observing wrongdoing that has not been reported or corrected can negatively influence how employees view the organization and their assessment of what to do about the perceived wrongdoing (in Phase 3). Two processes can occur—signaling or demoralization—which are not mutually exclusive. Phase 2 in the POB model has no parallel in the bystander intervention model, because the latter is not an organizational model.

Signaling.   Signaling theory (e.g., Lambert, 2000) holds that certain organizational actions can, sometimes unwittingly, cause employees or recruits to form desirable or undesirable attributions about the organization or to forecast events deemed related (Rynes & Barber,

1990). For example, during the recruiting process, compensation policies may influence, directly or indirectly, applicant attraction to the organization (Barber, Rau, & Simmering, 1996). Pay that is highly dependent on individual performance may signal a dynamic organization, which may attract a young, confident employee.

In the context of whistle-blowing, unreported or uncorrected wrongdoing may signal to employees that the organization would not correct wrongdoing if they reported it, because the existence of wrongdoing implies that the organization tolerates bad behavior. Research on sexual harassment is consistent with this notion. For example, "environments that do not discourage inappropriate and unwanted sexual behaviors actually inhibit reporting behavior ... if sexual harassment is tolerated by management and if reports are not taken seriously, targets may believe that the risks of reporting are too great" (e.g., Knapp, Faley, Ekeberg, & Dubois, 1997, pp. 694–695), or we would argue, that nothing would be done if wrongdoing were reported.

Formal policies to encourage reporting may appear to conflict with the occurrence of wrongdoing, and employees may dismiss them as "lip service." Anecdotally, signaling theory appears to be implicitly understood among the general public (most of whom are non-whistle-blowers); audiences often perceive whistle-blowers to be terribly naïve when they say that they really believed that management did not realize that wrongdoing was occurring and that once informed, correction would occur.

The extent to which wrongdoing will signal unresponsiveness will vary with the situation. For example, if the observer believes that no one else could know about the problem (e.g., the harasser has not bothered anyone else), then that is why it has not been reported or corrected. Or, the observer may believe that the wrongdoing is a very unusual event, but that normally the organization would take swift action when confronted with wrongdoing; in this situation; the mere occurrence of wrongdoing may not signal unresponsiveness at all. In contrast, if the observer believes that no one has reported the wrongdoing because nothing happened when previous wrongdoing was reported, or that the current problem is uncorrected despite management's knowing about it, then the current wrongdoing will signal to a greater extent that management tolerates wrongdoing.

Demoralization.   Research on employees who suffer sexual harassment has suggested that the health and psychological reactions to
experiencing this particular form of organizational wrongdoing are
substantial and negative (Fitzgerald, Drasgow, Hulin, Gelfand, &
Magley, 1997). In addition, wrongdoing detracts from the social and
psychological environment at work, even where the employee is not
the direct target (e.g., financial fraud or product safety problems);
thus, wrongdoing often demoralizes employees. For example, sexual
harassment was shown to have an "ambient" demoralizing effect;
employees who were not the harasser's target but who witnessed it
had lower levels of job satisfaction than did nonobservers (Glomb
et al., 1997). In fact, the path coefficient was larger than for those
who directly experienced the harassment, though both coefficients
were significant. The researchers' model (tested using structural
equation modeling) proposed that the direction of relationship is that
wrongdoing reduces satisfaction (i.e., not that satisfaction increases
the probability of interpretation that an act is wrongful) and their
results were consistent with this proposition. Further, experiencing direct or ambient wrongdoing also was associated with higher
levels of psychological distress symptoms, including anxiety, depression, and life dissatisfaction (Glomb et al., 1997). Later longitudinal
research confirmed the model (Glomb, Munson, Hulin, Bergman, &
Drasgow, 1999), and showed also that sexual harassment influences
work and job withdrawal. To the extent that these findings generalize to other types of wrongdoing, they suggest that organizations
that prevent wrongdoing will benefit not only from the avoidance of
the wrongdoing itself, but they will have more satisfied and committed employees, with lower levels of turnover and other withdrawal.

As with signaling, the extent of demoralization will likely depend
on situational, and perhaps other, factors. We propose that observers
who believe that wrongdoing has occurred but that it has been
corrected will likely be less demoralized than will people who believe
it is continuing despite authorities' awareness of it. They may reason
that in any organization mistakes are sometimes made, especially
by lower-level members, and fixing the problem is the hallmark of a
good organization.

Readers may point out that signaling and demoralization produce
negative affective reactions in organizational members and question
whether they are part of a *decision* process. We include them for two
reasons. First, individuals often face signals that conflict; for example,

they may witness very serious wrongdoing that others obviously know about, but they may also believe that the formal organization policy is not to tolerate wrongdoing, and that the organization could be endangered if it fails to correct wrongdoing. They still must decide how to interpret these signals, which will likely involve cognitive decision making. Compared with the signaling response, demoralization may be more affective in tone, but nonetheless will involve some cognitive sorting out of what is happening. Further, observers of wrongdoing still must decide what to do about the current wrongdoing, which involves a cognitive decision-making effort. The POB model proposes that organizational unresponsiveness and demoralization experienced in Phase 2 will discourage many employees from taking action, by affecting Phase 3.

In Figure 2.1, we note also that the observation of wrongdoing, and the extent to which it is perceived to be corrected or reported in Phase 1, are followed by Phase 3. As noted previously, nonobservers *cannot* proceed to Phase 3 because, by definition, observing wrongdoing is a necessary condition for whistle-blowing. Thus, the final outcome of "no wrongdoing to report" ends the process for them. But the process does not end there for observers who believe the wrongdoing has been reported or is in the process of being corrected. They can proceed to both Phase 2 and Phase 3, since they could decide to report the wrongdoing too. The model proposes they often will be less likely than other observers to do so, because they may believe no one has the responsibility to take further action (Phase 1), may see organizational signals that are less negative (Phase 2), may be less demoralized (Phase 2), and may answer the Phase 3 questions differently than do observers who believe that the wrongdoing has not been reported.

Finally, Figure 2.1 shows that Phase 3 involves decisions about whether to blow the whistle. Signaling and demoralization (Phase 2) may be manifested in variables other than whistle-blowing, such as observers' feeling a lack of satisfaction with or trust in their organizations, employee withdrawal, etc. Signaling and demoralization also may mediate some effects of Phase 1 processes on whistle-blowing (Phase 3). However, as will be discussed later, other variables and processes may have *other, direct* effects on Phase 3. For example, observers who have more proactive personalities (e.g., Bateman & Crant, 1993; Langer, 1983) may be more inclined than other observers of the same wrongdoing to report it.

Phase 3 As shown in **Figure** 2.1, in Phase 3, observers of wrong-doing must make decisions regarding whether it is their responsibility to act on wrongdoing and whether any action is available to them. These questions are analogous to those in the bystander intervention model, but in organizations, generally the decisions are more complex (Dozier & Miceli, 1985). Organization members usually have more time to act than do bystanders to emergencies. Further, more potential consequences, such as possible alienation from coworkers with whom one has worked for many years and disruption of career ambitions, must be considered (Dozier & Miceli, 1985). This assessment may be either a cognitive or an emotional process, or a combination thereof (Gundlach, Douglas, & Martinko, 2003).

If observers of wrongdoing believe either that they do not have responsibility, or that they do but that nothing they could do would make any difference, then they are less likely to blow the whistle, or to take any action, and the process ends, generally, without their taking action. If they do believe they are responsible and that potentially effective actions are available, they weigh the expected costs of blowing the whistle, such as the risk of retaliation, relative to expected benefits, such as the likelihood that reporting it will actually stop serious wrongdoing. They may consider alternative forms of whistle-blowing, such as putting the complaint in writing versus calling someone to discuss it; going to a trusted supervisor versus the board of directors; or remaining anonymous to the complaint recipient (e.g., an ombudsperson), identifying themselves to the complaint recipient but asking for confidentiality, or blowing the whistle more openly. If there are other actions, such as confronting a known wrongdoer directly and confidentially, they will weigh these costs and benefits as well. The POB model proposes that whistle-blowing (and its form) will depend on these decisions.

Utilizing the POB Model to Predict Whistle-Blowing

Various theories of behavior have been used to make predictions about which observers of wrongdoing are more likely to answer the Phase 1, Phase 2, and Phase 3 questions positively. We discuss them below, as we review results regarding specific predictor variables that have been studied empirically. For example, theories of power (e.g., Pfeffer, 1981; Pfeffer & Salancik, 1978), among other factors, are integrated into Phase 3 (Dozier & Miceli, 1985). Observers of wrongdoing who believe themselves to be more powerful are more likely to respond affirmatively to the Phase 3 questions (e.g., Miceli, Near, & Schwenk, 1991). For instance, those who hold important or credible positions— such as Sherron Watkins of Enron—may feel that they are obliged to act, that they can get someone to listen, and that they will escape negative consequences such as retaliation. As another example, moral intensity theory (e.g., Jones, 1991) provides a basis for predicting that the type of issue and its seriousness will affect the perception that wrongdoing has occurred—when the focal activity evokes moral intensity—and ultimately whether whistle-blowing will take place.

The POB model has been generally supported, but the correspondence with the bystander literature is imperfect, not surprisingly. For example, conflicting results have emerged regarding whether the number of other observers of organizational wrongdoing (perceived or actual) affect whistle-blowing, perhaps because of situational interactions (Miceli, Near, & Schwenk, 1991; Near & Miceli, 1996). As noted previously, whistle-blowers usually have much more time to think before acting than do witnesses to an emergency; further, interrelationships with other members of their employing organization would differ from those of strangers who might encounter street crime (Dozier & Miceli, 1985). Depending on the situation, other variables might also distinguish the emergency situation that is generally the focus of the bystander literature from the wrongdoing situation that is more usually examined in the whistle-blowing literature.

Results of Empirical Tests: Personal Variables

The POB model suggests many variables that may affect the decision to blow the whistle, and although research since the 1970s has produced some useful results (Near & Miceli, 1996), many hypotheses remain untested. These variables can be roughly categorized as "personal" (e.g., personality or dispositional factors, demographics), "situational" (e.g., the seriousness of the perceived wrongdoing or the type of wrongdoing), or "person by situation" (an example of this would be the fact that sexual harassment wrongdoing is usually directed against female employees, so that they are more likely to blow the whistle about this type of wrongdoing than are male employees). Although all readers might not classify all variables as we have here, our intent is simply to provide an easily understood classification scheme, rather than to propose that it is the only or the best possible scheme.

Most studies on "who blows the whistle?", including scenario studies, have focused somewhat more on situational variables, or have utilized samples that were somewhat homogeneous demographically, limiting tests of personal variables (e.g., Keenan, 2002a). We last summarized results from this research in 1996 (Near & Miceli, 1996).

In 2005, a comprehensive meta-analysis of studies of predictors of two different dependent variables—(a) self-reported actual whistle-blowing, and (b) intent to blow the whistle—was published (Mesmer-Magnus & Viswesvaran, 2005). The studies of actual whistle-blowing behavior relied on self-report data from respondents who said they had observed wrongdoing in their organizations during some specified time period (usually the last 12 months). The studies of intent to blow the whistle relied on the use of role-playing scenarios, which were presented to respondents with the instruction to indicate whether they would blow the whistle if they were confronted with the circumstances depicted in these hypothetical cases. Comparison of findings using the two measures of whistle-blowing showed different findings: the lists of predictors were not the same for the two measures. Mesmer-Magnus and Viswesvaran concluded that the findings from the two types of studies differed significantly, because of the difference in dependent variable; clearly method also differed for these two types of studies, although we would concur with the researchers that dependent variable was probably more important. On some research questions, there are very few studies that the researchers could actually use in their analysis, so we do not mean to imply that this finding holds for all questions (e.g., different studies used different variables to measure the whistle-blower's moral stance, so they could not be lumped together or directly compared). Nonetheless, this result makes it clear that whistle-blowing studies using survey methods may not yield findings that are directly comparable to those obtained from scenario research.

The discussion below presents studies by the phase in the POB model to which they most closely relate in order to make the theoretical linkage clearer. Where relevant, we summarize results from studies included in the Mesmer-Magnus and Viswesvaran meta-analysis (Table 2.1). We also summarize results from additional studies completed since publication of our last review in 1996, or the meta-analysis in 2005, and not covered in those two reviews, for

TABLE 2.1 Empirical Results Related to the Organization Member's Personal Characteristics That Predict Observation of Wrongdoing and Were Not Previously Reported in Near and Miceli (1996) or Mesmer-Magnus and Viswesvaran (2005)

Predictors	Studies[a]											
	A	B	C	D	E	F	G	H	I	J	K	L
Personality/dispositional												
Negative affectivity	+											
Demographic												
Marital status (married)	–	–	–	–	–	–	–	–	–			
Age			–	–	–	–	–	–	–	–		
Education			–	–	–	–	–	–	–	–		
Gender (male)											–	
Job situation												
Rank											–	
Pay	–											

Note: + = positive relationship; – = negative relationship; 0 = no significant relationship.

[a]Studies are listed in order of first appearance in the text: A. (Miceli et al., 2001b); B. (Lee et al., 2004); C. (Coles, 1986); D. (Dougherty et al., 1996); E. (Fain & Anderton, 1987); F. (Hesson-McInnis & Fitzgerald, 1997); G. (LaFontain & Tredeau, 1986); H. (S. E. Martin, 1984); I. (Schneider, 1982); J. (Tangri et al., 1982); K. (Everton, 1996); L. (Bergman et al., 2002).

whatever reason. In Chapter 3, we will continue with a discussion of situational factors, and person by situation interactions. Finally, we note that not all authors explicitly utilized the POB model, but for ease of communication, where variables relevant to the POB model were tested, they are included here.

Personal Variables Proposed to Affect Decisions in Phase 1

We know of very few studies that have treated the outcomes of Phase 1 (e.g., observation of perceived wrongdoing) as the dependent variable, and most have been limited to sexual harassment as the type of wrongdoing involved. Research in this area has focused largely on predictors of sexual harassment and whether the victim labeled the activities as sexual harassment. Sociologists note that deviant behavior is not really recognized as "deviant" until people "label" it as such (e.g., Merton, 1957). In addition, the effects on the victim (e.g., psychological stress resulting from the harassment) have been examined. Obviously, then, any conclusions must be viewed as preliminary and a great deal more study (e.g., of other types of wrongdoing) is needed.

Of course, each type of wrongdoing is in some way unique, but sexual harassment may differ from other types of wrongdoing. For example, the employee who reports the harassment is usually the person who suffered the harassment—unlike other types of wrongdoing where the employee may observe the event but not suffer most directly from its occurrence (e.g., Knapp et al., 1997). Further, the events surrounding the wrongdoing may be less ambiguous in the case of sexual harassment than in other cases of wrongdoing, because the employee directly observes the events. On the other hand, whether the events constitute sexual harassment and therefore wrongdoing may be more ambiguous than in other cases of wrongdoing. For example, accounting errors are probably less ambiguously wrong than repeated flirting, which may be viewed as sexual harassment in some contexts and not in others. For this reason, the importance of the labeling process is probably better recognized in research on sexual harassment than in research on other forms of wrongdoing.

As noted above, Phase 1 involves the prediction of which employees will believe that they have observed wrongdoing and that anyone is obliged to act. Thus, the outcomes are (a) observation of perceived wrongdoing or not—or labeling of an activity as wrongdoing—and (b) whether the wrongdoing is believed to have been previously reported or corrected. We know of no published study that examined the latter and separated such observers from other observers. Distinguishing this group in future studies may clarify some findings, because in some ways this group is predicted to behave like nonobservers, and in other ways like whistle-blowers and other observers.

Below we review studies in which the labeling of wrongdoing is the outcome variable of interest and the predictors include the potential whistle-blower's personality, moral judgment, and demographic characteristics, as well as the characteristics of the individual's job situation. Although the characteristics of the job situation can be classified as situational variables and regrouped with situational variables in Chapter 3, they are frequently measured as perceived by the potential whistle-blower and may vary with the individual. And, grouping them together with other individual variables is consistent with our organization scheme in our 1992 book, which may facilitate comparisons. In subsequent sections focusing on Phase 3, we review research in which whistle-blowing intent and actual whistle-blowing are the outcome variables of interest.

Personality or Dispositional Characteristics

Negative Affectivity.   As noted above, we know of only one study since 1996 (Miceli et al., 2001b) examining the relationship between observation of wrongdoing in general and dispositional characteristics; it focused on negative affectivity (Watson & Clark, 1984). Theory on negative affectivity clearly suggests a basis for predicting that different individuals will judge the same event to be more or less wrongful. Negative affectivity (NA) is an enduring disposition to experience subjective distress (Watson & Walker, 1996); people high in NA are more critical of themselves and others, and experience more stress, anxiety, anger, fear, and guilt (Watson & Clark, 1984). This trait influences the way employees perceive and react to objects and events in the work environment (e.g., Watson & Clark, 1984), in that they interpret neutral or ambiguous situations more negatively than do other people (Parkes, 1990). Hence, negative affectivity may influence perceptions that wrongdoing is occurring and that action is warranted, two key decisions in Phase 1. Consistent with this reasoning, preliminary empirical evidence suggests support for the model, in that observers of perceived wrongdoing had higher levels of negative affectivity than did nonobservers (Miceli et al., 2001b).

Moral Judgment and Values.   In our 1992 book, we discussed extensively the theory of moral judgment development (e.g., Rest, 1979) and how moral judgment would likely affect Phase 1. In general, the theory, applied to the POB, suggests that organization members with high levels of moral judgment development would be more inclined to judge a questionable act to be wrongful and deserving of action than would other members, thus increasing the likelihood of perceived (continuing) wrongdoing as an outcome. We described the existing research in our 1992 book, and in our 1996 review article. Unfortunately, we know of no research examining these propositions that has been completed since the prior review.

Studies of moral judgment and values have focused instead on their relative efficacy in predicting whistle-blowing intent or behavior, as summarized in the sections below on Phase 3 of the POB model.

Demographic Characteristics   Research on sexual harassment, one specific type of wrongdoing that occurs in organizations, sheds more light on the relevance of personal characteristics of the employee to whether she (less frequently he) observed the wrongdoing. Here, we must caution the reader that the type of wrongdoing may be extremely important. The variables that cause sexual harassment to occur or be directed at certain organization members, or particular observers to believe they have experienced it, may be very different from the variables that cause other types of wrongdoing or lead it to be perceived. For example, researchers have found that more "vulnerable" employees were more likely to experience sexual harassment, when compared to other employees (Fitzgerald, Drasgow, & Magley, 1999); the measures of vulnerability correspond to measures that we believe indicate low employee power (e.g., low hierarchical level). In contrast, more powerful employees may be more likely to witness serious financial wrongdoing, for example, because they have access by virtue of their positions to documentation than do less powerful employees. Thus, the type of wrongdoing observed, or its content, or the extent to which it is labeled as such, might depend in part on the observer's demographic characteristics.

Perceived sexual harassment varied with marital status, with married employees less vulnerable than others (Coles, 1986; Dougherty, Turban, Olson, Dwyer, & LaPrese, 1996; Fain & Anderton, 1987; Hesson-McInnis & Fitzgerald, 1997; LaFontain & Tredeau, 1986; S. E. Martin, 1984; Schneider, 1982; Tangri, Burt, & Johnson, 1982). It decreased with age (Coles, 1986; Dougherty et al., 1996; Fain & Anderton, 1987; Hesson-McInnis & Fitzgerald, 1997; LaFontain & Tredeau, 1986; S. E. Martin, 1984; Schneider, 1982; Tangri et al., 1982), and education level (Coles, 1986; Dougherty et al., 1996; Fain & Anderton, 1987; Hesson-McInnis & Fitzgerald, 1997; LaFontain & Tredeau, 1986; S. E. Martin, 1984; Schneider, 1982; Tangri et al., 1982). Thus, young, unmarried women with lower education levels may be seen as powerless targets by harassers, and hence they may be more likely to experience and perceive sexual harassment. Thus, we would say that these employees were more likely to observe wrongdoing, when compared to other employees. Yet, these employees may also be less likely to blow the whistle because they view themselves as power-less in the organization, and therefore less likely to be effective in stopping wrongdoing and more likely to suffer retaliation than other employees—but that is a separate question, addressed in Phase 3.

One study in which a research assistant asked student partici-pants to commit wrongdoing (i.e., to fudge the data purportedly to make the study publishable) found some evidence of a gender effect for labeling (Everton, 1996). Women viewed the research assistant as less likable and less ethical, and they labeled his actions as less acceptable, than did men.

Job Situation Characteristics   Sexual harassment has been shown to decrease with rank in the hierarchical level of the organization (Bergman, Langhout, Cortina, & Fitzgerald, 2002) and with employee's pay grade (Lee et al., 2004). This and all other studies of sexual harass-ment cited here measure harassment on the basis of the perception of the employee being harassed, unless otherwise specified.

Future Research Questions Regarding Phase 1   Future research is needed to identify other variables that predict whether employ-ees exposed to organizational wrongdoing actually label it as wrong-doing, apart from whether they then choose to blow the whistle on it. One source of information could be a qualitative analysis of anecdotes and case studies. The *Time* article suggested that Sherron Watkins and the other two whistle-blowers were perfectionist in tendency. Because many of their colleagues apparently saw the same evidence that confronted the whistle-blowers but noticed nothing amiss, we wonder whether the perfectionism caused these whistle-blowers to notice wrongdoing when others around them did not. Then, of course, empirical testing is needed.

Personal Variables Proposed to Affect Decisions in Phase 2

There has been very little research concerning Phase 2, other than that on sexual harassment. What has been done has provided sup-port for the prediction that observation of wrongdoing is demoraliz-ing and can signal unresponsiveness, and we will describe this work. Unfortunately, we are not aware of any studies that identify personal variables that affect signaling or demoralization; clearly research is needed. For example, are certain types of employees more likely to be demoralized by wrongdoing, or do different groups interpret signals differently?

Experiencing sexual harassment reduces job satisfaction and has other negative consequences for the victim (e.g., Glomb et al., 1999, 1997; Knapp et al., 1997; Magley, 2002). It is true that the target of sexual harassment may be more directly a victim than are those who observe other types of wrongdoing (Knapp et al., 1997). But research also shows that indirect (ambient) observation of sexual harassment directed toward others lowers job satisfaction and has other effects similar to those experienced by targets of the harassment (Glomb et al., 1999, 1997).

One study in the whistle-blowing literature, involving more than 1,000 military and civilian employees at a large military base, provided some support for the signaling hypothesis (Miceli et al., 2001b). Organizations can signal responsiveness by not allowing wrongdoing in the first place and responding quickly to correct it when it does occur. Consistent with this notion, employees who did not observe wrongdoing, inactive observers who believed the wrongdoing was being corrected without their action, and whistle-blowers using only internal channels had relatively high levels of self-efficacy for whistle-blowing (Miceli et al., 2001b), that is, beliefs that they could bring about change through whistle-blowing, such as belief that "if I were to report an illegal or improper act, I would get results." Inactive observers who did not believe that the wrongdoing was being corrected and whistle-blowers who used external channels (most of whom had first tried to get the problem corrected through internal channels), had lower levels of self-efficacy for whistle-blowing (Miceli et al., 2001b).

This study also provided some support for the demoralization hypothesis, to the extent that feeling demoralized is reflected in perceived organizational support, that is, "global beliefs concerning the extent to which an organization values their contributions and cares about their well-being" (Hutchinson, Sowa, Eisenberger, & Huntington, 1986, p. 500). If the observation of uncorrected wrongdoing is demoralizing, then we would expect that whistle-blowers and inactive observers who thought the wrongdoing was not being rectified (Miceli et al., 2001b) would have lower levels of perceived organizational support than would other employees (e.g., non-observers). Data supported this hypothesis.

If future research confirms the proposed causal directions, there are at least two important practical implications. First, resources dedicated toward developing and publicizing channels and training employees as to what is expected may be lost if the organization does not demonstrate prevention and correction. Second, organizations that prevent or swiftly correct wrongdoing can enjoy the perhaps unexpected side effects of better morale in general.

Personal Variables Proposed to Affect Decisions in Phase 3

In Phase 3, observers of perceived wrongdoing ask themselves whether they are responsible for doing something about the wrong-doing and whether there is an available action that might be effective in stopping wrongdoing. Observers of wrongdoing also must decide whether the costs of acting, including possible retaliation and time expended, outweigh the benefits likely to result, which may include the desired termination of the wrongdoing as well as cash awards and other benefits (Dozier & Miceli, 1985). As noted previously, power theories have been integrated within this phase of the POB model, because, for example, employees who have more power may be more likely to believe that they can both bring about change and escape retaliation (e.g., Near & Miceli, 1987). Some demographic character-istics, for example, may serve as indicators of power.

Most research examining characteristics of whistle-blowers has controlled for observation of wrongdoing, by comparing the char-acteristics of inactive observers and whistle-blowers versus those of nonobservers, or by providing scenarios describing the same wrongdoing to all respondents. Although we recognize that these are imperfect controls, they do help to sort out how people who believe they have witnessed organizational wrongdoing may differ in their reactions to it, depending on a number of variables. We exclude from our discussion two studies that did not compare whistle-blowers to others but instead considered differences among whistle-blowers; the first compared whistle-blowers who used external channels to those using internal channels (Dworkin & Baucus, 1998) and the second compared whistle-blowers who varied from one another in terms of the different types of wrongdoing that they reported (Near et al., 2004). Although these studies shed light on the whistle-blowing process, their results do not pertain to the POB model and predictors of whistle-blowing versus not blowing the whistle. Table 2.2 summarizes the recent studies relevant to Phase 3.

Personality or Dispositional Characteristics   In their meta-analysis, Mesmer-Magnus and Viswesvaran (2005) found no research involving personality or dispositional characteristics as predictors of whistle-blowing. In 1996, we cited several studies using personality variables, including tolerance for ambiguity, field dependence, internal locus of control, low self-esteem, and low self-monitoring. Positive results were found for all except internal locus of control. One study omitted from the 1992 and 1996 reviews and the 2005 meta-analysis reported results that may be relevant (Treviño & Youngblood, 1990). In that study, researchers asked MBA student participants to undertake a managerial in-basket task including some wrongdoing scenarios; whistle-blowing was among the types of responses that participants could select or write-in. Treviño and Youngblood found that, consistent with theory, internal locus of control predicted more ethical behavior, as classified by the researchers. Among those behaviors they categorized as more rather than less ethical was whistle-blowing.

Most of the prior results were based on respondents' answers to hypothetical questions concerning scenarios, in which the dependent variable was intent to blow the whistle if respondents were placed in a situation like that of the scenario. This variable is different from actual or self-reported whistle-blowing, and from intent to blow the whistle in response to perceived wrongdoing that respondents actually faced in their current work setting. Based on the results of the 2005 meta-analysis, we wonder whether these results would be the same if the outcome variable were actual whistle-blowing rather than intent to blow the whistle (Mesmer-Magnus & Viswesvaran, 2005).

Positive Affectivity.   Theory suggests that positive affectivity will affect whistle-blowing because observers who have high levels of positive affectivity may perceive they have greater chances for success in getting wrongdoing stopped and in avoiding retaliation, that is, that it will enhance the expected benefit-cost ratio (Miceli et al., 2001b). Only one known study has examined this hypothesis, and some support was found, in that whistle-blowers had higher levels of

TABLE 2.2   Empirical Results Related to the Observer's Personal Characteristics That Predict Whistle-Blowing or Whistle-Blowing Intent and Were Not Previously Reported in Near and Miceli (1996) or Mesmer-Magnus and Viswesvaran (2005)

Predictors	Studies[a]									
	A	B	C	D	E	F	G	H	I	J
Personality/dispositional										
Positive affectivity	+									
Internal locus of control		0							Mi	Mo
Self-esteem		0								
Proactive personality	+									
Relativism		0								
Idealism		0								
Authoritarianism						0				
Self-righteousness						0				
Moral judgment and values										
Internal religiosity								+	Mi	
Moral judgment										+
Demographic										
Marital status				0			0	0		
Age				+			+			
Tenure			+	0	+				Mi	
Education			+				+			−
Gender (male)					0	0	0	+	−	
Race (majority)					+					
Job situation										
Rank										
Pay			+	0						
Job performance							0			
Supervisory status				0			0	+		

Note: + = positive relationship; − = negative relationship; 0 = no significant relationship; Mi = mixed; Mo = moderator (interacted with another predictor).

[a] Studies are listed in order of first appearance in the text: A. (Miceli et al., 2001b); B. (Starkey, 1998); C. (Brewer & Selden, 1998); D. (Lee et al., 2004); E. (Goldman, 2001); F. (McCutcheon, 2000); G. (Rothschild & Miethe, 1999); H. (Miethe, 1999); I. (Wise, 1995); J. (Chiu, 2003).

positive affectivity than did inactive observers who believed that the wrongdoing had not been rectified (Miceli et al., 2001b).

Internal Orientation (Locus of Control).   Like positive affectivity, internal locus of control is predicted to increase whistle-blowing through enhancing the expected benefit-cost ratio. Two dissertations and one published study that included this variable—all based on scenarios—were not included in either review, and they yielded mixed results. When scenarios describing wrongdoing were presented to hospital employees, no relationship was found between employees' external orientation, or locus of control, and intent to blow the whistle (Starkey, 1998). In a second dissertation, one measure of internal locus of control, but not another, was significantly related to students' whistle-blowing intentions, when reacting to some scenarios but not others (Wise, 1995). In a scenario study, Chiu found that internal locus of control moderated the effect of ethical judgment on whistle-blowing by Chinese managers (Chiu, 2003).

Self-Esteem.   Self-esteem also should increase the expected benefit-cost ratio, because those with high dispositional self-esteem may be more confident in their abilities to persuade authorities to correct wrongdoing, and to avoid career-ending retaliation. But no relationship between self-esteem and intent to blow the whistle was found (Starkey, 1998).

Proactive Personality.   In their early theoretical and empirical work on proactive personality, Bateman and Crant (1993) proposed specifically that whistle-blowers would be more proactive than other persons who have observed wrongdoing. Proactive personality stems from people's need to control their surroundings, and it is reflected in the extent to which individuals take action to influence their environments (Bateman & Crant, 1993; Langer, 1983). Research shows that proactive personality is a narrowly focused personality trait that is consistently associated with two of the "Big Five" factors, Conscientiousness and Extraversion, yet it explains variance in organizational phenomena beyond that explained by the Big Five (Crant, 1995; Crant & Bateman, 2000; Seibert, Kraimer, & Crant, 2001). Proactivity has been shown to predict real estate sales success (Crant, 1995), supervisors' ratings of their subordinates' charismatic leadership (Crant &

Bateman, 2000), career salary, promotions, and satisfaction (Seibert, Crant, & Kraimer, 1999). However, one longitudinal study showed no relationship between proactivity and "voice" (Seibert et al., 2001); whistle-blowing is one way to voice concerns.

The "prototypic proactive personality" is "relatively unconstrained by situational forces, and ... effects environmental change" (Bateman & Crant, 1993, p. 105); thus, when highly proactive personalities observe wrongdoing, they will be more likely than other organizational members to blow the whistle (Crant, 1995). Other researchers have also suggested a linkage with "constructive dissent"; "when faced with a leader whose actions appear inappropriate, (high proactive) individuals bring the perceived inconsistencies to the manager's attention; and they actively oppose a decision they consider morally wrong" (Campbell, 2000, p. 54).

In terms of the POB model, observers with higher levels of proactive personality will believe that it is their responsibility to act, because they are more apt to see problems and try to solve them as part of their general approach to situations. Persons with high levels of proactivity will also be more likely to believe that actions are available to them, because they want to control their environment, and enjoy challenges and believe they are good at meeting them. Highly proactive persons also may believe they will succeed in getting wrongdoing stopped and that they will avoid retaliation and other costs, because they have succeeded in problem solving previously, and because they may be less sensitive to environmental cues suggesting otherwise than observers scoring lower on the proactivity scale.

Anecdotal evidence is consistent with these predictions. Annually, *Time* magazine selects a "Person of the Year," representing its Editorial Board's view as to which individual affected history most during that year (Lacayo & Ripley, 2002). In 2002, *Time* selected three Persons of the Year, Sherron Watkins, Coleen Rowley, and Cynthia Cooper, who blew the whistle on wrongdoing in Enron, the U.S. Federal Bureau of Investigation (FBI), and WorldCom, respectively. The reporters (Lacayo & Ripley, 2002) suggested that Sherron Watkins and the other two whistle-blowers were aggressive about pursuing situations that they thought were wrong, throughout their lives. The one controlled empirical study of which we are aware has shown that whistle-blowers (internal and external) have significantly more proactive personalities than do inactive observers, although the effect size is not large (Miceli et al., 2001b). Like the voice findings cited previously, these findings suggest that other factors may be involved. For example, highly proactive people may be more inclined to speak up and oppose wrongdoing, but this same disposition may lead them to be more ambitious and concerned about career success. If, like Sherron Watkins, observers with more proactive personalities believe that acting will truly help the organization, they might see no inconsistency between voicing concerns and managing their careers so they blow the whistle. But other proactive persons might see a conflict and resolve it in favor of proactively managing their career outcomes, saying nothing about the wrongdoing, or engaging in other proactive behaviors, such as information seeking, relationship building, and positive framing (e.g., Wanberg & Kammeyer-Mueller, 2000).

Relativism and Idealism.   Starkey proposed that two ethical dispositions, relativism and idealism, would be associated with whistle-blowing intent. But there was no relationship between these traits and hospital employees' intent to blow the whistle when they played the role of the wrongdoing observer in the scenarios provided (Starkey, 1998).

Authoritarianism and Self-Righteousness.   One scenario study not included in prior reviews considered whether the dispositional characteristics of authoritarianism and self-righteousness influence observers to blow the whistle (McCutcheon, 2000). Citing earlier work (Altemeyer, 1999; Falbo & Belk, 1985), McCutcheon noted that authoritarians "typically are very obedient to those in positions of authority and they are intolerant of ambiguity" (McCutcheon, 2000, p. 3); self-righteous people "are convinced that there is one correct answer to every problem and they are eager to criticize alternative behaviors" (McCutcheon, 2000, p. 2). Although McCutcheon did not explicitly describe the theory linking these characteristics to whistle-blowing, in terms of our model, authoritarians may believe that they are not responsible for acting on wrongdoing (especially by a higher-up), thus decreasing whistle-blowing. In contrast, self-righteous employees may believe that not only are they responsible, they have no choice but to blow the whistle, increasing whistle-blowing. However, none of the measures of these variables was related to whistle-blowing intent.

One interesting feature of this study was that "a close acquaintance" also rated each respondent's intent. There was a significant correlation (.37) between the self-rated intent and acquaintance-rated intent scores, providing some evidence of the meaningfulness of the self-rated intent measure.

Moral Judgment and Values.   The media sometimes report anecdotes in which whistle-blowers attribute their action at least partially to their religious or moral beliefs (e.g., Bates, 1999). As of 1996, research results suggested that whistle-blowing was related to values about whistle-blowing, but not consistently related to moral judgment, as reported in three studies. At that time we found one study each in which respondents said that they engaged in whistle-blowing because they felt morally compelled to do so, because doing so fit with their religious beliefs, or because whistle-blowing was socially responsible.

In the meta-analysis of studies completed before 2005, Mesmer-Magnus and Viswesvaran found that ethical judgment was unrelated to actual whistle-blowing ($r = -.08$) in two studies, and positively related to whistle-blowing intent ($r = .45$) in four studies (Mesmer-Magnus & Viswesvaran, 2005). Religiosity was not examined.

Other studies not included in prior reviews or the meta-analysis may be of interest. In one study (McNeely & Meglino, 1994), agents' value of concern for others and empathy predicted prosocial behaviors directed at specific individuals; however, whether this finding would extend to the prosocial behavior of whistle-blowing and to situations in which specific individuals are not known or the target is not an individual (such as society at large, or a principle) is unclear.

Citing a recent literature review (Loe, Ferrell, & Mansfield, 2000), Ashkanasy, Windsor, and Treviño (2006) noted that "only a few studies of ethical decision-making and behavior in organizations have studied the influence of CMD (cognitive moral development)" (p. 451). We found five studies that included measures of moral judgment and values and whistle-blowing, and were not included in earlier reviews or the meta-analysis. First, in a scenario-based dissertation (Wise, 1995), intrinsic religiosity was significantly related to students' whistle-blowing intentions, when reacting to some scenarios but not others. Second, in a scenario-based study of Chinese managers, moral judgment showed main effects in predicting whistle-blowing intent, as well as an interaction effect with internal locus of control (Chiu, 2003). Third, in a broad survey based on data from diverse samples, the quantitative survey measures of moral behavior were unrelated to actual whistle-blowing, but qualitative interview data, coded later by researchers, indicated that 79% of whistle-blowers said their personal values entered into their decision to blow the whistle (Rothschild & Miethe, 1999). Fourth, MBA students' cognitive moral development as measured by the Defining Issues Test (Rest, 1979) was associated with more ethical decision making (including intended whistle-blowing) to in-basket scenario wrongdoing (Treviño & Youngblood, 1990). This finding was replicated in a fifth study (Ashkanasy et al., 2006); this study also utilized scenarios with MBA participants.

Results from the meta-analysis and the qualitative data suggest to us that employees believe that they would blow the whistle in the future or have blown the whistle in the past because of their values and that moral reasoning may predict how people say they would behave or how others should behave. But statistical evidence is scant that employees have actually blown the whistle because of moral reasoning or values. We recognize that too little research has been completed to view this conclusion as anything but tentative, but it fascinates us, because it flies in the face of conventional wisdom. On the other hand, there is evidence that whistle-blowers do feel more "morally compelled" to report the wrongdoing than do inactive observers (Miceli, Near, & Schwenk, 1991). This evidence suggests that something in the situation, for example, the nature of wrongdoing, knowledge of someone being hurt by the wrongdoing, or other circumstances, may influence—or interact with personal characteristics to influence—whistle-blowing.

A review of the research investigating the linkages between religiosity and the broader classification of ethical behavior revealed that, similarly, there was no general relationship (Weaver & Agle, 2002). However, Weaver and Agle (2002, p. 95) proposed that personal and contextual variables such as role expectations may play important roles in "the religion-behavior matrix." Thus, future research could utilize their framework to develop theory regarding the potential relationships to whistle-blowing.

Demographic Characteristics Empirical research prior to 1996 showed some tendency of whistle-blowers to be relatively powerful employees, for example, they were supervisors or higher rank, and more senior, with higher pay and performance (Near & Miceli, 1996). We know of no published study that showed that whistle-blowers had little power (junior, nonsupervisory, low-paid employees, for example) relative to observers who did not blow the whistle. Nonetheless, in many studies, there was no relationship between whistle-blowing and demographic or position variables, so we cannot conclude that whistle-blowers are always more likely to be powerful employees.

In the 2005 meta-analysis (Mesmer-Magnus & Viswesvaran, 2005), age was correlated with whistle-blowing intent in three studies ($r = .19$), but not tested in studies of actual whistle-blowing. Gender was unrelated to whistle-blowing intent in two studies ($r = -.05$) but being male was related to actual whistle-blowing ($r = .13$), despite the popular view that women are more likely than men to engage in dissent (Alford, 2003). The correlation between education and whistle-blowing was zero in three studies of whistle-blowing intent and six studies of actual whistle-blowing. Tenure on the job was also unrelated to whistle-blowing intent and only weakly related to actual whistle-blowing ($r = .10$).

Findings in studies not included in the meta-analysis are similar. Although two studies reported a positive correlation with age and years of service to the organization (Brewer & Selden, 1998; Miethe, 1999), another reported no relationship to actual self-reported whistle-blowing (Lee et al., 2004). Another study using scenarios reported no relationship between age and ethical decision making, though this may have been a function of range restriction due to reliance on an MBA student sample (Ashkanasy et al., 2006). Age (included as a control variable) was related to whistle-blowing intentions with some scenarios but not with others (Wise, 1995). In a sample of police and civilian employees, the number of years of service at current agency was unrelated to self-reported whistle-blowing frequency or hypothetical willingness to blow the whistle (Rothwell & Baldwin, 2006, 2007).

Education was positively correlated with whistle-blowing in two studies (Brewer & Selden, 1998; Miethe, 1999). Marital status was not significantly related to actual whistle-blowing in large surveys using diverse but nonrandom samples (Miethe, 1999; Rothschild & Miethe, 1999).

Media reports have called attention to the role of gender in whistle-blowing. For example, in the *Time* article on the three Persons of the Year, Lacayo and Ripley (2002) observed that "there has been talk that their gender is not a coincidence; that women, as outsiders, have less at stake in their organizations and so might be more willing to expose weaknesses. They (the three whistle-blowers) don't think so. As it happens, studies have shown that women are actually a bit less likely than men to be whistle-blowers." Although the authors cited no sources, they could have been referring to earlier reviews of the academic literature (Miceli & Near, 1992; Near & Miceli, 1996). Like the meta-analysis, these reviews identified *no* studies of whistle-blowing and similar behaviors (e.g., reporting shoplifters) in which women were more likely to report wrongdoing, several in which men were more likely to report, and several studies showing no significant gender differences.

The findings on gender from studies not included in prior reviews also are mixed. Miethe found that female employees in the 1993 MSPB sample were underrepresented among whistle-blowers (Miethe, 1999), but they used a univariate analysis, not controlling for other independent variables. A scenario-based dissertation involving college students (not included in the prior review) found that, with some scenarios, women registered higher whistle-blowing intentions than did men (Wise, 1995), but another scenario study reported just the opposite (Ashkanasy et al., 2006). More recent studies (Goldman, 2001; McCutcheon, 2000; Rothschild & Miethe, 1999) have found no gender differences.

We know of no study documenting the investment effect (covarying with gender) proposed by the journalists. Contrary to their proposition, research has suggested that those with *less* at stake more frequently are inactive observers than are those with greater investment (e.g., Miceli & Near, 1984) or that the relationship is curvilinear (Somers & Casal, 1994). People with less time or other investment in their organization may have less to lose if retaliated against for whistle-blowing. But they may be less capable of getting powerful others to act due to lower credibility or perceived value to the organization and may care less about whether the wrongdoing is corrected. They may find it easier to leave an organization where conditions are unacceptable, because they do not forfeit as much in accumulated benefits, may have more transferable or current skills, may face less age discrimination, or other reasons. Therefore, they may elect to leave rather than take on the often costly battle of whistle-blowing; research indicates that exit is often chosen in lieu of voice in response to an intolerable situation (Hirschman, 1970; Moore, 2000).

In fact, theory suggests that men will be somewhat more likely to report wrongdoing than will women, for at least three reasons (Miceli & Near, 1992). First, men may occupy positions where more serious wrongdoing is more likely to be observed, because they are more likely than women to hold higher-status positions (England, 1979), and differences in observation opportunity would affect Phase 1 of the model. Some evidence also suggests that supervisors are more knowledgeable about how to respond to wrongdoing or where to report it, but this effect is reduced at higher levels in the organization (Keenan, 1990), which would affect Phase 3 of the model.

Second, men may be more likely than women to be members of professions where whistle-blowing is encouraged as part of a code of ethics, for example, engineers or accountants (Phase 3). Third, whistle-blowing is often seen as deviant or nonconforming to formal or informal organizational norms against "finking" (Dozier & Miceli, 1985), while the majority may tacitly or explicitly endorse "going along to get along," which could increase the perceived costs of action. Some research suggests that women may conform more to a majority opinion than do men (Costanzo & Shaw, 1966), though the evidence is not conclusive (Eagly, 1983). Obviously, gender roles and social pressures regarding appropriate behavior for men and women have changed since this research was conducted, so it is not clear that this effect would be observed today. Therefore, we do expect a slight apparent gender effect, but that this effect will disappear once the effects of wrongdoing observation, professional norms, and supervisory status are controlled.

Job Situation Characteristics
Job Variables.   As noted previously, because pay, performance, and professional or supervisory status, or role responsibility may reflect the power of the whistle-blower, which affects assessments of costs and benefits in Phase 3, these variables are likely to be positively correlated with whistle-blowing. There was some evidence to support all of them as predictors of whistle-blowing, as reported in the 1996 review (Near & Miceli, 1996).   In the 2005 review (Mesmer-Magnus & Viswesvaran, 2005), no studies of pay were included, but job level was weakly related to both whistle-blowing intent ($r = .10$) and actual whistle-blowing ($r = .08$). Job performance was related to actual whistle-blowing ($r = .11$) in two studies but less strongly to whistle-blowing intent in two studies ($r = .05$). Similarly, role

responsibility was related to whistle-blowing intent in four studies ($r = .15$) but less so to actual whistle-blowing in six studies ($r = .06$). Thus, these status variables showed weak or inconsistent relationships to whistle-blowing.

An effect for pay was found in one study (Brewer & Selden, 1998); in another, pay grade predicted observation of wrongdoing, which accounted for the apparent effects of pay grade on actual whistle-blowing (Lee et al., 2004). Supervisory status was unrelated to whistle-blowing (Lee et al., 2004). In an interview study relying on a national sample that was not randomly selected, the authors found no sociodemographic or job situation characteristics that distinguished whistle-blowers from "silent observers" (Rothschild & Miethe, 1999), including number of promotions and supervisory position. A recent study of police officers and civilian employees in the state of Georgia (Rothwell & Baldwin, 2007, p. 348) found that supervisory status was a significant predictor of self-reported frequency of whistle-blowing, measured as "how many times (a respondent) had reported minor violations, major violations, misdemeanors, and felonies," divided by the number of times the respondent had observed each type of misconduct, that is, four proportions were calculated. The authors also measured "willingness to report wrongdoing," because many respondents may not have observed wrongdoing. Supervisory status also predicted all of these types of wrongdoing, except felonies. Similar findings from this sample were reported elsewhere (Rothwell & Baldwin, 2006).

Satisfaction and Commitment to the Organization. Although satisfaction and commitment to the organization are influenced by the situation (e.g., Hodson, 2002), in 1996 we classified these as job situation characteristics variables (as a subcategory of personal characteristics) and continue it here for three reasons. First, this eases comparisons to that prior review. Second, affective reactions to the job or workplace may also be influenced by personal characteristics (e.g., Judge, Heller, & Mount, 2002), and scores will obviously vary from person to person, even within largely similar situations. Third, we want to distinguish these from situational characteristics perhaps of greatest interest relative to whistle-blowing—those pertaining to the wrongdoing itself and to the organization, as described in Chapter 3. Thus, we have continued the categorization from the prior review, but we agree with those who would argue that either classification could be justified.

Our earlier review (Near & Miceli, 1996) indicated that some studies showed whistle-blowers are more satisfied and committed than inactive observers and perceive the organization to be more just. In a more recent scenario study of whistle-blowing, there was no relationship between whistle-blowing and job satisfaction or organizational commitment (Sims & Keenan, 1998). This study was one of two that Mesmer-Magnus and Viswesvaran included in their meta-analysis of job satisfaction and intent to blow the whistle, in which the average correlation was zero. In the two studies of actual whistle-blowing, job satisfaction was correlated more strongly ($r = .19$). They also found eight studies of organization commitment and whistle-blowing intent, but the correlation was again essentially zero, as was also the case in the single study listed in the 1996 review. If future research demonstrates that job satisfaction is correlated with actual whistle-blowing, we would then want to know the causal direction of the relationship. We believe it is possible that more satisfied employees who observe wrongdoing feel compelled to blow the whistle and equally plausible that whistle-blowers feel job satisfaction either because of pride that their organization reacted well to their whistle-blowing or because they feel cognitive dissonance such that they conclude that after doing something so stressful and difficult as whistle-blowing, they must have cared about the organization for which they undertook this challenge. It actually seems to us that the relationship is most likely recursive, with job satisfaction and whistle-blowing causing one another. All of these ideas are speculative and would require empirical testing in order to get reliable answers to these questions.

Future Research Questions Regarding Phase 3

Optimism.   Research on positive psychology implies that other dispositions would affect whistle-blowing or would interact with events to do so. Proactivity is likely related to positive organizational behavior (Luthans, 2002). And research on subjective well-being or happiness (Diener, 2000) suggests that both events and how people interpret them (i.e., because of their dispositions or demographic characteristics) affect happiness. One such disposition is optimism (Seligman & Csikszentmihalyi, 2000); people high in optimism tend to have better moods and to be more persevering and successful (Peterson, 2000). This suggests that, although some optimists may not correctly perceive wrongdoing, those optimists who believe they have seen wrongdoing will be more likely to take action to get it corrected and push back if they encounter resistance.

Hope, Gratitude, and Generativity.   Among other dispositions examined in the positive psychology literature are hope, gratitude, and generativity (concern for future generations) (Giacalone, Jurkiewicz, & Dunn, 2005). We can speculate about these dispositions, though we are aware of no published research on whistle-blowing that has included them. Specifically, we would propose that higher levels of hope and generativity might increase whistle-blowing among observers of wrongdoing, because these qualities would increase felt responsibility for acting and/or expectations of net benefits from whistle-blowing (Phase 3 of the POB model). However, the role of gratitude might be more complex. For example, as described in the literature on prosocial behavior (e.g., Brief & Motowidlo, 1986), gratitude toward the organization may disincline an observer of questionable activity to view it as wrongdoing and to act on it. On the other hand, if a grateful observer believes that the organization is a victim of wrongdoing committed by some of its members, such as in the case of Watkins (at Enron), she may be more likely to want to help the organization by calling attention to the problem. Or, if the grateful observer believes that the organization really does want the information so that it can self-correct, the employee may feel compelled by the norm of reciprocity (e.g., Gouldner, 1960) to return the good treatment that she or he is grateful to have received from the munificent employer.

Obviously, much remains to be done to determine all the personal factors that affect whether whistle-blowing will occur in a given situation. Despite the incompleteness of the literature, we believe it is worthwhile to suggest implications of what is known, for research, for law and public policy, and for managerial practice.

Summary

Throughout this chapter, we have described theory and empirical research, and offered some specific directions for future research. One general implication of existing theory and research is clearly that there are many untested ideas that may prove fruitful in helping to understand "who blows the whistle, and why do they do so?" The

positive psychology literature, particularly the literature on dispositions such as hope, optimism, and generativity, should be integrated
into empirical tests. For example, is there an inverted U relationship
between optimism and whistle-blowing, as the literature discussed
earlier seems to suggest? As another example, although employees
with children may have higher levels of generativity, as they have a
very salient reason to be concerned for the effects of their actions
(or inactions) on future generations, will high generativity trans-
late into greater whistle-blowing (because the costs of inaction and
the sense of responsibility for stopping harm to others are great)?
Or, will this make the risks of dissenting so high (e.g., the fear that
one will lose one's job over reporting wrongdoing, and will not be able
to support his or her family) that the employee cannot justify, in his
or her own mind, taking those risks? Clearly, research is needed to
address these questions.

As long as society, organizations, and organizational members
continue to view whistle-blowing as negative—something about
which to feel shame or guilt—we will continue to experience unethical corporate behavior. Valid whistle-blowing, executed appropriately, can be a positive experience for all involved, and provides the
opportunity to stem what appears to be a veritable tidal wave of
recent corporate wrongdoing.

3

Situational Predictors of Whistle-Blowing and Recent Theoretical Developments

> On a Boeing Co. assembly line in Kansas in 2000, (an employee) saw workers drilling extra holes in the long aluminum ribs that make up the skeleton of a jetliner's fuselage. That was the only way the workers could attach the pieces, because some of their pre-drilled holes didn't match those on the airframe ... Whether questionable parts ended up in hundreds of Boeing 737s is the subject of a bitter dispute between the aerospace company and (three) whistle-blowers. The two sides also have enormously different views on what that could mean for the safety of the jets ... Under the U.S. False Claims Act, plaintiffs who prove the government was defrauded—more than two dozen jets went to the U.S. military—could receive monetary damages along with the government.
>
> After the whistle-blowers notified federal authorities in 2002, the FAA and the Pentagon looked into their charges. Each said its investigation cleared the airplane parts and found no reports of problems from military or civilian operators of Boeing jets. The Department of Transportation's inspector general also dismissed the charges. (Graves & Goo, 2006, p. A01)

The Boeing case, which is still pending at the time of this writing, illustrates several situational factors that could have motivated the whistle-blowers to act, such as the extent to which observers judge problems to be serious (e.g., a safety hazard that could put passengers' lives at risk), and the availability of financial incentives for whistle-blowing. The organization, and complaint recipients outside the organization, of course, could disagree with the whistle-blower, as in the Boeing case. But the case was reopened in 2005 by the Federal Aviation Administration, after experts provided new reports indicating that practices at Boeing and its supplier "were seriously flawed" (Graves & Goo, 2006, p. A01).

The purposes of this chapter are (a) to review and discuss empirical results pertaining to situational predictors of whistle-blowing, and (b) to describe recent theoretical developments that might be integrated with the POB to provide a richer theoretical model for predicting when whistle-blowing will take place. Obviously, this chapter takes up where Chapter 2 left off, because it is difficult to separate personal and situational variables that encourage a person to blow the whistle.

Empirical Results Testing the POB Model

Situational Variables Proposed to Affect Decisions in Phase 1

Table 3.1 summarizes the findings of studies that examined situational variables that are proposed to affect decisions in Phase 1. As noted previously, there are several possible outcomes: observing wrongdoing or not, and observing wrongdoing that is believed to be corrected or reported, or not. For the most part, studies of whistle-blowing on wrongdoing other than sexual harassment have not examined these outcomes.

A recent conceptual article (Henik, in press) provided a rationale for proposing some situational variables that may affect decisions in Phase 1. For example, citing prior research (e.g., Fiske & Tetlock, 1997), Henik argued that "taboo tradeoffs" are "decisions that pit a sacred value, like life or liberty, against a secular value, like profit or efficiency" (p. 5). She suggested that wrongdoing that appears to involve perceived taboo trade-offs, such as toxic dumping to reduce waste disposal costs, provokes greater anger than other types of wrongdoing, and that this may in turn result in whistle-blowing, depending on some other situational conditions. Empirical research testing her propositions was underway at the time of this writing.

Characteristics of the Perceived Wrongdoing   Research on sexual harassment provides some guidance about possible differences between the experiences of nonobservers and those of others. As noted previously, empirical attention has been devoted to the question of how employees define certain actions to be sexual harassment, that is, the labeling process by which employees decide that what they have experienced actually constituted sexual harassment.

Sexual harassment research shows that more explicit and extreme sexual harassment is related to the perception that harassment occurred

TABLE 3.1 Empirical Results Related to Situational Characteristics That Predict Observation or Labeling of Wrongdoing and Were Not Previously Reported in Near and Miceli (1996) or Mesmer-Magnus and Viswesvaran (2005)

Predictors	Studies[a]													
	A	B	C	D	E	F	G	H	I	J	K	L	M	N
Seriousness of (frequency of) (or explicit, extreme) wrongdoing	+	+	+	+	+	+								
Organizational level of the wrongdoer						+								
Organizational climate (tolerance of wrongdoing)				+			+	+	+	+	+			
Perceived general fairness												−, I		
Perceived ethics program follow-through												−, I		
Cultural values of individualism and/or uncertainty avoidance (on seeing minor fraud as wrong)													−	−
Cultural values of individualism and/or uncertainty avoidance (on seeing major fraud and/or harm to others as wrong)													+	+

Note: + = positive relationship; − = negative relationship; 0 = no significant relationship; M = mixed; I = interaction.
[a]Studies are listed in order of first appearance in the text: A. (Fitzgerald & Ormerod, 1991); B. (Gutek et al., 1983); C. (Reilly et al., 1982); D. (Bergman et al., 2002); E. (Brooks & Perot, 1991); F. (Lee et al., 2004). G. (Fitzgerald, Drasgow et al., 1997); H. (Hulin et al., 1996); I. (Timmerman & Bajema, 2000); J. (Williams et al., 1999); K. (Near et al., 2004); L. (Treviño & Weaver, 2001); M. (Sims & Keenan, 1999); N. (Keenan, 2007).

(Fitzgerald & Ormerod, 1991; Gutek, Morasch, & Cohen, 1983; Reilly, Carpenter, Dull, & Bartlett, 1982). That is, employees are more likely to "label" their experience as sexual harassment where triggering events are explicit, clear, or severe. Frequency of sexually harassing behavior was found to increase perceived offensiveness, a mediating variable which directly predicted reporting of the harassment (Bergman et al., 2002; Brooks & Perot, 1991). These findings suggest that it is the perceived seriousness (i.e., frequency, offensiveness, explicitness) of the sexual harassment that causes employees to label their experience as harassing, a necessary first step to blowing the whistle.

Frequency and length of sexual harassment was related to whether respondents labeled their experiences as either felonious or nonfelonious sexual harassment; organizational level of the harasser was also related to whether respondents labeled their experiences as nonfelonious harassment (Lee et al., 2004). Thus, these conditions of the wrongdoing affected the employee's perception that the behavior that was observed actually constituted wrongdoing, representing Phase 1 of the model. Lee et al. also found, among respondents who labeled the activity as harassment, that the frequency and length of sexual harassment was related to whether the employee decided to blow the whistle; ironically, organizational level of the harasser was inversely related to whether the employee decided to blow the whistle. Thus, Phase 3 actions were associated differently with the predictor variables than were Phase 1 actions. That is, the more serious sexual harassment committed by a *higher* level employee, the greater the extent to which the target labels the activity as felonious harassment. Of those who did label it as such (or as nonfelonious sexual harassment), the more harassment they experienced and the *lower* the level of the harasser, the more likely they were to blow the whistle. Whether the labeling findings would extend to other types of wrongdoing is an unanswered empirical question; the Phase 3 findings are discussed with those from other studies, below.

Current research on silence among employees has generally proposed that some employees remain silent in the face of clear evidence of organizational problems (e.g., Morrison & Milliken, 2003). But, in some situations, employees remain silent because they are not sure that a problem really exists—or at least, not a problem of such significant magnitude that it warrants mentioning. Employees may find the stimulus event to be ambiguous, and need to discuss it with coworkers or friends, or to search for confirming evidence before they are convinced that it constitutes actual organizational wrongdoing. The harassment literature implies that indicators of seriousness may reduce this ambiguity, but research is needed regarding other types of wrongdoing.

Characteristics of the Organization   The literature on sexual harassment has identified a characteristic of the organization that may later be shown to affect the assessment of wrongdoing in general, namely organizational tolerance of wrongdoing. An organizational climate tolerating harassment was shown to be related to the occurrence of harassment (Bergman et al., 2002; Fitzgerald, Drasgow et al., 1997; Hulin, Fitzgerald, & Drasgow, 1996; Timmerman & Bajema, 2000; Williams, Fitzgerald, & Drasgow, 1999). In our study of all types of wrongdoing at a large military base, we asked inactive observers, who observed wrongdoing but did not report it, why they did not do so. Of a checklist of several reasons, 10% indicated that they did not do so because "nothing *would* be done," compared to 43% who said "nothing *could* be done," and others who cited many other reasons for not reporting (Near et al., 2004). We believe that this category comes closest to reflecting a sense that the organization tolerates wrongdoing, so that reporting wrongdoing would not have any effect. If wrongdoing becomes commonplace within an organization and is simply tolerated, then employees who perceive an activity, such as fraud, may no longer judge it to be wrong. The wrongdoing becomes "normalized," a point we discuss below, and—because it is not perceived to be wrong or labeled as such in Phase 1—the employee does not take the further step of blowing the whistle in Phase 3.

One study (Treviño & Weaver, 2001) examined the effects of perceived general fairness in the organization and perceived ethics program follow-through. Survey data from more than 1,700 members of four business organizations indicated that both factors were negatively related to observation of perceived wrongdoing. Further, a significant interaction involving these factors indicated that perceived follow-through had less impact when the organization was generally perceived as fair.

Characteristics of the Country or Culture   Although we focus primarily on the United States, whistle-blowing occurs throughout the world, and has been noted in the following countries:

- Australia (e.g., Anonymous, 2002; Callahan, Dworkin, & Lewis, 2004; De Maria, 1997)
- Canada (e.g., Laver, 1996; Thiessen, 1998)
- Croatia (e.g., Tavakoli et al., 2003)
- Great Britain (e.g., Anonymous, 2002; Callahan et al., 2004; De Maria, 1997; Dobson, 1998; Figg, 2000; Lewis, 2002)
- Hong Kong (e.g., Chua, 1998; Near & Miceli, 1988)
- India (e.g., Keenan, 2002a)
- Ireland (e.g., Feldman, 2002)
- Israel (e.g., Day, 1996; Seagull, 1995)
- Jamaica (e.g., Sims & Keenan, 1999)
- Japan (e.g., Akabayashi, 2002; Yoshida, 2001)
- Korea (e.g., Park, Rehg, & Lee, 2005; Rehg & Parkhe, 2002)
- The Netherlands (e.g., Bates, 1999)
- New Zealand (e.g., Beattie, 2000)
- Russia (e.g., Knox, 1997)
- Somalia (e.g., Anonymous, 1996)
- South Africa (e.g., Camerer, 2001).

It is easy to imagine how country or culture characteristics could affect whether an observer believes she or he has witnessed wrong-doing, and whether anyone has the responsibility for reporting it (in Phase 1). Unfortunately, due to the paucity of research, it is too early to develop a taxonomy of country or cultural influences on the observation of wrongdoing. Such a taxonomy must also include a comprehensive treatment of legal, economic, and organizational conditions that may differ across countries, as all of these may affect wrongdoing assessment that may later lead to whistle-blowing. Recent attempts to specify such a taxonomy have focused primarily on cultural influences as predictors of whistle-blowing within countries (Rehg & Parkhe, 2002). The preliminary cross-cultural research that has been done on how wrongdoing is judged and whistle-blowing, while interesting, has relied heavily on scenario designs, in which participants are asked how they might behave if placed in a given situation, and has been limited by small samples.

Nonetheless, we agree with Keenan and his colleagues (e.g., Keenan, 2002a; Sims & Keenan, 1998, 1999; Tavakoli et al., 2003) that theories about cultural differences imply intriguing research questions in whistle-blowing contexts. Perhaps the best-known theory is that of Hofstede, who noted that management theories developed mainly in Great Britain and the United States are based on Western individualistic assumptions that may not apply for the majority of the world's population in other continents (e.g., Hofstede, 1980, 1999; Hofstede, Neuijen, Ohayv, & Sanders, 1990). The Hofstede model proposed that cultures vary across six key values dimensions, and has stimulated a great deal of recent research, some of which proposed alternations to the original dimensions (Sivakumar & Nakata, 2001). Although the Hofstede taxonomy and scales have been criticized (e.g., Yoo & Donthu, 2002), the developing research literature may inform research on whistle-blowing.

In one scenario-based study comparing U.S. managers' and Jamaican managers' stated propensity to blow the whistle (Sims & Keenan, 1999), hypotheses were derived from four of Hofstede's dimensions. Specifically, Sims and Keenan argued that U.S. culture would be rated as higher than Jamaican culture on individualism and uncertainty avoidance and about the same on masculinity and power distance. Consequently, they predicted that Jamaican and American managers would likely evaluate descriptions of wrongdoing differently. Although they did not measure Hofstede's dimensions directly, they did find significant differences between the two samples on some variables. Compared to U.S. managers, Jamaican managers viewed minor fraud as more immoral, and major fraud and harm to others as less immoral. Unfortunately, the differences between samples could not be reliably ascribed to cultural differences on Hofstede's dimensions, because the effects of other potential predictors (e.g., organizational characteristics) were not controlled. A similar study compared questionnaire responses of 70 U.S. managers with those of 75 Chinese managers (Keenan, 2007). Like the Jamaican culture, the Chinese culture is seen as less individualistic than the U.S. culture. Keenan found that, compared to U.S. managers, Chinese managers viewed minor fraud as more immoral, and harm to others as less immoral. There were no differences regarding major fraud perceptions.

A second study attempted to link the Hofstede model to ethical decision making; the authors provided preliminary evidence that culture scores on the "masculinity-femininity" dimension predicted negotiators' emphasis on justice versus caring (French & Weis, 2000). This dimension may affect whether questionable activity is judged to be wrongful and worthy of action (Phase 1 of the model), and it may also affect evaluations of the costs and benefits of action (Phase 3). Whether this finding can be extended to observation of wrongdoing and whistle-blowing remains to be explored. Previous research has linked moral development and whistle-blowing (e.g., Miceli & Near, 1992). There has been some discussion in the moral development literature as to whether the stages of moral development (Kohlberg, 1969) are gender neutral, and these could be related to or affected by the masculine-feminine dimension of the culture. Whereas Kohlberg argued that the highest stage of moral development would involve a "principled" conception of justice, Gilligan found that women were more likely to reach a stage of moral development where they focused on preserving relationships as the highest moral good; for example, they would be more likely to engage in questionable behavior to save a friend in life-threatening circumstances, than would men (Gilligan, 1982). She argued that Kohlberg's characterization of this stage as lower-level suggested a misinterpretation of the data because the decision to help a friend by committing some unethical behavior (e.g., stealing drugs from a drug store for a dying, penniless spouse) in fact represented the greatest level of altruism.

Given this argument, the question arises as to whether Hofstede's labeling of cultures as more masculine or feminine could be related to questions of moral development. Would employees in more "masculine" cultures (such as Japan and the United States) be more concerned with the validity of the specific charges raised by the whistle-blower? Would employees in "feminine" cultures (such as France) be concerned more for the consequences of the alleged wrongdoing on people in society (e.g., political corruption may be viewed as inevitable and relatively minor in consequence), or the consequences of whistle-blowing on people in the organization (e.g., "finking" is an uncaring and hence "bad" thing to do to one's colleagues)? In other words, would the focus be on relational issues in more feminine cultures rather than on following the rules or focusing exclusively on legal issues? These and many other questions derived from Hofstede's model could be examined.

Situational Characteristics Proposed to
Affect Decisions in Phase 2

We know of only one whistle-blowing study that examined signaling and demoralization in Phase 2 (Miceli et al., 2001b), and we described it in Chapter 2. This study, however, examined only whether those who witnessed uncorrected wrongdoing had lower self-efficacy for whistle-blowing and lower perceived organizational support, that is, wrongdoing was a zero-one variable. The study did not examine whether certain situations, such as more serious wrongdoing, were more likely to signal unresponsiveness or were more demoralizing than others. Future research should identify the characteristics that tend to produce greater signaling or demoralization effects.

Situational Characteristics Proposed to Affect Decisions in Phase 3

Table 3.2 summarizes the findings of studies that examined situational variables that are proposed to affect decisions in Phase 3. As noted previously, there are several possible outcomes: whistle-blowing (through various channels), other actions, or no actions. Generally, studies of whistle-blowing have focused on whistle-blowing and no action.

Characteristics of the Perceived Wrongdoing   In Phase 3, observers must decide whether they have responsibility for taking action and whether potentially effective actions are available. If so, then they must assess the costs and benefits of acting. As described below, many theories suggest that situational variables are likely to affect these decisions. Consistent with these theories, studies published before the mid-1990s showed that many characteristics of the wrongdoing are related to whistle-blowing (Near & Miceli, 1996), although many inconsistencies in findings were noted. Below we focus on research since that time, summarizing findings from the meta-analysis we have previously described (Mesmer-Magnus & Viswesvaran, 2005) and describing additional studies.

Seriousness or Magnitude of Wrongdoing.   Power theories suggest that more serious wrongdoing is more likely to be reported (Miceli & Near, 1992), because others may be more likely to agree with and support the observer, which gives him or her more power to become the whistle-blower. Serious wrongdoing is less ambiguous, and the observer may believe that prospective complaint recipients, especially those outside the organization, such as regulators, will consider it to be worthy of their time and intervention, also giving the observer more power. As noted in Chapter 2, Phase 3 of the POB

TABLE 3.2   Empirical Results Related to Situational Characteristics That Predict Whistle-Blowing and Were Not Previously Reported in Near and Miceli (1996) or Mesmer-Magnus and Viswesvaran (2005)

Predictors	Studies[a]																			
	A	B	C	D	E	F	G	H	I	J	K	L	M	N	O	P	Q	R	S	T
Seriousness of (frequency of, or explicit, extreme) wrongdoing	+	+	+	M	+	+	+													
Type of wrongdoing							+	+												
Wrongdoer power or status low			+			0	+													
Supportiveness of organization climate or culture						+			M	M	M	M								
Perceived general fairness													+, I							
Perceived ethics program follow-through														+, I						
Low distributive justice in general (with external whistle-blowing as the dependent variable)															+					
Low procedural justice in general (with external whistle-blowing as the dependent variable)																+				
Distributive justice of whistle-blowing channels (with internal whistle-blowing as the dependent variable)																	+			

Procedural justice of whistle-blowing channels (with internal whistle-blowing as the dependent variable)			+		
Interactional justice of whistle-blowing channels (with internal whistle-blowing as the dependent variable)			+		
Industry (public vs. private organization)	+	+			
Individualism, uncertainty avoidance, and other societal tendencies	M	M	M		

Note: + = positive relationship; − = negative relationship; 0 = no significant relationship; M = mixed; I = interaction. In the case of the categorical variable "type of wrongdoing," any significant relationship is noted with +. The category "supervisory support and quality of evidence," discussed in the text, is not included in this table, because we know of no studies not included in prior reviews or the meta-analysis.

[a]Studies are listed in order of first appearance in the text: A. (Bergman et al., 2002); B. (Brooks & Perot, 1991); C. (Lee et al., 2004); D. (King, 1997); E. (Wise, 1995); F. (Starkey, 1998); G. (Miethe, 1999); H. (Near et al., 2004); I. (Treviño & Youngblood, 1990); J. (Ashkanasy et al., 2006); K. (Kelley et al., 2005); L. (Rothwell & Baldwin, 2006, 2007); M. (Treviño & Weaver, 2001); N. (Goldman, 2001); O. (Seifert, 2006); P. (Brewer, 1996); Q. (Rothschild & Miethe, 1999); R. (Sims & Keenan, 1999); S. (Tavakoli et al., 2003); T. (Keenan, 2007).

model proposes that factors that increase one's sense of responsibility for reporting—as seriousness might—and improve the prospective benefit-cost ratio—as power might—will increase the likelihood that an observer will act on it.

As was shown in the Near and Miceli (1996) review, the seriousness or magnitude of wrongdoing generally has been found to be associated with whistle-blowing. In the meta-analysis of whistle-blowing intent and actual whistle-blowing (Mesmer-Magnus & Viswesvaran, 2005), seriousness of wrongdoing was correlated with both whistle-blowing intent ($r = .16$) and actual whistle-blowing ($r = .13$). Research not included in those reviews, and research completed since then, has further supported this finding.

Perceived offensiveness of sexually harassing behavior can be viewed as a form of wrongdoing seriousness. In two studies, it was shown to predict reporting of the harassment (Bergman et al., 2002; Brooks & Perot, 1991). Finally, a study of whistle-blowing about sexual harassment found that predictors of whistle-blowing were similar to those seen in studies where the whistle-blowing concerned other types of wrongdoing (Lee et al., 2004). These are indicators of wrongdoing seriousness, and they included frequency and length of sexual harassment, number of types of sexual harassment, and having multiple harassers.

Studies of other types of wrongdoing have also examined seriousness. In a field study, hospital nurses reviewed scenarios; wrongdoing severity, that is, the nurses' perception of danger or risk, was associated with greater reporting of wrongdoing to the supervisor, as prescribed by the organization, but not to other channels (King, 1997). Respondents indicated that they did not consider reporting to the supervisor to be whistle-blowing, but rather to be using the chain of command to report concerns about possible wrongdoing; in this industry, this kind of reporting was seen as legitimate and normal—and not whistle-blowing (King, 1994). It should be noted, however, that research has yet to establish whether employees in general view reporting wrongdoing to supervisors as meaningfully different from other types of whistle-blowing, particularly where supervisors are perceived as being involved in the wrongdoing in some way.

Two dissertations have explored seriousness. In a scenario-based study, students expressed higher levels of intentions to blow the whistle when the wrongdoing was serious (Wise, 1995). Similar results were obtained with hospital workers (Starkey, 1998). Finally, in a book reporting results from a series of studies conducted with diverse samples, Miethe noted that "severe misconduct" was related to both reporting in general and external whistle-blowing in particular across his samples (Miethe, 1999). Wrongdoing that was frequent was associated with whistle-blowing, and wrongdoing "systemic" to the organization (measured as frequent and expensive) was related to external whistle-blowing (Miethe, 1999).

Type of Wrongdoing.   Results from a study of differences in whistle-blowing by type of wrongdoing indicated that rates of whistle-blowing varied significantly by type of wrongdoing (Near et al., 2004). In particular, employees who observed wrongdoing involving mismanagement, sexual harassment, or unspecified legal violations were significantly more likely to blow the whistle than employees who observed stealing, waste, safety problems, or discrimination; those who did not blow the whistle varied significantly as to their reason for not doing so. Further, type of wrongdoing was significantly associated with cost of wrongdoing and quality of evidence of the wrongdoing—both of which are variables found to predict whistle-blowing in earlier studies (Miceli & Near, 1992). Type of wrongdoing was not significantly related to whether the whistle-blower was identified or anonymous, whether the whistle-blower thought the job required whistle-blowing in cases of observed wrongdoing, or frequency of wrongdoing. Similarly, Miethe found that wrongdoing involving public health issues or a prohibited personnel practice was related to both reporting of wrongdoing and external whistle-blowing while counterproductive work activity was inversely related to both reporting and external wrongdoing (Miethe, 1999).

We propose that type of wrongdoing is related to whistle-blowing because of its effects on other variables. Different kinds of wrongdoing vary in systematic ways: the seriousness—which may be reflected in their frequency, length of time that they continue, and dollar amount of damage; whether they harm the society as a whole, only a few individuals in the organization, or some other parties; and so on. If we could control all the sources of variance on which types of wrongdoing vary, we think that the type of wrongdoing would no longer explain additional variance in whistle-blowing. It may, however, be impossible to determine all the ways in which types of wrongdoing may vary. Further, it is a difficult test to make, because most samples of employees have been too small to permit controlling for 10 or more dummy variables representing different types of wrongdoing, as well as the additional characteristics (e.g., seriousness) that might be systematically associated with those types. For the time being, we believe that our earlier results, showing significant differences by type, should be viewed as tentative, and that more research is needed to understand the processes through which the type of wrongdoing affects whistle-blowing.

Wrongdoer Power or Status.   In our earlier review, results were mixed concerning the relationship between wrongdoer power and whistle-blowing (Near & Miceli, 1996), although external whistle-blowing was associated with low social status of the wrongdoer. Results obtained since then have been similarly conflicting. One field survey showed that the organization level of harassers predicted whistle-blowing in response to sexual harassers (inverse relationship) (Lee et al., 2004). In a scenario-based study of other types of wrongdoing, however, there was no relationship between hospital employees' intentions to blow the whistle and culprit power (Starkey, 1998).

Closeness of the wrongdoer to the whistle-blower might also be an indication of personal power of the wrongdoer over the whistle-blower. Miethe argued that employees who considered wrongdoers as close friends or coworkers, or as direct work supervisors, or who otherwise had a stake in the firm, would be less likely to report the wrongdoing but—if they did so—would be more likely to use internal channels to report the close friend or coworker and external channels to report the supervisor, and less likely to use external whistle-blowing if they had a stake in the firm (Miethe, 1999). In Phase 3, blowing the whistle on a friend might be very costly; the whistle-blower would likely lose the friendship. But seemingly contrary to this prediction, closeness was found to be *positively* correlated ($r = .45$) with intent to blow the whistle, though no studies were cited in the meta-analysis of its relationship to actual whistle-blowing (Mesmer-Magnus & Viswesvaran, 2005). The authors speculated that people closer to the wrongdoer may have better evidence of wrongdoing. This implies that closeness positively affects Phase 1 (whether the individual labels the questionable activity as wrongful and believes wrongdoing has occurred), but it may negatively affect Phase 3 (which includes only those who believe they have seen wrongdoing), if at all. Or, there may be two different dimensions of closeness that have different effects—proximity to the whistle-blower and emotional connection to him or her.

Supervisor Support and Quality of Evidence. The POB model suggests that supervisory support and better, clearer evidence of wrongdoing will increase whistle-blowing, because both will increase the likelihood that powerful others will be convinced and take appropriate action, thus enhancing the benefit-cost ratio. The Boeing case cited at the beginning of this chapter illustrates this problem clearly. Although the evidence of assembly line workers changing the specifications of the work was clear, investigators questioned whether this would affect the actual performance of the jets. We wonder whether whistle-blowers who reported misdeeds for which there was clearer evidence of performance effects would have received greater commendation for their reporting of possible wrongdoing.

In our earlier review of the literature, we found that supervisory support and evidence quality predicted whistle-blowing, and that the choice to use external channels was associated with having better-quality evidence. In the meta-analysis results (Mesmer-Magnus & Viswesvaran, 2005), supervisor support was positively corre-lated with whistle-blowing intent ($r = .28$) but negatively correlated with actual whistle-blowing ($r = -.12$), "suggesting that supervisor support may facilitate one's decision to blow the whistle, but work to inhibit behaviors required to actually blow it" (Mesmer-Magnus & Viswesvaran, 2005, p. 11). Evidence of wrongdoing was only slightly related to whistle-blowing. The relationship was negative when the dependent variable was intent to blow the whistle ($r = -.06$) but positive when the dependent variable was actual whistle-blowing ($r = .06$).

Characteristics of the Organization In our earlier review, we concluded that observers of wrongdoing were more likely to blow the whistle on it in organizations that supported whistle-blowing. Organizations with higher rates of whistle-blowing seemed to be high performing, to have slack resources, and to be relatively non-bureaucratic. Group size was positively related to whistle-blowing, but quality of supervisor was not. This finding regarding group size was inconsistent with the POB model's diffusion of responsi-bility hypothesis that suggested that whistle-blowing would be less likely in a larger group. However, these findings were based on a very limited number of studies, sometimes only one, that examined one or more of these variables. Below we describe more recent findings concerning characteristics of the organization.

Organizational Climate or Culture of Supportiveness for Whistle-Blowing.   Our review also identified some research showing that more threatening climate (measured as shared employee percep-tions aggregated at the organizational level) was associated with more *external* whistle-blowing, rather than less whistle-blowing. In the 2005 meta-analysis (Mesmer-Magnus & Viswesvaran, 2005), results showed that organizational climate for whistle-blowing was more strongly related to whistle-blowing intent ($r = .28$) than to actual whistle-blowing ($r = .10$); threat of retaliation was negatively correlated with whistle-blowing intent ($r = -.27$) but unrelated to actual whistle-blowing ($r = .04$); finally, organizational size was not strongly associated with either whistle-blowing intent ($r = -.10$) or actual whistle-blowing ($r = .09$).

Several studies not included in prior reviews or the meta-analysis examined the relationship between (a) hypothetical, perceived, or actual organizational climate or culture, and (b) whistle-blowing when wrongdoing is presented or perceived. First, as we will describe in more depth in the later sections on country and culture variables, several scenario studies by Keenan and colleagues included a perceived "organizational propensity (to encourage or discourage whistle-blowing)" variable. Second, consistent with the prosocial model, an in-basket study (Treviño & Youngblood, 1990) showed that "vicarious reward" (scenarios in which whistle-blowers were rewarded) led to hypothetical ethical decision-making behavior (a variable that included potential whistle-blowing), though enhanc-ing respondents' "outcome expectancies" (beliefs about managers' likely responses), but "vicarious punishment" (scenarios in which wrongdoers were disciplined after someone reported the wrongdoing) had no significant effect. Third, in a similar study (Ashkanasy et al., 2006), conditions of the rewarding of unethical behavior or the pun-ishment of ethical behavior influenced outcome expectations, but they did not affect ethical decision making. In this and the Treviño and Youngblood study, however, the dependent variable included other hypothetical choices in addition to whistle-blowing. So, more research is needed to clarify whether similar results would be obtained if the dependent variable were more focused on whistle-blowing.

Fourth, a scenario-based dissertation found a positive relationship between the supportiveness of organizational climate for whistle-blowing and hospital employees' intentions to blow the whistle (Starkey, 1998). Fifth, in a scenario-based master's thesis involving 219 undergraduate and master's-level students (Kelley, Sabin, & Wyrwich, 2005), two significant effects were found. There was a main effect for threat of retaliation that varied by type of whistle-blowing: threat decreased internal whistle-blowing intentions but did not affect external whistle-blowing intentions. In addition, there was a significant interaction between two situational conditions: threat of retaliation *increased* whistle-blowing intentions in low moral intensity situations (i.e., as manipulated by the experimenter), and had no effect in high moral intensity situations. Although the measures were not described, it appeared (from the tables) that moral intensity as manipulated had some elements in common with seriousness or magnitude of wrongdoing.

Finally, the relationship between several measures of whistle-blowing and five organization climates were investigated (Rothwell & Baldwin, 2006, 2007). The authors used the Ethical Climate Questionnaire (Cullen, Victor, & Bronson, 1993), which measures climates for law and rules, friendship or team-interest, social responsibility, company profit or efficiency, and independence. Generally, ethical climates failed to predict self-reported whistle-blowing (Rothwell & Baldwin, 2006). For the police subsample, whistle-blowing frequency was related only to climate for company profit or efficiency, and for minor violations of the law only. For the combined sample (including civilians), company profit climate was positively related (which might have been attributable to the police findings), and social responsibility climate was negatively related, to whistle-blowing frequency for minor violations only. There were no observed significant climate (or other) predictors of whistle-blowing for major violations. For the vignette (hypothetical) dependent variable, friendship or teamwork climate predicted willingness to blow the whistle in the police subsample. It should be noted that the climate measures were individual-level perceptions; it is not known whether these results would differ if a measure reflecting the extent to which individuals in the same unit or subunit agreed about the climate, or another independent measure of climate, were used.

Justice Perceptions.   Although researchers have noted that the justice of whistle-blowing channels may be related to the satisfaction of the outcomes of the whistle-blowing process (e.g., Near et al., 1993), empirical and, particularly, experimental investigations of the role of justice in whistle-blowing have been rare (Seifert, 2006). Two studies not labeled as "whistle-blowing" studies reported interesting and relevant findings linking justice perceptions to whistle-blowing.

First, a survey study described previously (Treviño & Weaver, 2001, p. 651) revealed that "when employees perceive general organizational justice and ethics program follow-through, there is ... greater willingness to report problems." Further, these two factors interacted.

Second, a study of actual external whistle-blowing (Goldman, 2001) examined two types of justice. Goldman (2001) hypothesized that negative relationships existed between a worker's filing of a discrimination claim and both distributive justice and procedural justice. Distributive and procedural justice referred to perceptions of practices within a worker's place of employment or former place of employment, as predictors of actual claims. All nine types of claims measured (e.g., three types were "filed a written 'charge' with the EEOC, state or local fair employment practice office") constituted external whistle-blowing, as we define it. The decision to claim was a dichotomous score equal to zero if respondents said they took none of the nine actions, and equal to one if respondents said they took one or more of those nine actions. Goldman found support for both hypotheses.

A third study, a doctoral dissertation in the accounting field (Seifert, 2006), tested hypotheses linking justice and whistle-blowing also. A between-subject scenario or vignette study (Seifert, 2006) examined whether managerial accountants and internal auditors were influenced by the presence or absence of distributive justice, procedural justice, and interactional justice of the complaint channel. Using the whistle-blowing policies and procedures of a company that won a 2004 award in the United Kingdom as the "Most Whistle-blowing Friendly Culture" (Procter & Gamble) as a guide, Seifert constructed vignettes illustrating either high or low levels of each type of justice. In the high distributive justice, the complaint was investigated and wrongdoing stopped. The high procedural justice condition portrayed whistle-blowing procedures as consistent with policy, that reporting is anonymous, and that the company would protect the whistle-blower retaliation. (We would note that if anonymity is assured, by definition, retaliation could not occur.) In the high interactional justice condition, the supervisor of the focal person was portrayed as explaining the whistle-blowing policies and showing politeness, dignity, and respect toward prospective whistle-blowers. Respondents were asked to rate the likelihood that the focal person in the scenario would report the CFO who engaged in fraud to others in the company. Seifert found that all three types of justice were positively associated with the perceived likelihood rating.

Seifert expected and found relationships that at first glance appear opposite to those found by Goldman. However, the justice perceptions Seifert investigated pertained to the whistle-blowing channel, and her dependent measure of whistle-blowing was limited to hypothetical internal whistle-blowing. One interpretation that can reconcile the findings is that greater justice in the organization or in whistle-blowing channels encourages observers of wrongdoing to report it to someone powerful within the organization, but if observers believe the organization or its reporting channels are unjust, they report wrongdoing externally. Similar findings, with different measures of threatening climate and culture, were described in research included in our 1992 book. An alternative interpretation might be that, in the Goldman study, respondents were reacting primarily to the degree of injustice of the wrongdoing itself, rather than to injustice of the organization in general or of whistle-blowing channels. If so, the Goldman findings may in that way be similar to the effect of seriousness of wrongdoing found consistently in multiple studies.

Industry Type, Public versus Private Organization.   Recent research has suggested that there may be effects of industry on whistle-blowing—specifically, for example, that whistle-blowers cluster in the public rather than private or not-for-profit sectors (Near & Miceli, 1996). What may manifest itself as an apparent industry effect may be personal or situational, or a combination of both. Also, research shows that organizational culture is "strongly influenced by the characteristics of the industry in which the company operates" (Gordon, 1991, p. 396); therefore, industry may also influence whistle-blowing through its effects on organizational culture.

The Public Service Motivation effect (Perry & Wise, 1990) suggests that individuals are drawn to work in the public sector because of their wish to serve the public; in terms of the model, in Phase 3, observers may feel more responsible for acting on wrongdoing. Thus, a selection effect (e.g., organizational recruiters may search for people who appear to share these values) or self-selection effect (e.g., job seekers choose organizations where they believe their values will be supported) could occur, thus reflecting lower costs and increased benefits of blowing the whistle in certain organizations. If so, either could produce more whistle-blowing in the public sector than in the private sector, because whistle-blowing may be seen as consistent with serving the public or society-at-large (as opposed to disloyalty to the employer). Consistent with this notion, an examination of whistle-blowing incidents described in articles appearing in 30 major newspapers over a 7-year period showed that 70% of the incidents occurred in the public sector, a number much higher than would be expected, given that only about 20% of the U.S. workforce was employed in the public sector during that period (Brewer, 1996). Interview research with whistle-blowers solicited across the United States yielded the same conclusion (Rothschild & Miethe, 1999).

Alternative explanations could be offered and examined empirically. For example, certain laws ostensibly protect some public sector employees but not private sector employees from retaliation for whistle-blowing. This might explain a greater incidence of whistle-blowing among public employees. However, we know of no empirical research testing this proposition, and many observers have questioned the extent to which these paper protections work as intended, suggesting that the question of legal protections is complex (e.g., Devine, 1997). Chapter 6 explores the status of whistle-blowers' legal protections. As another example, there could have been sampling error resulting from possibly greater scrutiny by the media of whistle-blowing cases in public organizations than in business firms during the time periods of the newspaper and interview studies. Further, because the interview study did not use a random sample, its results may not be representative of the broader population.

Characteristics of the Country or Culture   Country and culture variables were not included in our 1996 review, so the following summary identifies another new set of dimensions added by recent research. In some cultures, the term "whistle-blower" is viewed as derogatory, having a "snitch" connotation, whereas in others, "bell-ringer" or "lighthouse keeper" are preferred (Johnson, 2002). If so, observers may feel that their responsibility (in Phase 3) is to remain quiet and "loyal" to their employers, or that the risk of severe retaliation is high.

As a countervailing influence, various nongovernmental organizations (NGOs) have focused on the goal of reducing corruption, including the American Bar Association, the Ethics Resource Center, the Government Accountability Project, and Transparency International. Governmental agencies, including USAID, OECD, the Department of Commerce, the World Bank, and the Asian Development Bank, have embraced support for whistle-blowing as a way to reduce corruption, thereby improving the functioning of democracies around the world (Johnson, 2002). Clearly, by their encouragement of whistle-blowing, these institutions serve to legitimize it, in such a way that it may be more fully accepted even in cultures that traditionally have viewed the reporting of wrongdoing as akin to snitching.

The question of whether dimensions from the Hofstede model (discussed earlier) might be relevant to whistle-blowing has been raised. As noted earlier, Sims and Keenan (1999) argued that U.S. culture would be rated as higher than Jamaican culture on individualism and uncertainty avoidance and about the same on masculinity and power distance. The authors expected these differences to affect whistle-blowing. Although Jamaican and U.S. managers viewed both major and minor fraud differently, they differed in their stated likelihood to blow the whistle only for major fraud, in which scenarios U.S. managers said that they would be more likely to blow the whistle than did Jamaican managers. Other findings reported by Sims and Keenan were that U.S. managers rated "organizational propensity" to encourage whistle-blowing (a variable that seems similar to organizational climate) lower than did Jamaican managers. Ratings of their own individual "propensity" to blow the whistle and fear of retaliation did not differ significantly across groups. Unfortunately, this study (Sims & Keenan, 1999) did not include measures of whistle-blowing actions, and each group was smaller than 45 managers, limiting the statistical power of the study.

One scenario study not included in prior reviews compared the values on some of Hofstede's dimensions of U.S. and Croatian managers (Tavakoli et al., 2003). The authors proposed that, compared to Americans, Croatians would score low on individualism and masculinity, but high on uncertainty avoidance and power distance, and that these cultural differences would lead to the differences in whistle-blowing intent between the two samples of managers. They found that American managers' individual belief systems ("individual propensity") and perceived organizational climates ("organizational propensity") supported blowing the whistle to a greater extent than those of Croatian managers, who were significantly more likely to fear retaliation than U.S. managers. Americans were significantly more likely than Croatians to say that they would blow the whistle in scenarios involving major fraud, but not those involving minor fraud or harm to others.

In his similar study of Chinese versus American managers' perceptions described previously (Keenan, 2007), Keenan found that American managers were more approving of whistle-blowing ("individual propensity") and they said they would be more likely to blow the whistle on all three types of wrongdoing. But Chinese managers saw their organizations as more encouraging of whistle-blowing ("organizational propensity").

It has been proposed that whistle-blowing would be less common in collectivist cultures, where members might be more likely to judge the whistle-blower as a traitor to the employer and coworkers than in individualistic cultures (Rehg & Parkhe, 2002). In other words, collectivistic cultures may view whistle-blowing as an attack on the collectivity, meaning the organization itself and its members. But it is also possible that individualistic cultures would be *less* supportive, because the collectivistic culture would value the benefit to society of whistle-blowing (e.g., to protect the public from unsafe products or financial fraud) above any concern for the potential repercussions for an employer viewed as harming society. Preliminary research on whistle-blowing in South Korea (Park et al., 2005), which Hofstede characterized as a collectivistic culture, has examined conditions under which whistle-blowing occurs, but has focused only on samples drawn from South Korea, so no comparative data are available.

Other research questions related to societal culture can easily be envisioned. The potential role of organizational culture should also be considered. For example, one study showed that the organization's effects were stronger than the society's effects on member behavior, although the researchers found that both were important (Hofstede et al., 1990). It is possible also that one effect might moderate the other, in other contexts. Unfortunately, this study did not include whistle-blowing or organizational dissent variables. Thus, much could be learned from investigation of whistle-blowing in settings outside North America.

One conceptual paper (Rehg & Parkhe, 2002) developed theoretical predictions about possible interactions among organizational culture and societal culture. Whistle-blowing may be less likely in cultures where high power distance exists, such as India, because there is greater pressure to conform to accepted organizational practices (Rehg & Parkhe, 2002). In such cultures, employees may have a greater fear of retaliation for blowing the whistle, though no support for this proposition emerged in preliminary studies (Keenan, 2002a).

However, it may be that high power distance alone has no impact, but that it exacerbates any existing pressures to conform in organizations. Pressure to conform in organizations is emphasized when the structure is bureaucratic (Weinstein, 1979). This suggests an interaction effect between societal cultural differences (high power distance versus low power distance) and organizational structure (highly bureaucratic versus low bureaucratic), such that Rehg and Parkhe expected *lower* levels of whistle-blowing in highly bureaucratic organizations in high power distance cultures, and *higher* whistle-blowing levels in lower power distance countries, regardless of bureaucracy levels in the organizations, and in low bureaucratic organizations in higher power distance countries.

Finally, one situational variable that may influence whistle-blowing in different ways in different cultures is corporate ethics programs. Recommendations for particular ethics programs features (e.g., codes of ethics) are based largely on experience in Western countries, which may not be applicable to other societies (Weaver, 2001).

Person by Situation Interactions Proposed to Affect Decisions

Phase 1 The only studies examining person by situation interactions that we could find involved sexual harassment as the wrongdoing (i.e., the dependent variable). As indicated in Table 3.3, these studies showed that gender interacted with a number of situational variables to predict the occurrence of, or the labeling of, sexual harassment.

Observer's Gender and Male Domination.   Women were more likely to encounter sexually harassing situations when they worked in a mostly male environment (Coles, 1986; Ellis, Barak, & Pinto, 1991; Fain & Anderton, 1987; Fitzgerald, Drasgow et al., 1997; Fritz, 1989; Gutek & Cohen, 1987; S. E. Martin, 1984; Schneider, 1982), worked with male supervisors (Gutek, 1985), or performed stereotypically male tasks (Coles, 1986; Gutek, 1985; Gutek & Dunwoody, 1987; Koss,

TABLE 3.3   Empirical Results Related to Personal Characteristic by Situational Characteristic Interactions That Predict Sexual Harassment and Were Not Previously Reported in Near and Miceli (1996) or Mesmer-Magnus and Viswesvaran (2005)

Predictors	Studies[a]													
	A	B	C	D	E	F	G	H	I	J	K	L	M	N
Female observer, male-majority environment	+	+	+	+	+	+	+	+						
Female observer, male supervisor									+					
Female observer, male tasks	+								+	+	+	+	+	
Female observer, organization tolerance of harassment														+

Note: + = positive relationship; − = negative relationship; 0 = no significant relationship; M = mixed.

[a]Studies are listed in order of first appearance in the text: A. (Coles, 1986); B. (Ellis et al., 1991); C. (Fain & Anderton, 1987); D. (Fitzgerald, Swan, & Magley, 1997); E. (Fritz, 1989); F. (Gutek & Cohen, 1987); G. (S. E. Martin, 1984); H. (Schneider, 1982); I. (Gutek, 1985); J. (Gutek & Dunwoody, 1987); K. (Koss et al., 1994); L. (LaFontain & Tredeau, 1986); M. (U. S. Merit Systems Protection Board, 1988); N. (Fitzgerald et al., 1999).

Goodman, Browne, Fitzgerald, Keita, & Russo, 1994; LaFontain & Tredeau, 1986; U. S. Merit Systems Protection Board, 1988). This may have occurred because these situations created greater tolerance of sexual harassment.

Observer's Gender and Tolerance of Harassment.   In one study, organizational tolerance of sexual harassment in general and job gender context together affected level and frequency of sexual harassment (Fitzgerald et al., 1999). Job gender context was measured as the degree to which the respondent believed his or her job was usually held by a person of the same gender or that personnel of the same gender holding this job was uncommon; supervisor's sex; and gender ratio among coworkers.

Phases 2 and 3   We are not aware of any published studies examining the role of person by situation interactions in the signaling and demoralization processes (Phase 2). Regarding Phase 3, we know of no studies of the effects of person by situation interactions on whistle-blowing, given that the employee has observed wrongdoing.

Recent Theoretical Developments: Integration with the POB Model

Three new models seem to us to offer possibilities for extending and refining the POB model, and we consider each of these below. They are the social information processing model, the constructive deviance model, and the normalization of wrongdoing model.

Social Information Processing (SIP) Model of Whistle-Blowing

A recently developed model (Gundlach et al., 2003) predicting when whistle-blowing will occur is based on the social information processing approach (Salancik & Pfeffer, 1978). The SIP model proposed that additional variables affect the cost-benefit analysis of blowing the whistle, including the whistle-blower's attributions about why the wrongdoer acted and the wrongdoer's attempt to influence the whistle-blower through impression management. In addition, they proposed some other processes, particularly those involving the emotions of the employee who observes questionable activity. Below we provide an overview of the model. Organizational members engage in wrongdoing for many reasons, including environmental pressures or need for wrongdoing (e.g., opportunity or resource scarcity); "rational choices" to engage in wrongdoing in the face of low probability of being caught (e.g., when regulators are not vigilant) or suffering stiff penalties; and "predisposition" of the organization (e.g., past history) or its managers toward wrongdoing (e.g., Baucus, 1994). There may be pressure from leaders, through role modeling and authorization of corruption (e.g., Brief et al., 2001), or from changes such as during a merger when chains of command or operations are disrupted (Grimsley, 2000). The perceived reasons for wrongdoing—and the attributions observers make—may influence observers' reactions to it, according to the SIP model (Gundlach et al., 2003).

Gundlach and colleagues argued that whistle-blowers who attribute the wrongdoing to internal actions of a stable nature, that are

controllable and intentional, will view the wrongdoer as responsible
for the wrongdoing, and therefore the wrongdoing is deserving of
reporting. Further, to the extent that the wrongdoer does not take
steps to manage the impression made, the potential whistle-blower
is likely to feel anger and resentment, and to move to actually blow
the whistle. This reaction may be tempered by fear, however, if the
whistle-blower views the wrongdoer as powerful.

In their conceptual discussion of the social information processing model, Gundlach et al. (2003) argued that characteristics of the
wrongdoer influence the whistle-blower's view of the wrongdoing,
but some of the characteristics they cited also pertain to the nature
of the wrongdoing, including whether the outcomes are under the
control of the wrongdoer or stable, reflecting whether the wrongdoer
engages in this wrongdoing more than once. Other characteristics
pertain only to the wrongdoer, including whether the wrongdoing
was intentional or caused by internal characteristics rather than
external pressures. Finally, they argued that the wrongdoer's
attempt to manage the potential whistle-blower's impressions of the
wrongdoing will influence whether the individual decides to actually blow the whistle; again, this process may relate to characteristics
of the wrongdoing as well as the wrongdoer. It is highly plausible
that all of these variables do indeed influence whistle-blowing, but
we know of no published empirical tests of these propositions to date
(Gundlach et al., 2003).

Like the POB model, the SIP model proposes a decision sequence,
in which the potential whistle-blower considers costs and benefits
of each step. Observers who view the wrongdoer as responsible for
the wrongdoing (by attributing the wrongdoing to internal, stable,
and controllable causes) are more likely to see the wrongdoing as
deserving of reporting (Gundlach et al., 2003). Wrongdoers who
do not take steps to manage impressions will provoke more anger
and resentment and ultimately more whistle-blowing, unless the
wrongdoers are powerful and therefore feared.

The SIP model offers important theoretical advances: it proposes a
number of testable propositions, describes systematically the hypothesized role of the whistle-blower's emotions in deciding whether
to blow the whistle, and describes potential causes of wrongdoer
impression management, such as the expected or perceived attributions that other employees may make about the wrongdoer's responsibility for wrongdoing. Yet the SIP model does not explicitly include

other variables found to affect whether organization members perceive wrongdoing and engage in whistle-blowing, for example, other wrongdoing attributes and organization culture, climate, and reward systems (e.g., Miceli & Near, 1984, 1985; Miceli, Near, and Schwenk, 1991; Morrison & Milliken, 2000). Therefore, we believe that future research integrating this model with the POB model and testing the resulting propositions would be very valuable.

Two other theories have been developed since the SIP model was published, and since the last major revision of the POB model. We believe that these theories have the potential to provide significant insight into and guide future research on whistle-blowing, although they have not yet been tested in whistle-blowing contexts. Specifically, they might be used to elucidate how pressures for conformity to norms can affect observers' judgments in both Phase 1 and Phase 3, although neither was developed entirely with the goal of explaining whistle-blowing. These theories are the theory of constructive deviance and the theory of normalization of collective corruption.

Whistle-Blowing as Constructive Deviance

Many instances of whistle-blowing should be viewed as "beneficial deviant behavior" in response to norms of silence about wrongdoing (Warren, 2003). But determining what constitutes wrongdoing is problematic: saying that something is wrong only if it violates organizational norms is inadequate, because organizational norms sometimes support fraud, pollution, or other bad behavior that conflict with norms of other groups, such as society (Spreitzer & Sonenshein, 2004; Warren, 2003). Declaring behavior wrong only if it violates societal laws is inadequate, because that standard fails to consider immoral behavior or conflicts between nations' laws (Warren, 2003). Warren proposed using the construct of "hypernorms" (Donaldson & Dunfee, 1994, 1999), which are "globally held beliefs and values ... (that) ... encompass basic principles needed for the development and survival of essential background institutions in societies" (Warren, 2003, p. 628).

Warren provided a 2 × 2 classification schema for behavior as to (a) its support for or deviance from hypernorms, where deviance from hypernorms is viewed as destructive because these norms are beneficial for essential institutions, and (b) its support for or deviance from reference group norms, where the reference group is lower than global, such as a work group, or the organization. "Constructive conformity" supports both hypernorms and reference group norms (e.g., providing excellent customer service), and "constructive deviance"—which "includes certain types of whistle-blowing"—is behavior that conforms to hypernorms but deviates from reference group norms (e.g., in a situation like the Enron case, reporting financial wrongdoing to the Securities and Exchange Commission, or protesting racism in an organization where members refuse to acknowledge it) (Warren, 2003, p. 628). "Destructive deviance" is behavior that deviates from both hypernorms and reference group norms (e.g., embezzlement), while "destructive conformity" is behavior that deviates from hypernorms but falls within reference group norms (e.g., selling unsafe products). Of course, the appropriateness of these examples depends on the norms in the organization.

In terms of the POB whistle-blowing model, norms can affect both Phase 1 and Phase 2. For example, activity or omissions constituting constructive conformity would generate few outcomes of perceived wrongdoing, because there is no activity or behavior triggering a process that would cause members to believe that wrongdoing occurred; there is no violation of norms of appropriate behavior at any level. In contrast, serious wrongdoing such as chemical pollution of the company's surroundings that leads to serious illness violates widely shared norms, but company leadership may want the pollution ignored or tolerated (as dramatized in the film *Erin Brockovich*). Employees who are aware of such a situation might view it as violating hypernorms and thus define the activity as wrongful (Phase 1), but they may be unlikely to blow the whistle on it because they anticipate high potential costs and a low likelihood of success in challenging the organizational norms (Phase 3), resulting in destructive conformity. Warren's model thus provides potential bases for better understanding how employees come to define activity as wrongdoing and act on it, and these bases should be explored in future research.

The Normalization of Wrongdoing and Whistle-Blowing

Firms that engage in illegal corporate behavior are likely to do so again (Baucus & Baucus, 1997), perhaps because wrongdoing has become so accepted that it seems "normal." The model of normalization of collective corruption explains how the wrongdoing process can be *normalized* in such a way that it becomes part of everyday organizational structures and processes, viewed by organizational members as appropriate or legitimate behavior, and socialized into newcomers (Ashforth & Anand, 2003). In this model, normalization leads to inappropriate acceptance of wrongdoing through three interdependent processes: institutionalization, rationalization, and socialization.

Institutionalization begins when the collective corruption is initiated; as it continues, it is embedded in organizational memory, structures, and processes and routinized in ongoing operations, becoming accepted as part of the normative culture of the organization, adapted to and enacted "mindlessly" (Anand, Ashforth, & Joshi, 2004). Institutionalization is more likely when organization norms against the deviant behavior are not strong, rigid, obvious, or unambiguous (Robinson & Kraatz, 1998). The effect of institutionalization is self-censorship: organization members do not even see the wrongdoing; they have become inured to it through institutionalization (i.e., Phase 1 in Figure 2.1) so it does not occur to them to blow the whistle (i.e., Phase 3 in Figure 2.1). Because of institutionalization, some of the participants in field studies of whistle-blowing who claim not to have observed wrongdoing may have indeed observed wrongdoing but not labeled it as such. Similarly, a recent series of laboratory studies suggest a "slippery slope" phenomenon or "boiling frog syndrome": participants were less likely to notice cheating that increased gradually than abruptly increasing cheating (Gino & Bazerman, 2007; Pomeroy, 2007).

The second process ensues when organization members do not see themselves as corrupt because they rationalize it through any of eight mechanisms (Anand et al., 2004; Ashforth & Anand, 2003). They may: (a) persuade themselves that the action is not really illegal, and therefore not wrong; (b) deny their responsibility, believing that they have no other choice except to engage in corruption; (c) deny that anyone is injured by their actions; or (d) argue that if injury occurred, the victim deserved it for some reason. They may: (e) engage in social weighting, condemning those who engage in criticism or arguing that their corrupt actions are no worse than those of others in their referent group; or (f) argue that corruption is required because of higher loyalties, perhaps to employees who would lose their jobs if the firm died. Finally, they could: (g) defend themselves from a social equity position or "metaphor of the ledger"

(Ashforth & Anand, 2003), meaning that they deserve to engage in this "minor" deviant behavior because of accrued credits for good behavior; or (h) refocus attention toward their good works and away from their misdeeds, in a process of instrumental rationalizing (e.g., Robinson & Kraatz, 1998). The first mechanism, rationalizing that the action was not really wrong, applies to the judgment, in Phase 1, that no wrongdoing occurred; the remaining actions apply to Phase 3 of Figure 2.1, because all of them require the recognition that wrongdoing has occurred. Obviously, if the focal member is the sole wrongdoer, Phases 2 and 3 of the POB model make little sense for him or her, because one could simply stop his or her own wrong-doing, rather than feel bad about the fact that the organization has not corrected one's own wrongdoing, or report oneself. So we refer here only to wrongdoing in which others are also involved.

Collective corruption is by definition a group practice and new members must be socialized to collude in the wrongdoing, as they come to identify with their organization role and feel commitment to their peers. Four mechanisms may come into play (Ashforth & Anand, 2003): (a) *co-optation* by rewards linked to their collusion with the corruption, sometimes with rewards that are so subtle that they are not even aware that their initial attitudes toward the corruption have changed; (b) *incrementalism*, in which they escalate commitment to the corruption over time; (c) *compromise* by selecting the wrongdoing that represents the "lesser of two evils" (e.g., when polluters rationalize that their actions allow the firm to survive, thereby preventing layoffs of employees); or (d) *coercion* into wrong-doing through fear. Of these four mechanisms, co-optation might occur in Phase 1, resulting in the employee not even recognizing that wrongdoing has occurred; the remaining three mechanisms apply to Phase 3 of Figure 2.1. Socialization for wrongdoing is more likely in organizations in which there is high turnover, weak culture, and socialization practices that do not prescribe clear norms against wrongdoing (Robinson & Kraatz, 1998).

We interpret this model to mean that collective corruption encourages normalization of wrongdoing, but that collective corruption does not always automatically lead to normalization of wrongdoing. Corruption is defined as "misuse of an organizational position or authority for personal or organization (or subunit) gain, where misuse in turn refers to departures from accepted societal norms" (Anand et al., 2004, p. 40). Corruption is one type of wrongdoing,

but we see no theoretical reason to propose that normalization processes could not apply to other types of wrongdoing so we will use
the term "wrongdoing" rather than "corruption" in our discussion.

The model does not explicitly distinguish a case where multiple
members of a group actively engage in corruption from a case where
one member engages directly and actively in corruption and the
others know about it but do nothing to stop it, or even help to cover it
up. Picture a situation where one member engages in shady accounting practices that benefit both them and the organization (e.g.,
Enron). If other members of the group do not directly benefit from
the financial misdeed but do benefit indirectly because they are seen
as supportive of this wrongdoer, we believe that their collusion in not
reporting the wrongdoing to anyone represents collective corruption. Clearly there are differences in the magnitude of the collective
corruption—and these differences in magnitude may well be due to
the strength of the normalization process. This is an important definitional problem, because if collective corruption includes cases of
cover-up (i.e., non-whistle-blowing) then a great many wrongdoing
situations—perhaps most—constitute collective corruption. If so,
wrongdoing can be said to be collective when: (a) there is evidence
that more than one active wrongdoer is involved; and (b) multiple
parties are aware of wrongdoing but at least some do not act to
stop it.

Processes of normalization of wrongdoing are important because
they affect both Phase 1 and Phase 3 of observers' judgments. First,
normalization can cause observers of wrongdoing to not even "see" the
wrongdoing when it occurs, because they have become accustomed to
the organization's norms of what constitutes wrongdoing, through
institutionalization. Thus, procedures, systems, and other variables
that facilitate institutionalization constitute characteristics that bring
about a process that affects Phase 1 of the whistle-blowing model.
Second, normalization can also cause observers of wrongdoing, who
believe that they have observed wrongdoing, not to take action and
blow the whistle because they believe that doing so would be useless
or dangerous. Thus, normalization affects both the "labeling" of
wrongdoing and the specific decision to blow the whistle.

We believe that empirical study of the effects of normalization
of wrongdoing on whistle-blowing could yield important results.
Further, the normalization model offers suggestions for how the
cycle of normalization can be broken, and a recent paper (Misangyi,

Weaver, & Elms, in press) suggests that market control and anti-corruption government control have not been particularly effective, and that appeals to enact appropriate moral identities (through framing) may also be needed. In some sense, this is similar to making hypernorms more salient, for example, by pointing out that some activity violates a universal standard and thus cannot be tolerated by moral people.

Specific propositions from these perspectives should be articulated and examined empirically. For example, it has been suggested that financial incentives for desired behavior may in fact undermine it (Misangyi et al., in press), yet in whistle-blowing contexts it is not clear that this is true. Some research (explored more thoroughly in Chapters 6 and 7) suggests that offering financial incentives for whistle-blowing may help offset some of its expected risks and costs. An integration of these models, and articulating of specific propositions, may offer some insight into possible conditions that must be present in order for incentives to have desired effects. Also, the measurement of behaviors in question is critical both for conceptual clarity and for practical reasons. It is possible that someone could be moved by incentives to act on wrongdoing, while also (a) believing or claiming that the incentives had no effect, or (b) feeling or reporting unhappiness about doing so, greater cynicism, adverse effects on some aspect of moral identity, or other negative consequences. These effects could also be temporary. From a practical perspective, the most critical dependent variable is whether one acts to try to stop wrongdoing. If appropriately administered financial rewards encourage employees to act responsibly, it may well be that offering them is the right thing to do, even if employees report feeling more cynical as a result. But clearly more research is needed before drawing these conclusions.

Summary

In 1996, we concluded that

empirical research to date has not shown that whistle-blowers are inherently different from those organization members who observe wrongdoing but chose not to report it. In other words, there is no evidence that whistle-blowers are typically crackpots. Basically, whistle-blowers are employees who are in the wrong place at the wrong time—that is, they have the opportunity to observe wrongdoing, often because of the nature of their jobs. Although it is premature to draw conclusions, there is some evidence that if the wrongdoing is sufficiently serious and if potential whistle-blowers believe they can successfully cause the termination of the wrongdoing, they will act. Organizations can encourage the use of internal channels to blow the whistle by providing sufficient information to employees about the use of these channels and providing reassurance that they will not suffer retaliation if they use the internal channels. Preliminary research evidence indicates that whistle-blowers use external channels when they don't know about the internal channels and when they think the external channels will afford them protection from retaliation. (Near & Miceli, 1996, p. 515)

Since 1996, our conclusion is largely the same, except that we now have a bit more evidence suggesting that individual variables play a stronger role than previously thought. But we are disappointed that, although a massive amount of information dealing with whistle-blowing has been published since 1996, most of it is anecdotal. Very little controlled research on whistle-blowing has been published, particularly in the top journals; with more research, we might have more new directions to report. Further, there is evidence that changes in the legal and possibly the social environment are influencing the behavior of both organizations and potential whistle-blowers, suggesting that findings from earlier periods may no longer apply. Finally, we recommend that future research direct more attention to the question of type of wrongdoing and industry as larger characteristics that may be confounded with other situational characteristics of the whistle-blowing context, as well as with individual characteristics of whistle-blowers.

4

A Model of the Predictors and Outcomes of Retaliation

The case of Sheila White recently reached the U.S. Supreme Court. White was a former forklift operator for Burlington Northern Santa Fe Corp. The *Wall Street Journal* reported some of the facts of the case:

> In 1997, (White) complained her foreman was sexually harassing her. He was suspended for 10 days. She was reassigned to dirtier track work, though her job classification stayed the same. After she filed retaliation charges with the EEOC, a supervisor suspended Ms. White for insubordination. She was reinstated with back pay, but her lawyers contend the altered duties and suspension were illegal retaliation. Burlington Northern Santa Fe disagrees. "It can't be that every judgment call a supervisor makes is the basis for a federal retaliation lawsuit," says Carter G. Phillips, a Sidley Austin LLP managing partner in Washington, D.C., who represents the Fort Worth, Texas, railroad. (Lublin, 2006, p. B4)

The Supreme Court ruled unanimously that White had experienced retaliation and that the company's reinstating her and awarding back pay did not fully address the problem (Lane, 2006b). Because the case "expands the legal rights of millions of workers," employers will be paying increasing attention to retaliation issues (Lane, 2006a, p. A16).

As Sheila White's case illustrates, retaliation is a very important issue. As noted in the first chapter, we define retaliation against whistle-blowers to be undesirable action taken against a whistle-blower—and in direct response to the whistle-blowing. Yet prior research shows that retaliation does not occur in every case, and the extent or type of retaliation may vary from case to case. The previous chapters have focused on the prediction of when whistle-blowing will occur. But a very different question is: once whistle-blowing has occurred, under what circumstances might a whistle-blower experience or avoid retaliation?

In this chapter, we describe a model of the predictors of retaliation. We describe how theories of power, particularly resource dependence theory, suggest predictors of retaliation against whistle-blowers and reactions of whistle-blowers to retaliation. Then, we review existing research examining when and why organizations engage in retaliation against whistle-blowers. We discuss research concerning the consequences of retaliation for whistle-blowers. We begin with a model of the causes of retaliation.

A Model Predicting Retaliation

As depicted in Figure 4.1, the primary theoretical perspective used to predict retaliation concerns power relationships among the social actors involved. These actors are the whistle-blower(s), the wrongdoer(s), the complaint recipient(s) who hears the charge of wrongdoing, and the top management team.

From this perspective, the power context of the social actors predicts retaliation. But, because power relationships may change over

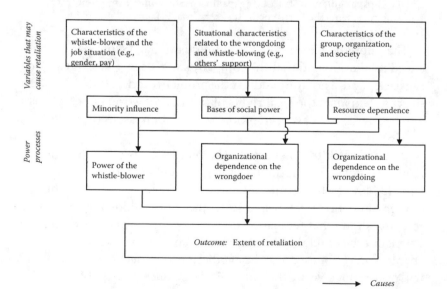

Figure 4.1   A model of the predictors of retaliation.

time, delineating the interaction effects may be difficult. Further, as will be explained below, one power theory suggests that, in addition to the social actors, the nature of the wrongdoing itself plays a role. Finally, the societal culture and regulatory environment in which the organization operates is important; for example, laws against retaliation and the extent to which they are enforced may influence the extent to which it occurs. However, we will address the legal issues in Chapter 6.

Three theories of power suggest means by which these power shifts might occur (e.g., Miceli & Near, 1992). All of these are discussed thoroughly in our 1996 review article, and in subsequent work (e.g., Miceli & Near, 2007) so we consider them only briefly here. All three theories of power provide bases for predicting that retaliation against whistle-blowers is inversely related to their power and credibility (Near & Miceli, 1987). First, from the view of *minority influence theory* (e.g., Moscovici, 1976; Nemeth, 1979), group members who take a position not held by the majority (e.g., whistle-blowers) are more influential if they appear credible, confident, competent, and objective (e.g., Miceli & Near, 1992). Second, people who have more *bases of social power*, such as expert power or referent power (French & Raven, 1959), are more powerful than others. Thus, depending on the number of bases and the nature of the bases of power, both whistle-blowers and wrongdoers can be powerful, as are the top management team and, in some cases, complaint recipients. Third, in *resource dependence theory* (Pfeffer & Salancik, 1978) organizational members have power when the organization depends on them for some resource; thus, whistle-blowers are relatively powerful if the organization depends on them and if the organization does not depend on continuation of the wrongdoing or on the wrongdoer (Near & Miceli, 1987). Wrongdoers are relatively powerful if the organization depends on them.

All three theories can be used to identify variables that reflect the *power of the whistle-blower*, often measured in terms of the individual's status in the organization, or dependence of the organization on the individual, as a resource to the organization. All other factors being equal, for example, whistle-blowers with little power can be ignored or retaliated against more easily and with fewer negative consequences to the organization, than can those who hold high-level positions or have special expertise that is needed and hard to replace, who are well respected for their experience and competence.

In addition, the social bases of power theory and resource dependence theory have a second important implication for predicting retaliation against whistle-blowers: that the more powerful the wrongdoer, or more dependent the organization is on the wrongdoer—all other factors being equal—the more retaliation will be directed toward the whistle-blower, in a misguided attempt to "protect" the wrongdoer by silencing, isolating, or getting rid of the whistle-blower, or sending a message to other would-be whistle-blowers. The *wrongdoer's power* is often measured in terms of the wrongdoer's status in the organization, which reflects legitimate or other bases of power, or the dependence of the organization on the individual.

Finally, resource dependence theory offers a third implication: that the greater the organizational dependence on the wrongdoing, the more it resists stopping or changing it, and one means of resistance is to retaliate. The *organization's dependence on the wrongdoing* is often assumed to be the inverse of the seriousness of the wrongdoing, measured in terms of cost, frequency, seriousness, or likely harm to insiders or outsiders. The rationale here is that the organization would not knowingly continue serious wrongdoing unless the benefits exceeded the costs of discovery, in terms of legal costs or foregone reputation or legitimacy.

We believe that the whistle-blower's power must be considered in the context of the relative power of the wrongdoer and the dependence of the organization on continuation of the wrongdoing. Where the organization depends heavily on the wrongdoer or the wrongdoing itself, even a whistle-blower with high status may not have sufficient relative power to escape retaliation. For example, if the "dependency scores" of the organization are greater for the wrongdoer and the wrongdoing (say 7 on a scale from 1 to 10) than for the whistle-blower (say 5 on that same scale) then we might predict that the whistle-blower is more likely to suffer retaliation than where the situation is reversed. We now turn our attention to the results of empirical studies that test or otherwise have implications for these theories.

Results of Empirical Studies Predicting Retaliation

In 1992 (Miceli & Near, 1992), we reviewed studies concerning predictors of retaliation; we updated this review in 1996 (Near & Miceli, 1996), and a meta-analysis of findings to date was published in 2005 (Mesmer-Magnus & Viswesvaran, 2005). We focus here on what has been learned since these reviews, which incorporates much of what we described in a recent chapter (Miceli & Near, 2007). At all times, as we explained in Chapter 1, retaliation has traditionally been measured as "comprehensiveness," that is, a sum of all the number of types of actual and threatened retaliation that the respondent checked from a list of possible retaliatory actions provided in the questionnaire.

Roughly following the general organization scheme used in previous chapters, we have classified the potential predictors of retaliation into three categories, as shown in Figure 4.1. The first comprises personal characteristics of the whistle-blower and of the job situation. The second category comprises situational characteristics pertaining to the wrongdoing and the whistle-blowing that influence the retaliation. These include characteristics of the particular wrongdoing and whistle-blowing situation itself (unique to those events). The third comprises situational characteristics relating to the organizational context in which it occurs. These are characteristics of the group and organization itself apart from the exact conditions of the wrongdoing and whistle-blowing, and of the society or cultural context.

Characteristics of the Whistle-Blower and the Job Situation

As shown in Figure 4.1, all three power theories suggest that some demographic variables would be related to retaliation. This would occur through their effects on the power of the whistle-blower, in actuality or as perceived by those who might retaliate.

Most of the studies completed prior to 1996 used data from surveys conducted by the MSPB, and the same items were used across multiple studies, allowing for replication of results. It should be remembered that the MSPB surveyed only public sector, federal-level (as opposed to state or local) employees. But the pre-1996 literature showed that no personal characteristics were consistently related to retaliation. Based on these results, the lack of relationship is quite striking: age, education, race, performance of the employee, pay, and role in the agency simply did not predict retaliation in a general way. Likewise, results of a recent meta-analysis (Mesmer-Magnus & Viswesvaran, 2005) showed that retaliation was only weakly correlated with the

Whistle-blowing in Organizations

TABLE 4.1   Empirical Results Related to the Characteristics of the Whistle-Blower and the Job Situation That Predict Retaliation and Were Not Previously Reported in Near and Miceli (1996) or Mesmer-Magnus and Viswesvaran (2005)

	Studies[a]			
Predictors	A	B	C	D
Demographic				
Marital status				0
Education				
Gender (male)	0		–	0
Race (minority)		+		
Job situation				
Pay	0			
Professional job status	0			
Job tenure	0			
Performance		–		

Note: + = positive relationship; – = negative relationship; 0 = no significant relationship.

[a] Studies are listed in order of first appearance in the text: A. (Rehg, 1998); B. (Miceli et al., 1999); C. (Rehg et al., 2004) and (Rehg et al., in press); D. (Rothschild & Miethe, 1999).

whistle-blower's education level ($r = .04$), job level ($r = -.07$) and role responsibility ($r = -.07$).

Table 4.1 summarizes the findings from research since the 1996 and 2005 reviews, which shows that, generally, this picture is unchanged in the federal sector. MSPB data gathered in 1992 from surveys of federal employees added a few personal variables not available in prior MSPB data sets. Generally, as in prior studies, personal and job situation variables were unrelated to retaliation comprehensiveness (Rehg, 1998); these included education, gender, pay, professional job status, and job tenure (Miceli et al., 1999). Consistent with the model, however, another study indicated that retaliation was more comprehensive when the whistle-blower was a member of a racial or ethnic group other than non-Hispanic whites and self-reported job performance was lower (Miceli et al., 1999). More recent research in a large military base found that only one demographic variable predicted retaliation. In this sample, women perceived greater retaliation than did men (Rehg et al., in press; Rehg et al., 2004).

Findings are similar outside the federal sector, although only one systematic study has been published, to our knowledge. An interview study involving employees of business and not-for-profit employees indicated that no personal characteristics insulated whistle-blowers from retaliation (Rothschild & Miethe, 1999).

From a practical standpoint, these findings can be viewed as encouraging, because—although retaliation against anyone is arguably problematic—it generally is not disproportionately directed at powerless people, who may have fewer resources to enable them to withstand or recover from it. However, we think the research is not sufficiently advanced to place much confidence in these findings in sectors other than the federal sector, and there have been studies showing that, in some cases, certain demographics mattered.

From a research standpoint, these findings are perplexing for at least two reasons. First, the model may be sound, but measurement issues may have weakened the studies' ability to test the hypotheses. Obviously, the demographic measures can be faulted for being at best indirect indicators of power; more direct measures could be used where conditions permit. The leverage that the individual has in the specific situation may be more important. For example, an auditor may have extremely high credibility and leverage about financial matters because his or her role and high performance may give him or her power, but if she or he complains of age discrimination, the financial and accounting expertise may be irrelevant and she or he may be retaliated against in the latter situation but not the former. As another example, a whistle-blower who is a good friend to a complaint recipient or has confidential information that recipient does not want shared may have more leverage than someone else to get the complaint recipient to act without punishing the whistle-blower, and these indicators of power are unlikely to be reflected in the variables in the published studies.

Other measurement issues may also be evident. In some cases, negative events interpreted as retaliation may not have occurred at all or could have occurred for reasons other than whistle-blowing. For example, a poorly performing individual could perceive that criticism or being passed over for promotion was due to his or her complaining about wrongdoing, when in fact there was no wrongdoing, and she or he was simply a nuisance. Some measures of retaliation had unknown reliability (Mesmer-Magnus & Viswesvaran, 2005). There is also a potential range restriction problem, in that whistle-blowers who were fired, or who were severely mistreated and quit, may have left the federal sector and if so, their data were not in the databases. Those who transferred within the federal sector, of course, could have been in the sample. On the other hand, if these problems were severe, the power to detect any significant relationships with any variable would have been compromised. But, as will be shown later, there have been consistently demonstrated relationships between the measures of retaliation and situational variables. This suggests that issues pertaining to the measurement of retaliation did not fully account for the nonrelationship with demographic variables.

Second, perhaps the model should be changed because, at least with regard to personal variables, it does not accurately describe the conditions leading to retaliation. Future research could explore whether demographics interact with situational variables. More specifically, demographics may interact with types of wrongdoing or with contextual variables to predict retaliation. For example, minorities may experience more retaliation than do other employees when they complain about race discrimination but not when they complain about other types of wrongdoing.

As another example, the gender context may interact with the gender of the whistle-blowers. Retaliation may be greater against female whistle-blowers when they occupy male-dominated positions or work in male-dominated organizations, as implied by a study in which female attorneys suffered greater levels of interpersonal mistreatment than did male attorneys (Cortina et al., 2002). Female whistle-blowers may experience no more retaliation than their male counterparts where the gender mix is more balanced or less when it is female-dominated.

Similarly, in a survey of civilian and military employees of a large military base, the predictors of retaliation were different for women than for men (Rehg et al., in press; Rehg et al., 2004). As noted by the authors, social role theory seems to provide a promising basis for research on these questions. Social role theory predicts that the gender-based societal division of labor reduces the influence of women in work groups, regardless of their status, and that women who violate gender expectations will be sanctioned (Carli & Eagly, 1999; Gutek, 1985). Roles assigned in society carry over to the workplace; people expect that these societal roles for women (e.g., acquiescent, not assertively vocal) be followed in the workplace, even if these expectations conflict with the role demands of the job and lead to ineffective job performance (Kidder & Parks, 2001). Thus, social role theory implies that women who blow the whistle in male-dominated contexts would violate these expectations of acquiescent behavior. Consequently, others may react more negatively and retaliate to a greater extent than when men blow the whistle.

Situational Characteristics Related to the Wrongdoing and Whistle-Blowing

In this section, we describe results pertaining to retaliation as a function of situational characteristics related to the wrongdoing and whistle-blowing. We begin by continuing from the last section our focus on the whistle-blower by discussing empirical results pertinent to the support that the whistle-blower receives from others in the organization. Results from recent work are summarized in Table 4.2.

TABLE 4.2 Empirical Results Related to the Situational Characteristics Relevant to the Wrongdoing and Whistle-Blowing That Predict Retaliation and Were Not Previously Reported in Near and Miceli (1996) or Mesmer-Magnus and Viswesvaran (2005)

Predictors	Studies[a]							
	A	B	C	D	E	F	G	H
Top management support	−	−						
Middle-management or supervisor support	−	−						
Coworker support	0	0	−					
Wrongdoer power or status		+		+	+			
Seriousness of wrongdoing	M	+			0	+		
Type of wrongdoing		+					+	
External whistle-blowing channels	+	+	+					+
Person by situation interaction: external channels and whistle-blower gender		+						

Note: + = positive relationship; − = negative relationship; 0 = no significant relationship; M = mixed. In the case of the categorical variable "type of wrong-doing" and the interaction, any significant relationship is noted with +.

[a] Studies are listed in order of first appearance in the text: A. (Miceli et al., 1999); B. (Rehg et al., 2004) and (Rehg et al., in press); C. (Rehg, 1998); D. (Cortina & Magley, 2003); E. (Lee et al., 2004); F. (Rothschild & Miethe, 1999); G. (Near et al., 2004); H. (Dworkin & Baucus, 1998).

Support for the Whistle-Blower from Others in the Organization
Support from others in the organization is likely to decrease retaliation through at least two power processes, as depicted in Figure 4.1. The presence of at least one other person who deviates from norms considerably reduces the pressure to conform to the majority view (e.g., Moscovici, 1976; Nemeth, 1979). Coworkers or managers may support the whistle-blower because they like the whistle-blower (referent power), or respect his or her expertise, for example, when an engineer reports safety violations, or through other bases. In addition, coworker or management support may enhance the whistle-blower's legitimate power.

Management Support.   As indicated in the 1996 review, and consistent with the model, retaliation was *negatively* related to top-management support and middle-management (or supervisor) support, in multiple studies. Results of the meta-analysis (Mesmer-Magnus & Viswesvaran, 2005) showed that retaliation was negatively related to supervisor support at all levels ($r = -.39$).

More recent work shows similar findings. One study involved a comparison of MSPB regression results from three samples drawn from the same organizations over time; the first two of these samples were also included in the previous reviews, so they should not be viewed as independent (Miceli et al., 1999). Results indicated that the relationship between lack of management support and retaliation increased over time ($\beta = .18$ in 1980, .33 in 1983, and .29 in 1992). In the same study, lack of supervisor support was also related to retaliation ($\beta = .26$ in 1980, .40 in 1983, and .16 in 1992). A more recent study of retaliation among whistle-blowers at a large military base also produced findings indicating that lack of support from management and supervisor were the strongest predictors of retaliation (Rehg et al., in press; Rehg et al., 2004).

Coworker Support.   In both the 1996 review and the 2005 meta-analysis, coworker support was unrelated to retaliation, a finding that has been replicated in more recent studies (Miceli et al., 1999; Rehg et al., in press; Rehg et al., 2004). However, in his dissertation comparing regression results based on all three time periods of the MSPB data (1980, 1983, and 1992), Rehg found that coworker support was a significant predictor of retaliation in the 1992 data, where retaliation comprehensiveness could be measured more broadly than in the earlier two surveys (Rehg, 1998). He added four more types of retaliation to the checklist of variables used in the first two surveys: (a) verbal harassment/intimidation, (b) denial of an award, (c) being fired, and (d) being shunned by coworkers; clearly two of the four new types represented forms of reprisal that could be used by coworkers more easily than some of the types on the traditional checklist. With the revised retaliation measure taken as the dependent variable, coworker lack of support was a significant predictor, though not quite as strong as supervisor lack of support or management lack of support. Nonetheless, these results suggest that lack of coworker support is more likely to influence reprisal when reprisal itself is more broadly defined.

In addition, as described in Chapter 1, Rehg (1998) proposed that, from this measure of overall retaliation, two relatively independent dimensions of retaliation could be separated: informal and formal retaliation. Informal retaliation, coworker alienation, and negative behaviors toward the whistle-blower are important outcomes of whistle-blowing processes (Dobson, 1998). Using the 1992 MSPB data set, Rehg found mixed support for his model. Specifically, he found that suffering *informal* retaliation but not formal retaliation was significantly associated with lack of coworker support and lack of higher management support, but not with supervisor support. He found that suffering *formal* retaliation exclusively (i.e., no informal retaliation) was significantly associated with lack of higher-level management support but not with supervisor or coworker support. Finally, suffering both forms of retaliation was significantly related to lack of higher-level management support and lack of support from a supervisor but was unrelated to lack of support from coworkers. These results suggest that retaliation processes vary, depending on the source of the retaliation; future research should separate informal from formal retaliation.

Characteristics of the Wrongdoer(s)   Another situational dynamic concerns the power of another key player in the process—the wrongdoer(s). As depicted in Figure 4.1, wrongdoer power can be examined through two of the same theories as those applied to the whistle-blower—French's and Raven's bases of social power theory (French & Raven, 1959), and resource dependence theory. We view minority influence theory as having less potential for deriving predictions about the wrongdoer's power, to the extent that the situation involves organizational wrongdoing that appears to be tolerated by the top management team, that is, tolerating or ignoring wrong-doing—and not speaking out—reflect majority views. However, we recognize that there may be some situations where both the wrong-doer *and* the whistle-blower may be a "deviant" in the sense of resist-ing majority influence, for example, in the case of embezzlement.

In their review of the literature prior to 1996, Near and Miceli pointed out that wrongdoer power might be an important part of the equation predicting retaliation, but cited no findings on that point because this variable had not been examined empirically (Near & Miceli, 1996). Nor did Mesmer-Magnus and Viswesvaran list wrong-doer power as a predictor of retaliation in their 2005 meta-analysis (Mesmer-Magnus & Viswesvaran, 2005). Since that time, wrongdoer power was shown to predict retaliation in three studies (Cortina & Magley, 2003; Lee et al., 2004; Rehg et al., in press; Rehg et al., 2004).

Characteristics of the Wrongdoing In Chapter 3 we noted that characteristics of wrongdoing, such as its seriousness, were related to whether whistle-blowing would occur. As shown in Figure 4.1, power theories suggest that wrongdoing characteristics play a role in retaliation as well. One central dynamic concerns the effects of the organization's dependence on the continuation of the wrongdoing on retaliation, as derived from resource dependence theory (Pfeffer & Salancik, 1978).

Seriousness of Wrongdoing. The power model of whistle-blowing suggests that if organizations engage in serious wrongdoing—and thus leave themselves open to detection and sanction—they do so because continuation of this wrongdoing is very important to their continued success or even survival. Obviously, to some extent the power of the wrongdoer(s) cannot be separated from the seriousness of the wrongdoing; for example, financial wrongdoing may be more serious and the organization may be more dependent on it, where top management is involved (as in the case of Enron), than where it is isolated in one lower-level department or division. A study of a large military base produced findings showing that wrongdoing serious-ness and wrongdoer power loaded in the same factor (Rehg et al., in press; Rehg et al., 2004).

Research results on the question of whether wrongdoing serious-ness or magnitude is related to retaliation have been mixed (Near &

Miceli, 1996), perhaps in part because different measures of wrong-doing seriousness have been used, as noted in an earlier chapter. In the 2005 meta-analysis (Mesmer-Magnus & Viswesvaran, 2005), retaliation was correlated significantly with both seriousness of wrongdoing ($r = .13$) and frequency of wrongdoing ($r = .30$). Research conducted since these two reviews has also produced mixed results. In the study of predictors of retaliation in the MSPB data comparing regression results from the same sample of federal agencies over time (Miceli et al., 1999), seriousness of wrongdoing was significantly related to retaliation in only one of the three time periods, 1983 ($\beta = .13$); in the remaining two time periods, the relationship was not significant ($\beta = .06$ in 1980 and .09 in 1992). In another study, retali-ation was associated with significant wrongdoing by the organiza-tion (Rothschild & Miethe, 1999). A factor reflecting wrongdoing seriousness and wrongdoer power significantly predicted retaliation (Rehg et al., in press; Rehg et al., 2004).

Finally, in a study of whistle-blowing about sexual harassment (Lee et al., 2004), the number of types of wrongdoing (including both felonious sexual harassment and nonfelonious sexual harassment) did not predict retaliation. At this point, we conclude that serious wrongdoing, measured in a variety of ways, seems to predict retalia-tion, but that further research is needed to verify the breadth, depth, and causal direction of this relationship.

Type of Wrongdoing.   In general, organizations are less dependent on certain types of wrongdoing, for example, that involves sexual harassment by one individual against a given individual, or embezzle-ment, than on other types, for example, wrongdoing that may increase revenues (temporarily at least), as in the case of addictive cigarettes. Neither prior review included this variable. In a multivariate study of retaliation at a large military base (Rehg et al., in press; Rehg et al., 2004), the researchers did not directly examine type of wrongdoing, but they found that wrongdoing that harmed insiders, which can be related to the type of wrongdoing, predicted retaliation.

In the only known systematic investigation of the relationship between a full range of types of wrongdoing and the comprehensive-ness of retaliation (Near et al., 2004), the authors noted that previous research suggested that cost of the wrongdoing predicted retaliation comprehensiveness (Near & Miceli, 1996). Therefore, they argued, if cost of the wrongdoing is associated with type of wrongdoing, then type of wrongdoing may account for the apparent relationship with retaliation, not cost alone. Type of wrongdoing was found to be significantly associated with retaliation, with retaliation being significantly higher against whistle-blowers who reported legal violations than against those who reported waste (Near et al., 2004).

Why this occurred could not be ascertained given the limitations of the data in that study. We would speculate that this finding occurred because waste does not benefit anyone, including top management. Why waste would occur in the first place, since there is no apparent benefit, is unknown; we can speculate that one reason is the persons involved in the waste are simply not competent enough to do the job efficiently. Or, perhaps waste occurs because organization systems are designed incompetently and reward waste, or staffing for oversight is inadequate, or because conflicting goals exist (e.g., when a budget system requires managers to spend or lose resources at year-end, to make organizational accounting less complicated; or managers overspend because they believe they otherwise will be allocated less money in the next fiscal year, or because the allocator does not have time to assess and compare real needs across units). Therefore, whistle-blowers who report waste are seen as doing a service for the organization, rather than harming it. In contrast, whistle-blowing about other types of wrongdoing—many of which might have been illegal—is probably more embarrassing for the organization, because it implies managerial malfeasance and harm to others, including outsiders. Whistle-blowing on illegal activity can open the door to fines, negative publicity, increased regulation, or even criminal prosecution—consequences we have frequently seen in such recent cases as Tyco, WorldCom, and Enron. In any event, research is needed to examine these speculations.

Whistle-Blowing Channels   Another possible predictor of retaliation is the choice of channels; as discussed in Chapter 3, most whistle-blowers who used external channels also used internal channels, usually before they used external channels (Rehg et al., in press; Rehg et al., 2004). The power model suggests two scenarios: in the first, external reporting leads to more retaliation, and in the second, more retaliation leads to external reporting. In either case, the organization may be resisting changing the original wrongdoing as well. An internal whistle-blower may feel that the complaint of wrongdoing has been ignored and decide to escalate the complaint to someone external with more power, in order to bring pressure on the organization. Because external channels may be very threatening to the organization, it may direct greater retaliation only after the external whistle-blowing, such as their supervisors, to discourage this power play. An alternative scenario is the following, in which the direction of causation may be different. Some employees who blow the whistle internally may experience comprehensive retaliation, and this then may cause them to make external reports, to get more power to avoid more retaliation, and/or to vindicate the whistle-blowing action, by bringing the attention of external authorities to the matter. For example, employees who believe promotions have been denied unfairly may try to resolve problems internally, but experience substantial punishment for speaking up, so they then may file discrimination charges with a state civil rights agency. In either scenario, we would expect that external reporting would be associated with retaliation.

Research prior to 2005 was consistent with this prediction. Whistle-blowers who used external channels were found to be more likely to suffer retaliation than those who used internal channels alone (Near & Miceli, 1996). In fact, the average correlation between retaliation and use of external channels was .17 in the meta-analysis (Mesmer-Magnus & Viswesvaran, 2005).

Results from studies not included in those reviews have been generally consistent. In the study comparing regression results over time from the same federal agencies, use of external channels predicted retaliation in 1980 ($\beta = .12$) and 1992 ($\beta = .15$), but was not tested in 1983 (Miceli et al., 1999). In a secondary analysis of MSPB data, Rehg found that whistle-blowers who experienced both informal and formal retaliation were more likely to have used external channels to report wrongdoing ($\beta = .14$), although the causal direction of this relationship could not be determined from the cross-sectional data (Rehg, 1998). A comparison of legal cases showed that whistle-blowers who used external channels rather than internal channels alone were more likely to suffer retaliation (measured as a zero-one variable), usually by delayed firing rather than firing immediately after the whistle-blowing (Dworkin & Baucus, 1998). This study also showed that external whistle-blowers were more likely to have had superior evidence of wrongdoing and to have been *less* effective in changing the organization. This study used data from legal cases, coded by the researchers; these data, by their nature, came from a small number of whistle-blowers who had filed lawsuits, in which "success" was measured on the basis of facts cited in the legal case and interpreted by the researchers. This result differed from those findings obtained through survey data, in which the respondent was asked about perceived success of the whistle-blowing effort in changing the organization. In fact, the average correlation between "success" of the whistle-blowing in changing the organization's actions and retaliation was –.20 (Mesmer-Magnus & Viswesvaran, 2005), across multiple studies, but cause-effect relations could not be ascertained. We wish to stress that both methods relied on very small samples; in our view there has not been sufficient research on this point for definite conclusions to be reached.

Future research could examine the extent to which varying methods of disclosure are seen as more procedurally just or unjust (Miceli & Near, 1997), and whether this predicts retaliation. Here we are not referring to a legal standard but rather to shared beliefs about justice. For example, is it a universally held belief that the whistle-blower must first talk to the perceived wrongdoer, to give him or her the chance to make corrections, before reporting wrongdoing to authorities, such that retaliation seems justified when the whistle-blowers' actions don't seem "fair"? Does a greater power differential between the parties affect this belief?

Person by Situation Interactions That Predict Retaliation   Person by situation interactions have not been examined frequently. In the study of a large military base, the use of external channels was associated with retaliation against female employees but not male employees (Rehg et al., in press; Rehg et al., 2004).

We now turn to an additional set of situational characteristics that were related to whether whistle-blowing occurs: the characteristics of the group, organization, and society. The power model suggests that some variables in this category of characteristics also may influence retaliation.

Characteristics of the Group, Organization, and Society   The power model in Figure 4.1 suggests that characteristics of the group, organization, and society influence retaliation. The minority influence literature suggests a number of variables that influence the relative power of the majority and the minority, but to our knowledge, no studies have examined these variables in a whistle-blowing context, so we will not discuss them. The bases of social power would be less relevant here since they pertain primarily to individuals rather than to entities; we can conceive of situations where group variables may be relevant, for example, that the greater the distance between the expertise of the group and that of the whistle-blower, the more powerful the individual may be. But again, there is virtually no research on group variables in whistle-blowing, so we have little to say here. The third theory, resource dependence theory, suggests many organizational and societal variables that lessen the organization's dependence on the whistle-blower and increase its dependence on the wrongdoing or the wrongdoer will increase retaliation, and these have been the focus of some research on retaliation. Because there is greater theoretical development than empirical research, there are too few studies to list in a table.

Organizational Climate or Culture.   Does an organization culture that emphasizes compliance discourage wrongdoing, thereby reducing the need for whistle-blowing, enhancing the perception that management would respond to complaints, and preventing retaliation? This may seem self-evident, at least to those involved in compliance and legal enforcement, as illustrated in the following anecdote.

When James Derouin, partner and environmental and natural resources practice group leader in the Phoenix office of law firm Steptoe & Johnson LLP, was hired as outside counsel for one of Exxon's companies 25 years ago, they told him: "If you do anything that is illegal, improper or unethical on our behalf, we'll fire you." The executives ticked off a detailed list of do's and don'ts—for example, don't send us Christmas presents; a card will suffice. "Yes, the company later had its problems, but the management culture I dealt with in the '70s was incredibly demanding in terms of compliance and rectitude, and it gave me a great deal of faith in representing them," Derouin says. "That's how blunt you need to be. When you're not, it creates the suspicion that there are loopholes" (Krell, 2002, p. 22).

But it has been suggested that emphasis on compliance creates so much bureaucracy or over-controls employees that it undermines the development of ethical values, good decision making, and trust in management (e.g., Pfeffer, 1994). There is some evidence that this can occur (e.g., Pfeffer, 1994; Treviño, Weaver, Gibson, & Toffler, 1999; Weaver & Treviño, 1999). Where it does, wrongdoing and retaliation may occur with greater frequency.

Thus, bureaucracy may present a double-edged sword. On the one hand, bureaucratic organizations with rules requiring compliance with ethical behavior may discourage wrongdoing, thereby pre-empting the need for whistle-blowing. Further, when wrongdoing does occur, they may have very clear rules and policies about how to rectify the situation. For example, Kerr and Slocum contrasted reward systems in organizational cultures that were hierarchically based versus those that were performance-based (Kerr & Slocum, 2005). In the hierarchically based culture, which supported loyalty to the firm, if wrongdoing and retaliation against whistle-blowers were specifically proscribed then we would expect compliance with these norms—but if the norms against wrongdoing and retaliation were not specific and strong, we might expect that other members of the organization would engage in retaliation against whistle-blowers out of loyalty to the firm. Similarly, in firms with performance-based reward systems, if the wrongdoer was seen as harming the bottom line and the whistle-blower as improving the bottom line, we would expect greater support of the whistle-blower and less support of the wrongdoer. Alternatively, if the wrongdoing was viewed as support-ing firm performance and whistle-blowing as detracting from it, we might expect less support for or even outright reprisal against the whistle-blower. Thus, there could be cases where either a hierarchi-cally based reward system (probably more common in a bureaucratic structure) or a performance-based reward system (perhaps more common in an organic or nonbureaucratic structure) could discour-age wrongdoing and encourage whistle-blowing.

On the other hand, when whistle-blowers do question managerial decisions in bureaucracies, they challenge the authority structure along with the particular decision in question. Because of the impor-tance of the authority structure to the operation of bureaucracy (Weber, 1947), its primacy cannot be questioned by subordinates. In a now-classic book, a sociologist argued that bureaucracies would be more likely to engage in retaliation than would less bureaucratic orga-nizations because bureaucracies could not permit any second guess-ing of managerial decisions (Weinstein, 1979). Bureaucracies also may find change more difficult than do other organizations, and they may also be slower to terminate wrongdoing and change operations (Near & Miceli, 1996). For these reasons, we would expect retaliation to be greater in organizations where the bureaucracy has become so rigid that it is dysfunctional or in organizations that do not support change, relative to other types of organizations, and regardless of the whistle-blowing situation. Often these two categories of organization overlap, as suggested by the threat-rigidity hypothesis proposed by Staw and colleagues (Staw, Sandelands, & Dutton, 1981).

Consistent with this reasoning, research in various kinds of organizations, including several large and bureaucratic firms and government agencies, suggests higher rates of retaliation against whistle-blowers in certain organizations compared to others (Miethe, 1999). It should be noted that not all government bureaucracies have "bureaucratic structures"—nor do all private sector firms *not* have bureaucratic structures. The layperson's popular use of the term "bureaucracy" differs from the technical definition of "bureaucratic structure," which originated with Max Weber in the late 1800s (Weber, 1947); it is this second usage that we are following here. Miethe did not systematically compare organizations with more bureaucratic structures to those with less bureaucratic structures, but noted only that different patterns appeared in government agencies than in firms. From his results, it is difficult to tell whether retaliation would in fact be more likely in organizations with more bureaucratic structures.

On the other hand, to the extent that bureaucracies provide greater procedural justice, they may be less likely to tolerate retaliation than organizations in which managers can do anything they please as long as they "meet the numbers." Some bureaucratic mechanisms that can enhance procedural justice include rules forbidding wrongdoing and retaliation that are actually part of the culture rather than "window dressing," or avenues for appeal, such as grievance procedures or ombudspersons. According to institutional theory (e.g., Scott, 2001), adoption of employee protections occurs as a response to changes in civil rights and other laws, and "to the broader normative climate that often precedes and accompanies changes in the law" (Martin, 2000, p. 213). Further, "organizations that adopted these procedures before being legally required to do so tended to be large corporations, public organizations, and organizations with a strong link to the public sector, such as federal contractors. These organizations were said to adopt the procedures because their size and visibility to external constituents made them more vulnerable to legal and public attack" (Martin, 2000, p. 213).

For example, the U.S. military seems to have adopted racial integration more quickly and with fewer instances of retaliation than did private industry following World War II. This is not to say that the change process was easy. One possibility is that change driven from the top down and in line with procedural rules governing its implementation may be easier than other types of changes. Research on the "dual core" model of change suggests that structural and strategic organization change is more effective when driven from the top, whereas technological change and product innovations may be more effective when they are suggested from the bottom up, through the organization chart (Daft, 1978). To extrapolate from this model, we might propose that organizations that explicitly proscribe retaliation are less likely to experience high rates of retaliation—and that such proscriptions are more readily accepted by managers used to following rules, because they are accustomed to living in bureaucratic structures. Clearly, more research is needed to test these propositions.

Another important area that has been largely unexplored in published empirical research concerns the effectiveness of actions organizations have taken or could take to reduce the incidence of retaliation and enhance the climate and culture to encourage reporting of wrongdoing. Research concerning corporate ethics practices may be helpful in this regard. Results of a usefulness analysis of the effects of environmental influences and management commitment to corporate ethics indicated that scope of the ethics program was unrelated to the top management's commitment to ethics but was instead related to environmental pressures to adopt a program of broad scope (Weaver, Treviño, & Cochran, 1999b). On the other hand, top management commitment to ethics was significantly related to the strength of the compliance orientation and the values orientation toward ethics in the organization, whereas environmental pressure was not. We interpret these findings to mean that management involvement in ethics seemed to be related to the depth of the corporate ethics program but environmental pressure was related to its breadth.

Further, these authors found in a second study that top management commitment to ethics was significantly related to institution of an ethics program that was integrated with the rest of the organization's structure and culture, while top management commitment to performance was significantly related to the institution of an ethics program that was decoupled or not integrated with the organization's structure and culture (Weaver, Treviño, & Cochran, 1999c). We extrapolate from these two studies to suggest that an ethics program that discourages wrongdoing and encourages whistle-blowing might require more depth than breadth in the corporate ethics program—and that therefore top management commitment to ethics would be the variable most likely to make this happen. Beyond this, the top management commitment would increase the integration between this ethics program and the larger culture of the organization, thereby increasing the likelihood of supported whistle-blowing, without retaliation. Unfortunately, in a third study, these authors seemed to conclude that many firms have low-cost symbolic ethics programs but that there is large variance in the extent to which these programs exert influence in those firms (Weaver, Treviño, & Cochran, 1999a).

Some recent research in the sociology literature on sexual harassment and other discrimination (e.g., Dobbin & Kelly, 2007; Kalev & Dobbin, 2006; Kalev, Kelly, & Dobbin, 2006) has yielded some very interesting findings. This research examines, among other things, the extent to which women and minorities are becoming better represented in jobs dominated by men and nonminority whites. The research is pertinent to whistle-blowing because it deals with organizational change processes to correct or avoid wrongdoing and inequity, and some of the research focuses on which types of employer practices are relatively effective in fostering change. One study of EEO-1 filings (forms filed annually by large employers), survey data, and other information revealed that affirmative action "compliance reviews, which alter organizational routines, had stronger and more lasting effects than lawsuits, which create disincentives to discriminate" (Kalev & Dobbin, 2006, p. 856). Other research has shown that grievance procedures have been implemented in response to "landmarks" in harassment law, and this has been attributed to the influence of human resource professionals rather than attorneys (Dobbin & Kelly, 2007). Finally, assigning responsibility for change to a manager and other efforts to establish responsibility for diversity were more effective in producing change than were diversity training and diversity evaluations, with efforts to reduce the social isolation of underrepresented groups (e.g., through better mentoring) scoring between these other two approaches (Kalev et al., 2006).

The studies of ethics programs, and those from the sociology literature, did not focus on whistle-blowing per se, so we do not know the extent to which these findings would generalize to organizations trying to create strong ethics programs focused on encouraging whistle-blowing and discouraging retaliation, but there is no inherent reason why these findings would not generalize in this way. What we do lack is more specific information about the "best practices" that make whistle-blowing programs work well.

In organizations in which top management is genuinely committed to encouraging internal reports, there is little guidance to offer as to which concrete steps will "work" when employees are fearful or reluctant to come forward. For example, what types of training have proven useful, or not useful, in reducing the perceived threat of retaliation and improving managerial responses to wrongdoing and whistle-blowing? Which complaint channels are more trusted, and why? Should employees always be encouraged first to report problems to a supervisor, or does some form of ombudsperson approach work more effectively? Can a 360-degree appraisal system generate suggestions for operational improvement, including responses to wrongdoing, in a nonthreatening way? And do the answers to any of these questions depend on situational conditions, such as the demographics of the workforce?

Societal, Country, or Cultural Variables.   Weaver has argued that cross-cultural differences mean that ethics programs—one means that an organization may use as part of a strategy to reduce retaliation—need to differ as well if they are to be effective: no one form of ethics program will work in all countries (Weaver, 2001). This raises the question of what research shows, or has yet to explore, about the effects of societal characteristics on retaliation against whistle-blowers.

As noted in previous chapters, whistle-blowing has been documented or investigated in many countries, and in many of them, the term "whistle-blower" is viewed as derogatory; yet governmental and nongovernmental organizations (NGOs) have focused on the goal of reducing corruption. Clearly, by their encouragement of whistleblowing, they attempt to legitimize it, in a variety of cultures. To the extent that retaliation discourages future whistle-blowing, perhaps even more so in some cultures than in others, its effect needs to be understood in additional cultures, beyond the United States. Unfortunately, as noted previously, due to the dearth of cross-cultural research on retaliation (Rehg & Parkhe, 2002), it remains for future researchers to develop a taxonomy of cultural influences.

Nonetheless, we propose that theories about cultural differ-ence imply intriguing research questions about organizational and employee reactions to whistle-blowing. As noted in earlier chapters, probably the best-known model of cultural differences is Hofstede's (e.g., Hofstede, 1980; Hofstede, 1999; Hofstede et al., 1990). In brief, the Hofstede model proposes that cultures vary across six key oppos-ing values dimensions (e.g., collectivism versus individualism, and masculinity versus femininity). We suggest possible research direc-tions below, based largely on Hofstede, but other cultural typologies could also be used to develop hypotheses.

In cultures where high power distance exists (e.g., India), there is greater pressure to conform to accepted organizational practices; in such cultures, employees may have a greater fear of retaliation for blowing the whistle, though no support for this proposition emerged in a preliminary study (Keenan, 2002a). Because retaliation usually is initiated by higher-level supervisors, where power distance is greater, we expect stronger norms supporting the legitimacy of retaliation by supervisors and the acceptance of retaliation by subordinates. Pressure to conform in organizations is further emphasized when the structure is bureaucratic (Weinstein, 1979), so we could even picture an interaction effect between societal cultural differences (high power distance versus low power distance) and organizational structure (highly bureaucratic versus low bureaucratic), such that retaliation would be seen as much more legitimate when power distance was high and organizational structure was relatively bureaucratic.

A second cultural dimension that may have an influence is femininity-masculinity. For reasons described in Chapter 3, the question arises as to whether Hofstede's labeling of cultures as more masculine or feminine could be related to questions of moral devel-opment. Would employees in more "masculine" cultures (such as Japan and the United States) be more concerned with the validity of the specific charges raised by the whistle-blower, and retaliate more often where the charges are seen as frivolous? In contrast, might employees in "feminine" cultures (such as France) be concerned more for the consequences of the alleged wrongdoing on people in society (e.g., political corruption may be viewed as inevitable and relatively minor in consequence), or the consequences of whistle-blowing on people in the organization (e.g., "finking" is an uncaring and hence "bad" thing to do to one's colleagues)? In other words, would the focus be on relational issues in more feminine cultures rather than on following the rules or focusing exclusively on legal issues? If so, then there may be an interaction between the nature of the wrong-doing being reported, others' perceptions about the validity of the charges, and culture, in affecting retaliation. For example, where a whistle-blower reported that his or her employer was polluting the local water supply, and observers believed that the report was true and that the polluting endangered residents, she or he may be less likely to experience retaliation in "feminine" cultures, than under other conditions.

Again, predictions are further complicated because organizational culture may play a role, and it may be confounded with societal culture. Recent suggestions that some organizational cultures are more masculine or macho than others (e.g., Hacker, 2003) would suggest that employees of a masculine-gendered or cultured organization, located in a masculine society, would experience greater retaliation, because of concerns about the perceived illegitimacy of organizational dissent. However, this variable may also interact with others, as described previously.

Finally, we might wonder whether workers in more individualistic cultures would be *more* supportive of whistle-blowing than would collectivistic cultures, where members might be more likely to judge the whistle-blower as a traitor to the employer and coworkers. In other words, would collectivistic cultures view whistle-blowing as an attack on the collectivity, meaning the organization itself and its members? In collectivistic cultures, would retaliation against the whistle-blower then be viewed as a reasonable and expected—even legitimate—outcome? Or would individualistic cultures be *less* supportive, because the collectivistic culture would value the benefit to society of whistle-blowing (e.g., to protect the public from unsafe products or financial fraud) above any concern for the potential repercussions for an employer viewed as harming society—and therefore be less likely to view retaliation as normal and legitimate? Or would all of this depend on the victim of the wrongdoing, such that wrongdoing that harmed the family would be viewed as an attack on collectivist norms and retaliation against the whistle-blower rejected, whereas wrongdoing that harmed another country but aided the firm's interests might be viewed as supportive of collectivist norms, so that retaliation against whistle-blowers would be viewed as normatively legitimate? The complexity of untangling collectivist loyalties quickly becomes apparent in consideration of such scenarios.

These and other research questions related to the effects of societal culture on retaliation can easily be envisioned. The potential moderating role of organizational culture should also be considered. For example, a study comparing the strength of effects of societal culture and organizational culture (Hofstede et al., 1990) demonstrated that both the organization's effects and society's effects on member behavior were important. However, this study did not focus on whistle-blowing behavior or organizational dissent, so research is needed on this question. Although the Hofstede taxonomy and scales have been criticized (e.g., Yoo & Donthu, 2002), as the research literature develops, it may inform research on retaliation against whistle-blowers.

We have devoted much of this chapter to the predictors of retaliation. But the consequences of retaliation are also important. In the next section we address the question of why some instances of retaliation result in additional complaints or other actions.

Research Concerning the Outcomes or Consequences of Retaliation

Previous studies have focused more on antecedents or causes of retaliation than on outcomes or consequences. Outcomes may be overwhelmingly negative both for the person and for the organization, including its people, for example, other members and the wrongdoer; its culture, for example, the development of norms concerning wrongdoing; its profitability and reputation; the extent to which it is regulated; and even its survival. For example, the whistle-blower who experiences retaliation may not simply stop the protest; she or he may escalate the protest to a journalist or someone else outside the organization, causing more adverse publicity and other negative consequences. Past research has documented a correlation between retaliation and the use of external channels (e.g., Miceli & Near, 1984). Whistle-blowers and other organization members may become demoralized and contribute less to the organization or leave. The bottom line is clear: managers who wish to avoid public embarrassment should cease wrongdoing and not retaliate against whistle-blowers. Stonewalling, dissembling, and reprisal are not effective strategies for discouraging whistle-blowing. We therefore examine the research on the consequences of retaliation; all of it has focused on the effects on the whistle-blower. Obviously more research is needed to investigate consequences of retaliation for the organization.

Whistle-blowers may also experience stress, or other negative psychological or physical consequences. They may be less satisfied with their supervisors with remaining in the organization. They may become stigmatized if they stay. They may withdraw, including quitting the organization altogether. Retaliation may also covary with or lead to lower effectiveness at getting problems corrected; we will address effectiveness in Chapter 5. Finally, as noted previously, in response to retaliation, whistle-blowers may make reports about the original wrongdoing or reports about the retaliation to parties not previously involved, including parties outside the organization, such as the EEOC, the Audit Committee of the Board of Directors, or the media.

In some instances, for example, when the process extends over many weeks, months, or even years, it may be difficult to determine to what extent consequences are a function of retaliation, of the original whistle-blowing, or of another subsequent event. As we discussed in Chapters 2 and 3, wrongdoing alone can be stressful or demoralizing, and a lack of response to a whistle-blowing attempt can be as well. But we know that some preliminary research suggests that employees who see wrongdoing that is already being corrected are nearly as satisfied as nonobservers. And, obviously, if whistle-blowers are met with immediate positive response from the organization, that is, the wrongdoing is corrected and whistle-blowers are exclusively thanked or otherwise rewarded, there is little theoretical reason to believe that they would experience negative consequences, such as stress. This may suggest that any negative outcomes likely result from retaliation.

But nonresponse may lead to these negative consequences as well; for example, if the whistle-blower must continue to document wrongdoing or meet with other parties to problem solve, or convince other complaint recipients of wrongdoing, this time may be draining, and take him or her away from more enjoyable work activities or come from his or her personal time. This may be exhausting and tedious, for example, and put whistle-blowers in a position of conflict with people with whom they previously had easier or more enjoyable relationships. All of these conditions can easily cause dissatisfaction, felt stress, or physical problems such as depression or sleep disorders, even if there were no retaliatory events. And if retaliation also occurred, it might be that it, the whistle-blower's additional actions (e.g., documenting, meeting), and these other negative consequences are a function of the general resistance, rather than their being a result of retaliation itself.

Therefore, although researchers may not be able to trace the cause of dissatisfaction or other consequences to retaliation (as clearly separable from wrongdoing and whistle-blowing), it seems reasonable to assume that retaliation may covary with, if not cause, other consequences to some extent. And, if so, they will likely be much less than perfectly related, as they might be somewhat different manifestations of the results of the organization's resistance to change. We now consider each of these possible reactions in turn.

Psychosocial Effects

The psychosocial effects on whistle-blowers who suffer retaliation have not been studied systematically since the 1996 review, outside of the sexual harassment literature. Of those who experienced social retaliation in Cortina's and Magley's (2003) study, 84% experienced depression or anxiety and 84% experienced feelings of isolation or powerlessness. Social retaliation may also be related to whistle-blowers' longer-term reactions, including such negative consequences as severe psychological distress, leaving the organization, and avoiding whistle-blowing in the future no matter what the circumstances. So far as we know, no extant research has examined this question.

Aside from the negative effects of the wrongdoing itself and what can be a draining process of blowing the whistle to multiple parties (described previously), retaliation may add other negative consequences. Accounts in the popular press suggest that whistle-blowers often lose their jobs, their marriages, or their physical and mental health, as a result of the retaliation they have suffered.

Feelings toward the Supervisor

We know of two studies in which retaliation was investigated as a predictor of effects on the whistle-blower. In the first, retaliation had predicted negative feelings toward the supervisor (Cortina & Magley, 2003). In a study of military and civilian employees of a large military base, retaliation was again found to predict negative feelings toward the supervisor (Rehg et al., in press; Rehg et al., 2004). Thus, it appears that retaliation against whistle-blowers may backfire in the short term, reducing the quality of their working relationship to their supervisor.

Stigmatization of the Whistle-Blower

As reviewed above, research to date has considered whether coworker support predicts retaliation against whistle-blowers. Perhaps the causal direction predicted is wrong: perhaps whistle-blowers who suffer retaliation subsequently suffer stigmatization at the hands of their coworkers and other organization members. In an experiment, subjects were asked by a research assistant to engage in wrongdoing by providing data that would be consistent with the experimenter's hypothesis, and then observed as a "whistle-blower" (actually a confederate) reported the wrongdoer to the experimenter (Everton, 1996). Contrary to hypothesis, subjects did not rate the whistle-blowers who were rewarded, rather than punished, as more ethical or likable, or their actions as more acceptable. Nor did subjects rate the "whistle-blower" more favorably if they had been told that they themselves were similar to the whistle-blower. Although Everton did not predict this outcome, female subjects were more likely than male subjects to rate the whistle-blower favorably and the research assistant ("wrongdoer") unfavorably. Subject gender did not interact with "whistle-blower" gender to predict ratings of the "whistle-blower" (e.g., female subjects did not rate female "whistle-blowers" differently than did male subjects) nor was there a main effect for "whistle-blower" gender. Although this study provides little support, other research suggests that stigmatization deserves more attention.

Research on stigmatization (e.g., Goffman, 1963; Hewlin & Rosette, 2005; E. E. Jones, Farina, Hastorf, Markus, Miller, & Scott, 1984) may suggest other research directions relevant to retaliation. Organizational members may devalue the inputs of stigmatized members and label them as social deviants (Goffman, 1963). For example, stigmatized persons might be relegated to out-group status, given lower performance ratings, etc. Stigmatization occurs when social norms, such as those that may support wrongdoing, are violated (Hewlin & Rosette, 2005; E. E. Jones et al., 1984).

It may be that norms in most organizations would not support activities and omissions (e.g., failure to maintain adequate safety standards or to file required government forms) that society has deemed to be wrongful, such as unfair discrimination. In fact, it is often the person who objects to the wrongdoing, rather than the wrongdoer, who is stigmatized, suggesting that norms support wrong-doing or at least tolerate it (Hewlin & Rosette, 2005). Depending on the nature and source of the outward behaviors researchers consider to be evidence of stigmatization, they may also constitute retalia-tion by managers (or the organization as a whole), or by coworkers. Research to date is focused primarily on fear of being stigmatized and how its avoidance may lead to silence, which in turn facilitates the perpetuation of discrimination and other wrongdoing (Hewlin & Rosette, 2005). Seemingly, this research can also inform research on factors that may affect blowing the whistle; as the literature expands to the question of who experiences stigmatization after blowing the whistle, it can also inform research on the predictors and conse-quences of retaliation. Further, the three categories of factors pro-posed to affect the fear of stigmatization—organizational reward systems, organizational resistance to change, and individual power (Hewlin & Rosette, 2005)—may also affect the actual occurrence of stigmatization and retaliation against those who do act, as implied by our prior discussion.

External Reporting

As described previously, comprehensiveness of retaliation was found to be related to external whistle-blowing (e.g., Rehg et al., in press; Rehg et al., 2004). Future research should sort out which is the cause and which is the effect.

Summary

In this chapter, we discussed research concerning retaliation against whistle-blowers. We described how theories of power, particularly resource dependence theory, suggest predictors of retaliation against whistle-blowers and reactions of whistle-blowers to retaliation, and we reviewed existing research examining when and why organizations engage in retaliation against whistle-blowers and its short-term and long-term consequences for whistle-blowers. The methodological problems inherent in studying whistle-blowing and retaliation sometimes seem insurmountable; despite this we encourage researchers to continue their efforts in this regard, because the results matter, both for theory and for our practical understanding of the importance of dissent in organizations and society. In Chapter 5, we focus on the effectiveness of whistle-blowing in changing the wrongdoing.

5

What Predicts Whistle-Blowing Effectiveness? We Have a Lot to Learn

In April 2007, Keith Olbermann, host of the MSNBC news show *Countdown* and cohost of a radio show on the sports network ESPN, found himself in the midst of a controversy involving Don Imus, whose CBS radio show *Imus in the Morning* was simulcast on MSNBC (ESPN Radio, 2007). While watching a tape of the Rutgers University women's basketball team playing in the final national championship tournament game, Imus and his cohosts had made on-air racist and sexist comments about the players. After employees and viewers complained, and sponsors withdrew financial support for the show, MSNBC and CBS cancelled the Imus program, which had a "long history of inflammatory comments" (Associated Press, 2007).

As with many cases of wrongdoing that are eventually made public, there were internal whistle-blowers—such as Olbermann—who were unable to get management to take action to solve the problem in a timely way. A few days after the firing, on Olbermann's radio show, he described some of these efforts (ESPN Radio, 2007):

> There were people who were harassed—and I use the term broadly, as opposed to a specific set of sexual harassment things, although that was part of it. There were people who were harassed, women who were harassed there, by the whole staff of the Imus show, who went in and complained to the previous management at MSNBC. And the response to that was "OK, we're moving your desks." (laughs) So they had to move, rather than somebody wanting to touch Don Imus or the people there and say "You can't do this anymore," because there was no controlling him.

> And this problem accelerated over the years, and I, quite frankly, went in to management more than a year ago and said, "there's a breaking point coming; there's a tipping point coming here. It seems to be getting worse. They seem to be getting worse in terms of their behavior off the air and on the air, and we need to do something about that."

Unfortunately for all concerned, it took more than a year, and some very negative publicity and financial "hits," for MSNBC management to recognize that its whistle-blowers were right and to stop the wrongdoing. In contrast, the story of Dr. Nancy Hopkins has a very different ending.

Dr. Hopkins is a science professor at the prestigious Massachusetts Institute of Technology. In the early 1990s, she and other female science professors documented evidence of gender discrimination in resources, including lab space, salary levels, and other conditions of employment. When their report was shared with the dean, he did not greet it with hostility, nor did it become yet another report collecting dust on an academic shelf. Instead:

> (Dean Birgeneau) first addressed problems that can seriously impede productivity in research and teaching, and he redistributed more equally the benefits that signal institutional respect for faculty members. For example, a number of senior women who had been underpaid received salary increases; several women who had not received discretionary funds from the administration for years got money for research; some women got more space; and some got funds for renovations of their labs or offices. Birgeneau also worked with department heads to insure that female professors were asked to join committees involved in hiring new faculty members, and he helped several departments recruit new senior female professors.

> Those efforts have led to an increase in the number of female faculty members in science, most notably in tenured positions. They also have improved the professional lives of many tenured women. As one professor told me recently, "I had decided to leave M.I.T., but when they showed that they appreciated me and my area of research, I decided to stay. As a result of the dean's and the department head's actions over the past two years, we have become the No. 1 department in my field in the country. I am extremely happy here now." (Hopkins, 1999, p. 1)

The success story does not end there. The courageous whistle-blowers and organizational leaders at MIT shared the report with the public.

> The response to the report's release was unanticipated. Within days, the report and the administration's endorsement of its conclusions received front-page coverage in *The Boston Globe* and *The New York Times*. Numerous articles and editorials soon followed in newspapers around the country. I was invited to the White House, where President and Mrs. Clinton and Labor Secretary Alexis M. Herman praised the courage of the M.I.T. administration and the tenured female faculty members in science, and expressed their hope that M.I.T.'s handling of gender discrimination could serve as a model for other institutions. (Hopkins, 1999, p. 1)

Hopkins and her colleagues' experiences provide an exemplar of what the process of whistle-blowing is supposed to be. Ideally, wrongdoing would not occur in the first place, and second best, organizational leaders with the power to make changes would see problems quickly and correct them. Employees, particularly those who may be directly or indirectly harmed by the wrongdoing, should not have to find themselves bearing the additional burden of using their resources and risking ostracism or retaliation in order to correct organizational wrongdoing. But where whistle-blowing is necessary, it is good to know that whistle-blowers can be very effective not only in stopping the immediate wrongdoing, but in making long-term, comprehensive changes in the organization, and even in helping other people and organizations as well.

Previous chapters in this book described research on (a) the motivations of whistle-blowers, and why most employees stand by rather than report wrongdoing; (b) the consequences of whistle-blowing for the whistle-blower, such as retaliation (and in a few cases, awards). Research on the effectiveness of whistle-blowing is important for at least four reasons.

First, some top managers are sincere about wanting to correct and prevent wrongdoing, for ethical reasons (Weaver et al., 1999c), or because they are wise enough to realize that allowing wrongdoing ultimately hurts their organizations (Weaver et al., 1999b). But they may not know how to respond to valid whistle-blowing. Research can suggest ways to improve organizational responses. For example, if whistle-blowers are more effective when wrongdoing is easy to change, then organizations whose leaders are sincere can look hard at internal operations to find ways of: (a) dealing with more challenging or entrenched problems, and (b) encouraging employees to take on these challenges (Van Scotter et al., 2005).

Second, for those top managers who need more encouragement, research can help inform the work of legislators or legal scholars who are investigating ways in which legislators can write better laws giving organizations more incentive to act appropriately (e.g., Dworkin & Callahan, 2002). Legislators in the United States and elsewhere have traditionally focused primarily on providing protection from retaliation rather than on encouraging organizations to respond effectively to whistle-blowing complaints, with disappointing results (e.g., De Maria, 1997; Dworkin & Callahan, 2002; Miceli et al., 1999).

Third, research on effectiveness may help observers of perceived wrongdoing to assess the likelihood that the organization will stop or change objectionable practices, and may suggest strategies for increasing that likelihood. As Olbermann explained, he chose not to speak out on the air for complex reasons, including a concern that it would not correct the problem and might actually make things worse, for himself and for the less powerful people who worked for him. As he said, "you do not have to throw your own career under the bus to try to correct a situation. I've done that before. I made a mistake doing it. It was not fair to myself, and it was, more importantly, not fair to the people who were the victims of the situation that I found myself in and they, more importantly, found themselves in" (ESPN Radio, 2007). Thus, research that helps prospective whistle-blowers size up the situation, and that offers guidance on how best to proceed, may be practically useful.

Over the past 20 years, research findings have identified many factors predicting the decision to blow the whistle (and to a lesser extent, to whom) (Miceli & Near, 1992; Miceli et al., 2001b). One important factor is expected effectiveness. Research has demonstrated consistently that observers of perceived wrongdoing are more strongly influenced to blow the whistle by their perception that they will be successful in getting the wrongdoing stopped than by expected retaliation (e.g., U.S. Merit Systems Protection Board, 1981). But factors that affect the actual probability of terminating the wrongdoing have less frequently been explored (Miceli & Near, 2006; Perry, 1992; Van Scotter et al., 2005).

A fourth reason why whistle-blowing effectiveness is important is that it can improve the functioning of capital markets. At a meeting of a White House task force charged with responding to corporate accounting scandals, Federal Reserve Chairman Alan Greenspan argued that wrongdoing by corporate executives had "undermined the system by which free markets allocate capital to the highest and best use" (Pearlstein, 2004, p. D1). Further, in a follow-up memo, Greenspan "acknowledged that Wall Street was implicated in the accounting shenanigans. Wall Street analysts and money managers, he wrote, put executives under increasing pressure to meet elevated and unrealistic earnings expectations. And it was Wall Street bankers who lent their good names to misleading corporate bond offerings while structuring complex financial transactions whose purpose could only have been to inflate their clients' reported income while camouflaging liabilities" (Pearlstein, 2004, p. D1). Subsequently, SOX (Sarbanes-Oxley Act, 2002) was passed in response to these and related concerns; as will be discussed in Chapter 6, some of its provisions were designed to protect and encourage valid whistle-blowing (Dwyer, Carney, Borrus, Woellert, & Palmeri, 2002).

Therefore, the purpose of this chapter is to describe conditions that may enhance the effectiveness of whistle-blowing. We describe theory and empirical research and offer examples. Unfortunately, however, there are far fewer studies of whistle-blowers' effectiveness than of the predictors of whistle-blowing and retaliation. Specifically, we are aware of only two studies of effectiveness (Miceli & Near, 2002; Van Scotter et al., 2005) and one of resolution (Perry, 1992), which we discuss below. As a result, this chapter will likely raise more questions than it can possibly answer. So, we identify research needs; it is our hope that this may help researchers to identify more conditions that enhance whistle-blowers' success in getting problems solved. Ultimately, we hope that organizations will be able to eliminate the need for whistle-blowing, by proactively creating organizational cultures and systems that encourage ethical behavior and discourage wrongdoing.

As noted earlier, whistle-blowing is not exclusively an American phenomenon; it has been documented in many cultures (e.g., Miceli & Near, 2005a). However, to our knowledge, published studies of whistle-blowing in cultures outside the United States have focused only on the conditions leading to the reporting of wrongdoing or on the role of retaliation (e.g., Keenan, 2002a; Tavakoli et al., 2003). We know of no published international studies investigating the effectiveness of whistle-blowing. Therefore, we cannot say to what extent theorizing about, and empirical research examining, effectiveness based primarily on U.S. organizations and employees would be generalizable to other cultures. With this limitation in mind, we begin by describing theories predicting the effectiveness of whistle-blowing.

Power Theories and Whistle-Blowing Effectiveness

In Chapter 1, we defined effectiveness of whistle-blowing as "the extent to which the questionable or wrongful practice (or omission) is terminated at least partly because of whistle-blowing and within a reasonable time frame" (Near & Miceli, 1995, p. 681). This definition of effectiveness differs from that of the related construct of "resolution" (Perry, 1992), which indicates some sort of closure, as "when an authoritative source inside or outside the organization vindicates the whistleblower's position and punishes wrongdoers" (Perry, 1992, p. 311), in at least two key ways. First, *resolution* requires only that an authority agree with the whistle-blower to some extent, but *effectiveness* signifies that some authority has taken corrective action, that is, that when the whistle-blower is completely effective, the wrongdoing is stopped. Second, *effectiveness* does not require that the wrongdoers be punished, but this criterion is part of the definition of *resolution*. We infer from these differences that Perry's idea of resolution is influenced more heavily by conflict theory, whereas our idea of effectiveness is rooted more firmly in considerations of organizational change and variables that influence the change process, such as power. In discussing potential predictors of effectiveness, we compare results for the two studies of effectiveness in which we were coauthors to those obtained by Perry, when such comparisons are possible. So far as we know, no other studies of whistle-blowing effectiveness have been published thus far.

As with retaliation, we view effectiveness to be at least partly a function of power relationships, for the following general reason. The definition of whistle-blowing (provided in Chapter 1) implies that observers of perceived wrongdoing have no need to seek the intervention of others with power, if they believe they have sufficient power to stop perceived wrongdoing themselves. Therefore, whistle-blowers' effectiveness depends on their ability to influence parties who are powerful (Perry, 1992, 1993). Power is a property of relationships between one person and another, or one subunit of an organization and another (Clegg & Dunkerley, 1980); all of these parties can be considered "social actors." Consequently, power relationships among these actors and with regard to the wrongdoing itself, and whistle-blowers' views of them, are critical.

Below, we discuss how power theories can facilitate understanding of whistle-blowing effectiveness. Various theories of power have been tested as bases for predictions concerning whistle-blowing (e.g., Miceli & Near, 1992). In Chapter 4, we used these theories—particularly, resource dependence theory (Pfeffer & Salancik, 1978)—to predict retaliation by organizations against whistle-blowers. We have described elsewhere how the theory of resource dependence helps explain the conditions under which whistle-blowers are more effective in their quest to terminate the wrongdoing (Near & Miceli, 1995). Therefore, we summarize this discussion below.

As we noted previously, resource dependence theory holds that social actors who possess or control resources needed by other social actors have power over them (Pfeffer & Salancik, 1978). Because dependence is the opposite of power (Emerson, 1962), the social actors who need these resources are dependent on whoever can provide them. Although power derives from situations, it depends upon people, because people control activities, have followers or subordinates, and may be members of multiple coalitions (Salancik & Pfeffer, 1977). The unit of analysis can be any social actor—an individual, a group, an organization, or a larger collectivity (Emerson, 1962), although much of the empirical research focuses on relationships between organizations (Pfeffer & Salancik, 1978).

In applying resource dependence theory to effectiveness, we see that the willingness and ability of the organization to change the objectionable practice will be affected by the extent to which it depends on the whistle-blower(s), the wrongdoer(s), and the practice itself (e.g., to survive or profit) (Near & Miceli, 1995). Organizations may depend equally on these entities, or on one more than the others (Near & Miceli, 1985). The degree of dependence can vary over time and across situations so, when attempting to understand how effectiveness plays out, one must pay attention to a variety of variables (Van Scotter et al., 2005). We first consider those pertaining to the power of the whistle-blower.

The Power of the Whistle-Blower

Resource dependence theory posits that three key factors differentiate the power of organizational members. These are: (a) the hierarchical structure of organizations; (b) the specialization of labor; and (c) differences in the supply and demand for specific knowledge, skills, and abilities (Pfeffer & Salancik, 1978).

The first factor emanates from the hierarchy. The hierarchical structure of organizations conveys power because greater resources are controlled at higher levels. For example, compared to a first-level supervisor, a top manager controls larger budgets, can hire and fire more important employees, and makes more strategic decisions. Therefore, power is a function of structure (Pfeffer, 1981).

The second factor is the specialization of labor. Organizations depend on certain employees who have specialized knowledge and skills that are not easily replaced (Pfeffer & Salancik, 1978), rendering them influential relative to employees with less critical human capital. These key employees have greater latitude in how they accomplish their goals, how they interact with others, and how they use resources; also, their activities are harder to monitor (Jensen & Meckling, 1976).

The third factor is the differentiation of supply and demand. Employees supplying demanded resources are better able to benefit the organization and are therefore more powerful than those holding jobs where qualified substitutes are plentiful or few job openings exist in other organizations. For example, consider two lower-level employees for the CIA, both of whom are equally skilled in a language other than English. In the 1970s, during the peak of the cold war, the employee who was fluent in Russian was likely to have greater power than the employee who was fluent in Arabic. Today the reverse is true, but in the future both might be equally valuable languages to the CIA, depending on global political trends. Both employees might hold the same rank and tenure with the organization, and both might be equally proficient at their jobs, but the skills of the Arabic speaker are now in greater demand than are the skills of the Russian speaker, thereby giving the former greater power within the organization.

If employees are powerful because of these three factors, they will be more powerful as whistle-blowers, and sometimes, as complaint recipients such as senior audit staff, managers, or attorneys. Rational leaders of organizations would not want to risk losing or alienating such important and valuable employees by failing to respond appropriately to their reports of wrongdoing. According to agency theory, good agents (in this case, top managers or their designated complaint recipients), are primarily motivated out of concern for the principal's (in this case, the organization's) welfare, rather than for personal enrichment, career advancement, or some other motive that conflicts with that concern (Eisenhardt, 1989). Thus, generally, agency theory would predict that top managers who are good rather than poor agents strive to avoid alienating employees on whom the organization depends, because doing so would hurt the ability of the organization to meet its goals. Consequently, agents who hear the concerns of powerful employees may be inclined to do what they want, suggesting that more powerful employees would be more effective whistle-blowers. Of course, when the wrongdoer(s) also are people on whom the organization depends, good agents face more difficult decisions.

Despite the theoretical support, the limited research on effectiveness shows no relationship between whistle-blowing effectiveness and measures of the position power of whistle-blowers (e.g., supervisory positions, and those requiring higher levels of education, pay, or tenure) (Miceli & Near, 2002; Perry, 1991; Van Scotter et al., 2005). The problem with any list of power resources is that it assumes the same resources have utility in all situations, and it assumes that people are able to judge the utility of all resources in all situations. But resource dependence theory proposes that organizational power is not absolute; power normally is limited to specific types of actions and decisions in specific situations (Salancik & Pfeffer, 1978). Further, power relationships are dynamic; dependencies are determined by interactions and the flow of information and processes (Clegg & Dunkerley, 1980; Salancik & Pfeffer, 1978). Therefore, these general measures of position power may not suffice; resources that have utility in one situation will not have the same utility in all situations. If so, more effective whistle-blowers will be those who possess *relevant* power, that is, power in the specific situation surrounding the wrongdoing and whistle-blowing.

Whistle-blowers may have power because of characteristics of the specific situation, including both the wrongdoing and the nature of the organization itself. Situation-specific bases of power that we consider below include: (a) whether whistle-blowing is role-prescribed; (b) whether the complaint is viewed as valid or meritorious; (c) whether the whistle-blower feels self-efficacious in the context of the situation; and (d) whether the whistle-blower has leverage over the wrongdoer or complaint recipient.

Role-Prescribed Whistle-Blowing   One basis of situation-specific power is the extent to which whistle-blowing is supported by the organization (Perry, 1992). For example, internal auditors may be required to report suspected financial wrongdoing to their managers or the board of directors; faculty members may be required to report students' suspected academic dishonesty to a university honor panel. When whistle-blowing is specified in words by the organization to be part of one's job, rational organizational leaders seemingly would support whistle-blowing in actions. If so, whistle-blowing should be more effective when it is role-prescribed. But, as many whistle-blowers have learned through difficult experiences, what is said and what is done are not always consistent.

In a survey study using three samples of employees, role-prescribed whistle-blowers were more effective than were non-role-prescribed whistle-blowers in two samples (Miceli & Near, 2002); a measure of role-prescription was not included in the survey used with the third sample. In a later study of employees at a large military base (Van Scotter et al., 2005), role prescriptions were not significantly related to effectiveness. Therefore, future research is needed to determine whether role prescriptions matter across a wide variety of organizations and occupations, or whether they are important only in certain situations, and if so, why. One possibility is that role prescriptions supporting whistle-blowing will be more strongly associated with effectiveness when they are consistent with organizational actions as well as verbalized policies, and other members of the organization agree with whistle-blowers that whistle-blowing in the situation is role-prescribed.

Valid Complaints and Respectable Complaint Processes   Assessing validity empirically raises many issues, as discussed in Chapter 1. For example, perceptions of what constitutes wrongdoing may vary widely and may be influenced by the stake that the observer has in defining the activity or omission. The judgment involved in this process suggests that another related basis of situation-specific power is the extent to which whistle-blowing on the particular wrongdoing observed is viewed as credible or legitimate by other members of the organization. The most important other member in this process is the initial complaint recipient, because she or he will decide what action will be taken; of course, the whistle-blower may take the complaint to other parties at the same time or later, but for ease in communication we will refer here to the first complaint recipient.

Generally, the focus should be primarily not on the whistle-blower or his or her motives, but rather on the evidence of wrongdoing, because even persons who are disliked or who actually have bad motives may have identified wrongdoing that needs to be corrected. But in some cases, there may be little evidence other than the whistle-blower's assertions, and so the credibility of the whistle-blower may be the only basis others have for judging the case. But in other cases, a focus on the whistle-blower rather than on the wrongdoing may obscure the validity, or others may use this as an excuse to ignore the message.

One implication is that, if perceived validity is low, the whistle-blower will be ineffective, because there is no felt need to take action if the complaint recipient does not believe wrongdoing has taken place. Where wrongdoing has been perceived by the complaint recipient, if organizations are led by good agents acting in the best interests of the organization, they will want to eliminate wrongdoing quickly, because it can be quite costly to the organization, even apart from the effects on others. For example, $5 billion per year is lost due to employee theft, as is $200 to 300 billion per year in tax fraud (Miethe, 1999). More recent estimates attributed to the U.S. Department of Commerce and other sources are that employee theft costs employers $30 to 100 billion per year (Case, 2000) and is a causal factor in 30% of business failures (Maleng, 2004). As another example, product recalls and the related lost sales, as well as higher insurance rates, are very costly; for example, a salmonella scare cost Cadbury Schweppes to recall candy bars at a cost of nearly $40 million (Walsh, 2006). The costs sometimes can be avoided if contamination, or poor design or manufacture, is caught internally, early in the process.

The more convinced that the complaint recipient is that wrongdoing has occurred, then, the more reason there is for the organization to take corrective action, to avoid or reduce these risks and costs. This suggests that the greater the agreement between complaint recipients and whistle-blowers about the wrongdoing, the more effective that whistle-blowing will be, in getting it stopped. However, obviously, organizations vary with respect to commitment to high ethical standards; otherwise, wrongdoing would never occur or would quickly be stopped. Therefore, we would narrow the prediction. It seems reasonable to propose that, in well-managed organizations that are behaviorally committed to high ethical standards, whistle-blowers will probably be more effective when the internal party to whom the wrongdoing is reported agrees that the complaint's content is meritorious or valid. We would expect that this effect would be stronger when there is independent evidence that good management and maintenance of high ethical standards is part of the organizational operations. But this proposition has not been tested.

Several other factors may affect the judgment of the complaint recipient or in other ways give the whistle-blower greater power and consequently enable him or her to be more effective in stopping wrongdoing. These include evidence and corroboration by others, others' views of the whistle-blower's motives, and the process used. All of these factors are conceptually interrelated and may be shown empirically to be inseparable in some cases.

Evidence: Documentation and Corroboration.   Claims may be perceived as more legitimate when evidence of wrongdoing is well-documented (e.g., filed audit figures that show irregularities). Consequently, we could expect whistle-blowers to be more effective under these circumstances. The Hopkins-MIT case mentioned previously seems to illustrate the importance of having hard evidence of disparate treatment, although we cannot rule out other reasons why the whistle-blowing was effective. Similarly, the graphic photos of prisoner abuse at Abu Ghraib (e.g., Hersh, 2004) were difficult to ignore or recast as acceptable behavior.

Corroboration may also provide evidence that gives power to the whistle-blower. The support of other third parties who are not the complaint recipients, such as coworkers or managers, may influence the complaint recipient's judgment about whether the complaint is meritorious. When complaint recipients believe that others besides whistle-blowers have corroborated their stories, they may be more inclined to act. Consistent with this hypothesis, third-party verification of the complaint was related to issue resolution (Perry, 1992).

Others' Views of the Whistle-Blower's Motives.   As suggested earlier, one factor used to judge the whistle-blower's legitimacy may be perceived motive. Appearing to have lofty motives may make the whistle-blower seem more credible or admirable. Even an etiquette columnist, Miss Manners (the journalist Judith Martin), has noted that social disapproval of whistle-blowers depends on others' perceptions of motives: "(Miss Manners can) understand why innocent bystanders are indignant if the informants turn out to be wrong or motivated by less lofty impulses than those coming from the conscience ... Whistle-blowers who have proven to be both disinterested and correct are commended by society. Except that this tends to happen some time after they lose their jobs, their reputations, and their friends" (Martin, 2004, p. D6).

Whistle-blowers who are not the target of the wrongdoing may be viewed as more credible than are apparent victims, because their actions may be seen as less self-serving. For example, male whistle-blowers who object to discrimination or harassment against women may be respected more than if they complained on their own behalf. However, prior research has shown that people on whom wrongdoing has a direct effect are more likely to blow the whistle (Miceli & Near, 1992), so it is good to see that not being a target is not an essential requirement for effectiveness, as in the Hopkins-MIT case.

The Process Used.   Others judge not only the content or validity of the allegation itself, but also the process of blowing the whistle. For example, coworkers may agree with the whistle-blower that wrongdoing has occurred (i.e., the content of the complaint is seen as credible, legitimate, or valid), but may believe the whistle-blower was wrong in going over his or her boss's head to complain about it. In an organization where dissent and innovation are encouraged, whistle-blowing may be viewed with less alarm or disapproval than it would be viewed in an organization where the chain of command is viewed as inviolate. To the extent that the process used is viewed as legitimate, the whistle-blower gains more power and will likely be more effective. Whistle-blowers "perceived by co-workers as pursuing a legitimate claim by legitimate means" may be more likely to achieve resolution (Perry, 1992, p. 313). Perry found no support for this hypothesis, but this may have occurred because of low statistical power, due to small sample size.

The case of Keith Olbermann illustrates the difficulty of determining what process will be most effective, even when the whistle-blower is fairly powerful. In particular, the decision of when to escalate the complaint to an outsider is complicated, because the whistle-blower is focused on what will get change made—given that previous appeals to management have not worked—and less on retaliation against himself. As he described it in the following exchange with his radio cohost, Dan Patrick:

> DP: "Some (critics questioned) ... why you waited till Imus was out the door before you start to criticize him."
>
> KO: "...I didn't. In terms of doing it publicly—yeah, I did. I waited ... you do what you can do in that situation and not more ...Try to resolve the problem internally, give it a certain period of time, believe the assurances of your management—and if you can't, then you go public when you feel like you have to...

DP: "...but ... if Don Imus worked for Fox (Network)—and said what he said on Fox—you would have skewered him. Right?"

KO: "As I've said many times, there is a practicality about this business, and a compromise that you have to make ... Was I guilty of maybe not making as big a stink about this as I should have? Yeah. But ... if I had started to make Don Imus the 'Worst Person in the World' when I first wanted to ... there would have been a constant battle. I would have been happy to join that battle with him (but) there would have been a constant battle involving the people who work for me—my producers, my staff—who have no business being trotted out. And they would have been mentioned by name on Imus's show. They would have been mentioned by name; there would have been problems involving them internally; there would have been complaints about them. I didn't think I had a right to do that. And I thought I had a responsibility to my employers to go along with them, and after the management change about a year ago, I figured there was probably—something was going to happen. And finally, something did. Imus took care of it himself." (ESPN Radio, 2007)

In this case, it is hard to say whether good process ultimately stopped the wrongdoing, although it does appear that good process may have prevented some retaliation. Olbermann was powerful by virtue of at least three factors: (a) in his position as an on-air host on MSNBC, he has good and growing viewer ratings (and views on YouTube), and a recently renewed four-year contract (Goodman, 2007; Nevius, 2006); (b) as a white man, he was not a direct target of the final act of wrongdoing and possibly only an indirect target of some of the prior alleged wrongdoing, and thus may have seemed credible; and (c) the evidence of wrongdoing prior to the final incident was seemingly clear, and was judged by others within the organization to be objectionable. All of these factors should have enhanced his effectiveness in getting management to stop the wrongdoing, but they were insufficient, though they may have enabled him to blow the whistle and to escape at least some retaliation.

But the wrongdoer in this case also was powerful, bringing in millions in revenue to the network (Associated Press, 2007). The timing of management's decision to fire Imus suggests they were not persuaded at the time of the prior internal complaints. Rather, it occurred only after many sponsors, including American Express and Procter & Gamble, pulled their advertising on the Imus show or on MSNBC (Story, 2007), presumably because they were concerned that sponsorship might alienate their customers, and after some recurring guests indicated they would no longer appear on the show (Associated Press, 2007). Further, although we have no other evidence, Olbermann's account certainly raises the question of whether management was honestly committed to maintaining an ethical culture, a condition we have specified as important throughout this chapter. All of these observations suggest that concerted action by powerful outsiders may be necessary when management is reluctant to act. This case also illustrates the complexity of factors in the whistle-blowing process.

In summary, pending further empirical work, it seems reasonable to propose that, in well-managed organizations that are behaviorally committed to high ethical standards, whistle-blowers will be more effective when the persons besides the complaint recipient, that is, the authority to whom the wrongdoing is reported, agree that the complaint's content is meritorious or valid. We also expect that in such organizations, whistle-blowers will be more effective when they are not the targets of the wrongdoing and when they use processes judged to be fair or appropriate. The support of powerful outsiders may give more power to whistle-blowers as well. We now turn to other factors pertaining to whistle-blower power that may be associated with effectiveness.

Whistle-Blowing Self-Efficacy   Greater felt credibility or legitimacy (and hence, power) may be reflected in self-efficacy for whistle-blowing, that is, whistle-blowers' perceptions that reporting problems will get them corrected. For example, the employee who believes that telling the safety officer about a perceived hazard may not make a difference will likely be less effective than the person with higher self-efficacy (Van Scotter et al., 2005). This may occur because the whistle-blower is not valued by management, because she or he thinks the complaint recipient would not believe her or him, or because the whistle-blower has accurately perceived that management simply is not serious about correcting wrongdoing.

Whistle-blowing self-efficacy is more narrow and specific than is general self-efficacy, which is an individual's estimate of the knowledge, skills, abilities, and motivational force that he or she can bring to bear on a specific situation (Bandura, 1989). Thus, we expect that the higher the self-efficacy for whistle-blowing, the more effective the whistle-blower will be in getting it stopped. Preliminary support for this proposition was found in a study of employees at a military base (Van Scotter et al., 2005); for reasons noted earlier, we expect this to be more pronounced depending on the will of top management. We propose that, in well-managed organizations that are behaviorally committed to high ethical standards, whistle-blowers would be more effective when self-efficacy for whistle-blowing is high.

The Whistle-Blower's Leverage   Another basis of situation-specific power is the leverage that whistle-blowers believe they have over the parties who may be able to stop wrongdoing, that is, the complaint recipient or the wrongdoer (Van Scotter et al., 2005). A whistle-blower's leverage could arise from many legitimate or illegitimate sources, and may extend beyond workplace relationships. For example, a wrong-doer may be dependent because the whistle-blower is a close friend, or because she or he is bound by a norm of reciprocity (Gouldner, 1960) to return a prior favor, and may give up the wrongdoing once the whistle-blower has expressed concerns. Regardless of the source, we expect leverage to be associated with effectiveness, and prelimi-nary evidence supportive of this proposition has been reported (Van Scotter et al., 2005). Once again, we would expect the effect to be more pronounced in well-managed, ethical organizations.

Earlier, we indicated that the organization's ability or willingness to change wrongdoing would be influenced by three sets of power relations: its dependence on the whistle-blower, its dependence on wrongdoers, and its dependence on the wrongdoing itself. We now turn our attention to the second of these factors.

Organizational Dependence on Wrongdoers

As noted earlier, resource dependence theory suggests that whistle-blowers possessing more resources on which the organization depends will be more powerful than whistle-blowers possessing few needed resources. Therefore, all other factors being equal, they will be more effective in stopping wrongdoing than will other whistle-blowers in organizations in which top managers wish to do the right thing. But, as implied in the Olbermann-Imus case described earlier, one factor that may not be equal is the power of the wrongdoers. For the same reasons, unethical employees who control substantial resources will also be powerful. They will likely have opportunities to use organizational resources in important and questionable ways, and to pressure others to remain silent (Near & Miceli, 1995). One general implication is that the more powerful the wrongdoer, the harder it may be for the whistle-blower to get wrongdoing stopped—all other factors being equal.

Where organizations depend more heavily on wrongdoers, top management may be less willing (a) to alienate them by forcing the wrongdoing to stop, which could result in the wrongdoers' withdrawing critical resources, or (b) to fire them, thus removing both the wrongdoing and the wrongdoer, both of which appeared to be happening in the Olbermann-Imus case. Alternatively, wrongdoing may continue because high-level wrongdoers could be profiting from the wrongdoing and have the power to continue it. For example, Enron's chairman of the board, Kenneth Lay, seemingly ignored the initial warnings of the whistle-blower, Sherron Watkins, because of the power of the CEO, Jeffrey Skilling, who was allegedly the primary wrongdoer (Frey, 2002). Several months before Enron's problems became publicly known, she wrote a memo to the CEO, Ken Lay, raising questions about dubious partnerships (Associated Press, 2002). Watkins urged him to see the "house of cards" that was about to collapse, but he did not take the suggested actions. Instead, Enron's CFO, Andrew Fastow, sought legal advice on whether she could be fired (Associated Press, 2002). Her memo was later "discovered in a box of documents seized by investigators" (Frey, 2002, p. C1), as Enron fell. She was subsequently subpoenaed to testify before Congress about her memo. So, as in Olbermann's case, her internal whistle-blowing was ineffective, at least until powerful outsiders became involved independent of her actions. And, like Olbermann, Watkins may have perceived—correctly—that she could not mobilize these outsiders at the time in a way that would have changed the wrongdoing and avoided retaliation. As will be described in Chapter 6, SOX (Sarbanes-Oxley Act, 2002) was passed at least partly in response to this dilemma.

In the only known empirical investigation of "involvement of the dominant coalition in the target incident," the researcher predicted that it would be negatively associated with whistle-blowing issue resolution, but this hypothesis was not supported in his sample (Perry, 1992, pp. 311–312). Top management involvement also was not related to perceived effectiveness in a more recent study (Perry, 1992). Once again, however, this may have resulted from small sample size or other factors. Therefore, we recommend that researchers investigate whether whistle-blowers are more effective when wrongdoers are exclusively in lower levels of the hierarchy.

Organizational Dependence on the Wrongdoing

In addition, organizations may become dependent on certain processes, activities, or operations (Pfeffer & Salancik, 1978). Because
the organization depends on resources from the external environment for survival, it may also depend on continuation of the wrongdoing as a way to gain resources from the environment. For example,
an organization may use illegal behavior to reduce its dependence
on other organizations in its environment (Pfeffer & Salancik, 1978).
Organizations that depend on continuation of the wrongdoing for
their own survival are unlikely to terminate the wrongdoing when
confronted with the evidence. If we assume that organizations are
rational (Thompson, 1967) or "risk averse" in the terms of agency
theory (e.g., Jensen & Meckling, 1976), they normally would not
engage in risky behavior (e.g., serious wrongdoing) that could lead
to embarrassment or costly sanctions unless they had a vital need
or compelling reason to do so (Van Scotter et al., 2005). We expect
that organizations would not engage in "material" wrongdoing (i.e.,
costly) or long-term, "entrenched" wrongdoing unless top management considered it critical for the organization's survival. Therefore,
we predict that the more material and entrenched the wrongdoing,
the less effective the whistle-blower will be.

Material Wrongdoing The term "material" has been defined as
"sufficiently important to influence decisions made by reasonable
users of financial statements" (Whittington, Pany, Meigs, & Meigs,
1992, p. 47). If an organization chooses to engage in material wrongdoing, then the benefits of engaging in the risky behavior may be
perceived by managers to outweigh its costs (Near & Miceli, 1995).

Some research (Miceli & Near, 2002) has shown that the organization's dependence on continuation of the wrongdoing itself, as
reflected in the perceived materiality of wrongdoing, is negatively
related to whistle-blowing effectiveness. This may occur because top
management believes that the organization's survival depends on
the wrongdoing, or because the opportunity for wrongdoing and its
consequent benefits is too attractive to forego.

Similarly, Perry found that when greater change was "required by
the whistleblower's claims," the issue was less likely to be resolved
(Perry, 1992, pp. 311–312). However, in a more recent study (Van
Scotter et al., 2005), no relationship was found, which could suggest

once again that top management leadership is critical. In better-managed organizations whose leadership expects the highest ethical standards, serious or material wrongdoing may occur simply because top management is not aware it is occurring, and there may be zero tolerance for all wrongdoing and hence a willingness to correct it once management learns of it. Therefore, we believe future research should examine whether, in well-managed organizations and those behaviorally committed to high ethical standards, whistle-blowing effectiveness will not depend on materiality; in other organizations, whistle-blowers will be more effective when wrongdoing is less material or serious.

Entrenched Wrongdoing   Resource dependence theory suggests that when organizations (or individuals) become too dependent on a single supplier of important resources, that supplier gains power over them. When organizations engage in practices that are illegal or unethical, because they benefit the organization in some way, a similar situation occurs. Organizations that tolerate practices that improve profits, at least temporarily, become increasingly dependent upon them (e.g., Enron's refusal to discontinue questionable accounting practices because this would hurt its financial performance).

Organizational survival may depend on continuing the wrongdoing (Baucus & Baucus, 1997; Baucus & Near, 1991), and wrongdoing then becomes fully entrenched in the organization culture. Thus, it is harder for whistle-blowers to get changes made. The theory of normalization of wrongdoing described previously in this book provides another perspective that leads to similar predictions. To the extent that wrongdoing has become normalized, complaint recipients and others in the organization may not recognize it as an aberration or as objectionable activity. So when the whistle-blower complains about it, complaint recipients may simply believe that the whistle-blower is wrong. For reasons described in Chapter 3, the more entrenched the wrongdoing, the more likely it has become normalized, and if complaint recipients do not agree wrongdoing has occurred, they are unlikely to change the practice or omission, rendering whistle-blowing ineffective.

Consistent with these propositions, research using several large samples has shown that whistle-blowers were less effective when wrongdoing had occurred for a longer period of time (Miceli & Near, 2002). Results consistent with this reasoning have been found in a later study as well (Van Scotter et al., 2005). Thus, there is consistency in the early findings that wrongdoing entrenchment is significantly and negatively related to whistle-blowing effectiveness. No research has examined whether these results would be more pronounced in organizations that are *less* well-managed and ethical. In better organizations, we expect that there would likely be less entrenched wrongdoing in the first place, but where it occurred, managers would work harder to stop entrenched wrongdoing.

In summary, future research should consider other bases of whistle-blowers' situational power and organizational dependence on the wrongdoers and wrongdoing. From a methodological stand-point, multi-item measures should be used to enhance reliability and validity. Further, causal directions could be explored. Of course, this is more easily said than done, as described in Chapter 1.

Implications for Whistle-Blowers, Managers, and Public Policy

The basic premise of resource dependence theory is that organizations are dependent on a number of social actors for needed resources. We applied resource dependence theory to whistle-blowing and proposed that situation-specific power of the whistle-blower would be positively related to whistle-blowing effectiveness. Powerful whistle-blowers would be better able to persuade an organization to terminate wrong-doing or whistle-blowing would be effective because the organization's top managers, as good agents, would be concerned with alienating powerful and needed whistle-blowers.

We would hope that top managers, as ethical agents, would also be concerned with wrongdoing reported by less powerful whistle-blowers, because the merits of the case may be independent of who reports wrongdoing. But this may not be the case. As agents charged with defending the organization, they may focus first on the most powerful whistle-blowers or wrongdoers, or on continuation of wrongdoing that seems to help the organization more than it harms it. In other words, they may give greater strategic attention to those resources on which they depend most.

Unfortunately, there is very little research on whistle-blowing effec-tiveness; we hope this chapter will help to stimulate more research. One implication of existing research on effectiveness is that prospec-tive whistle-blowers should consider what bases of power they might possess, either over the wrongdoer (if an individual can be identified) or over the potential complaint recipient. Research using random samples of organizational members (as opposed to self-selected, extreme cases that tend to be reported in the media or are better known) shows that the most typical organizational response to the whistle-blower is to ignore him or her (Miceli & Near, 1992). Future research could explore the bases of power to determine which are the most valuable and useful to possess to overcome this typical response.

Research has also shown that the more that wrongdoing is entrenched, the more resistant the organization is to correcting it, once reported. One implication of this finding is that organizational leaders who are sincere about preventing and stopping wrongdoing should take steps to ensure that they are not satisfied with making minor changes to correct small problems. When important problems are identified, more resources must be devoted to taking the whistle-blowers' concerns seriously and finding ethical and managerially sound alternatives to the current operations. To encourage this, policy makers may also want to consider more incentives for correction or greater penalties for noncompliance or nonresponsiveness when problems are serious or of a greater magnitude.

One implication for public policy is that laws should be designed to enhance whistle-blower power in cases where allegations of wrongdoing seem to be valid. State and federal legislators have generally assumed that potential whistle-blowers could be encouraged to speak out if they were protected from retaliation, by law. In fact, changes in the law have not necessarily increased the incidence of whistle-blowing (Dworkin & Near, 1987, 1997; Miceli et al., 1999). Many factors, including the lack of "teeth" in the laws protecting whistle-blowers, have been identified (Dworkin & Callahan, 2002). Legal changes should be focused on these factors, including providing incentives to organizations to respond quickly to whistle-blowers and penalties for those who continue wrongdoing after being alerted.

A major change in U.S. law was made by the Sarbanes-Oxley corporate reform law (SOX) (Sarbanes-Oxley Act, 2002), which provided federal statutory protection to some private sector whistle-blowers. However, as of this writing, only three whistle-blowers have received a favorable judge's ruling since SOX took effect in 2002, according to one plaintiff's lawyer (Barakat, 2004). In a study of the effects of SOX on encouraging whistle-blowing, Moberly noted a comparison with rates under another federal law with whistle-blower protections—the

Occupational Safety and Health Act (Moberly, 2006). According to Moberly, 786 cases went to the Occupational Safety and Health Administration (OSHA) for investigation prior to September 30, 2006, of which 17 were found to have merit and another 106 were settled. He added, "the percentage of meritorious and settled cases for SOX is slightly lower than the percentage of successful claimants for other whistleblower statutes administered by OSHA, perhaps suggesting that the 'stronger' whistleblower protections of SOX do not result in more protections for whistleblowers" (Moberly, 2006, p. 1128). Whether and how this act will help whistle-blowers to be more effective should be examined empirically.

Summary

Researchers have focused considerable attention on two issues: what causes employees who observed organizational wrongdoing to blow the whistle, and what causes organizations to retaliate against the whistle-blower? Researchers have also analyzed case studies to examine the personal and career consequences of retaliation in depth (e.g., Alford, 2001). Less empirical attention has been paid to an equally important question: under what conditions is whistle-blowing most likely to be effective? As seen with the Abu Ghraib prison scandal in Iraq (e.g., Hersh, 2004), whistle-blowers who somehow get the message out effectively have much greater impact on the organization than those who do not. When the "message" is "heard," organizations often respond quickly to terminate their wrongdoing. When the message is buried, and the whistle-blower discredited, the wrongdoing may continue unabated. Research directed toward examining the role of power relationships—and especially the organization's dependence on the whistle-blower, the wrongdoer, and continuation of the wrongdoing—may help elucidate the conditions that increase whistle-blowing effectiveness.

6

The Legal Status of Whistle-Blowing

> In his 20 years as a pharmaceutical salesman, Douglas Durand thought he had seen it all. Then, in 1995, he signed on as vice president for sales at TAP Pharmaceutical Products Inc. in Lake Forest, Ill. Several months later, in disbelief, he listened to a conference call among his sales staff: They were openly discussing how to bribe urologists. Worried about a competing drug coming to market, they wanted to give a 2% "administration fee" up front to any doctor who agreed to prescribe TAP's new prostate cancer drug, Lupron. When one of Durand's regional managers fretted about getting caught, another quipped: "How do you think Doug would look in stripes?" Durand didn't say a word. "That conversation scared the heck out of me," he recalls. "I felt very vulnerable."
>
> Durand didn't end up in stripes. Far from it. To protect his good name and, as he puts it, to "cover his rear," Durand began gathering the inside dope on TAP and feeding it to one of the country's leading federal prosecutors. It was the first step in what would become a 6-year quest to expose massive fraud at the company. Durand's 200 pages of information were so damning that TAP pleaded guilty to conspiring with doctors to cheat the government. And last October, after negotiating a settlement for 2 years, federal prosecutors announced a record $875 million fine against the company. For his efforts, Durand won an unprecedented award of $77 million, or 14% of the settlement, as allowed under a federal whistle-blower statute. (Haddad & Barrett, 2002, p. 126)

The Durand case illustrates that whistle-blowers can receive large monetary rewards for reporting wrongdoing. Such rewards play an important role today in encouraging whistle-blowing. However, they also raise important questions such as: Are cash awards effective as an incentive to stop wrongdoing? Do they encourage the filing of frivolous suits, undermine the culture of trust that should exist in an organization, interfere with what should be essentially an ethical decision, or bring about other undesirable consequences?

Our 1992 book, *Blowing the Whistle*, included a chapter on the legal status of whistle-blowing at that time, including large cash incentives for whistle-blowing under the False Claims Act (FCA)

(Miceli & Near, 1992). Since then, there have been many significant legal developments. Probably the three most important are the passage of SOX (Sarbanes-Oxley Act, 2002), the adoption of false claim-type acts by a growing number of states (see appendix for citations), and the spread of whistle-blowing laws around the world. Of these, SOX is likely to have the biggest impact on U.S. business.

Because of the complexities of these laws, and to avoid redundancy with other sources, we have attempted here to highlight the most important changes in the laws, in terms familiar to nonlawyers. We have provided only a brief description of older laws discussed in more depth in the 1992 book.

In the United States, there are two primary models of specific whistle-blowing legislation: laws that focus on protection against retaliation, and laws aimed at encouraging whistle-blowing through incentives. Most state and federal laws, including SOX, are of the former variety. The False Claims Act and state equivalents, and the Corporate Sentencing Guidelines (CSG), are examples of the latter. All of the latter also protect the whistle-blower from retaliation. We will describe these models in turn.

Laws and Decisions That Focus on Protection against Retaliation

Federal Laws Designed to Address Specific Types of Wrongdoing

Initially, whistle-blowers were protected by courts interpreting laws designed to address a particular problem such as water pollution through the Clean Water Act, enacted in 1972, discrimination through Title VII of the Civil Rights Act of 1964, or labor relations through the National Labor Relations Act of 1935. Protected whistle-blowing under these laws must pertain to the subject for which the law was passed (e.g., water pollution or discrimination) but generally the report can be made within or outside the organization. Redress for retaliation must generally be initially pursued through a designated administrative agency. Courts, which can hear appeals of agency decisions, have liberally interpreted the protection to include a wide variety of whistle-blowing-related activities, including assisting in investigations and testifying. Remedies in these cases usually consist of reinstatement if the whistle-blower had been fired, and recovery of lost wages and benefits.

The Civil Service Reform Act and Related Developments   The Office of Special Counsel (OSC) was established under the Civil Service Reform Act of 1978 (CSRA) to, among other things, protect federal government employees from reprisal so they would feel free to report fraud, waste, and other wrongdoing they observed. Unlike the laws mentioned above, this was targeted specifically at protecting whistle-blowers. The Merit Systems Protection Board (MSPB) was authorized to hear and adjudicate reprisal complaints brought by whistle-blowers.

Despite this intent, the system proved not to be effective. Congress then passed the Whistleblower Protection Act of 1989 enacted to strengthen whistle-blower protection for federal workers (Miceli & Near, 1992, pp. 237–238). The act strengthened the Office of Special Counsel. It also allowed federal employees to pursue their own retaliation cases against agencies if the OSC refused to take them to the MSPB, and eased the burden of proof necessary to prove harassment due to whistle-blowing.

In addition to these laws, government employees enjoy some protections for their speech under the U.S. Constitution. Because the Constitution governs actions of the government, these protections do not apply to private sector employees' actions.

In 2006, a U.S. Supreme Court decision (*Garcetti v. Ceballos*) narrowed First Amendment speech protection for federal workers in whistle-blowing cases. The 2006 opinion reflected the appointment of a more conservative justice to the Court and, unlike the Court's decision the prior year when the Court's composition was different (the 2005 case is discussed below), the *Garcetti* Court in a 5–4 decision found in favor of the government employer. The majority refused to protect the prosecutor, who wrote a memo asking whether a sheriff's deputy had lied in an affidavit to get a search warrant, finding that when public employees make statements pursuant to their official duties, the employees are not speaking as citizens, and thus are not constitutionally protected from employer sanctions. It further noted that there are whistle-blower protection laws under which the plaintiff could have sought redress. This picked up on a theme the dissent argued in the 2005 case. As the *Garcetti* dissent noted, the ruling could silence potential public employee whistle-blowers who have information about government wrongdoing.

Following the *Garcetti* decision, the Senate passed legislation designed to overturn it and to grant better protection to federal whistle-blowers. Senate bill S. 494, passed by unanimous consent on June 22, 2006, as an amendment to the 2007 National Defense Authorization Act, is part of a move to reform the Whistleblower Protection Act (WPA), (one of the laws mentioned by the *Garzetti* Court), because the WPA is generally seen as ineffective, as was the CSRA. At the same time, the House passed even broader reform legislation designed to increase protection for federal employee whistle-blowers. At the time of this writing, differences between the two bills were due to be resolved in conference committee. If retained, the reforms will include increased protection through broader coverage of what constitutes retaliation to include punitive security clearance denial, retaliatory investigations, and gag orders. It would also bar the president from *ex post facto* reclassifying an employee as an "intelligence employee" and thereby restrict the individual's merit system protection rights after he or she has filed suit. The "reasonable belief" that wrongdoing occurred—the standard for virtually all whistle-blowing laws in order for the whistle-blower to be protected—would be restored. Additionally, coverage would be extended to national security employees and government contractors. Whistle-blowers could disclose classified information to members of Congress on relevant oversight committees or their staff. The Office of General Counsel would have greater authority to seek disciplinary measures against managers who retaliate. If enacted, government whistle-blowers could have jury trials, and jurisdiction would be restored to all circuit courts of appeal. According to GAP (Government Accountability Project), the federal circuit court of appeals, which currently hears appeals, has effectively gutted protection for whistle-blowers by refusing to protect them. Since 1994, the court had only found for one employee on appeal versus 119 against (GAP, 2006).

Sarbanes-Oxley Act   The Sarbanes-Oxley Act of 2002 (SOX) represents reification by the United States Congress of the importance of whistle-blowing in the control, detection, and deterrence of wrongdoing. It follows the dramatic growth of whistle-blowing laws in the 1980s and 1990s (Callahan & Dworkin, 2000; Dworkin, 2007a), along with a growing hostility and distrust of big business and government. However, it was the wrongdoing, scandals, and resultant publicity and anger brought on by the leaders of failed corporations such as Enron and WorldCom that were the particular impetus for the law.

Whistle-blowers were important in bringing the wrongdoing to light, in testifying before Congress in hearings about the law, and they play a crucial role in SOX enforcement. SOX has been controversial since its enactment and has been challenged on several grounds, including that it is unconstitutional (unsuccessfully) and that it is too costly, especially for small business (H. Brewer, 2006).

SOX recently had its 5-year anniversary, and opinions regarding it have become more positive. There is general consensus that it has forced greater oversight and accountability which, in turn, has restored confidence in the markets (Lublin & Scannell, 2007; G. Farrell, 2007). Costs are declining (Scannell, 2007), and at least one study indicates that the law is not driving good foreign companies to list on the London instead of the New York stock exchanges (Ip, 2007). Indeed, there is evidence that investors are willing to pay a sizeable premium for listings on the U.S. exchanges. What is not positive has been the effect on whistle-blowing and the protection afforded whistle-blowers (discussed below).

SOX, which applies to publicly traded companies, follows on the precedent established by the federal Corporate Sentencing Guidelines (CSG) and calls for companies to establish a code of ethics—which must apply to top corporate officers—and whistle-blowing procedures. The CSG encourage companies to establish whistle-blowing procedures through reduced fines and penalties for compliance and increased fines and penalties for failure to do so. A large number of companies responded to the guidelines by outsourcing the whistle-blowing to independently run hotlines.

Wrongdoing covered by SOX includes mail, wire, bank, and securities fraud. Further, several decisions have held that the alleged intentional fraud does not need to be material to the company's financial statement to be a protected disclosure. As with virtually every state statute, SOX does not require whistle-blowers to be right in order to be protected. They must merely reasonably believe that the information concerns a covered violation.

Internal and External Whistle-Blowing under SOX.   Unlike most of the state and federal whistle-blowing statutes, SOX specifies different report recipients for internal versus external whistle-blowing about the fraud in order for the whistle-blower to be protected. SOX states that an internal report (the most common type of initial whistle-blowing, as discussed earlier in the book) must go to someone with supervisory authority over the employee or to someone working for the employer who has the authority to investigate, discover, or terminate the wrongdoing. SOX also requires audit committees of the companies to establish whistle-blowing procedures whereby employees can anonymously submit issues of concern regarding questionable accounting or auditing matters (Sarbanes-Oxley Act, 2002). Further, it requires them to have procedures for retaining and treating the complaints. The requirement of an anonymous report recipient is unique among whistle-blowing statutes. Often the organization's response to this requirement has been to contract with an independent hotline company to receive the complaint.

At least 35 national companies offer hotlines, virtually all of which are privately held (Green 2004). They protect information about them as trade secrets, and it is difficult to determine their effectiveness. Another problem with the SOX encouragement of hotlines as the reporting mechanism of choice is that there is scant evidence that anonymity promotes whistle-blowing. Indeed, a recent study reported that whistle-blowing had gone down 20% since the passage of SOX (Dyck et al. 2007). One of the major providers of hotline services, The Network, Inc., reports that the number of reporters requesting anonymity has dropped from 78% to 48% in the past 20 years as employees become more comfortable about reporting (*CFO Magazine*, 2006). Drawbacks to anonymity are that it makes follow-up more difficult and anonymity is often difficult to maintain in light of who has access to the information about wrongdoing; because companies do not warn employees that anonymity cannot be guaranteed they may in fact have even broader liability than they would from the retaliation claim itself (Jernberg, 2003). Further, many employees do not trust that their reports will remain confidential and therefore do not use the hotline, making the promise of anonymity moot for some employees (*Metropolitan Corporate Counsel*, 2006).

The inevitable delay caused by reporting outside the organization means that follow-up is delayed, and that evidence may be lost (Jernberg, 2003). One provider reports that even though callers are urged to call back in a few weeks to see if there are additional questions, only about 30% do (Green, 2004). Because of these problems, many experts recommend that hotlines only be used in conjunction with other, in-house procedures such as ombudspersons, and Internet reporting.

A person who reports the suspected fraud externally must give the information to a federal regulatory or law enforcement agency, or to any member or committee of Congress. Like virtually all state statutes, SOX does not protect whistle-blowers who go to the media.

SOX's Antiretaliation Provisions.   SOX broadly defines retaliation to include discharging, demoting, suspending, threatening, harassing, "or in any other manner discriminat(ing)" against the whistle-blower (Sarbanes-Oxley Act, 2002, Section 1514A). This is both more specific and more inclusive than other whistle-blowing statutes. If the whistle-blower suffers retaliation for reporting, Section 806(a) gives the employee the right to bring a civil suit. However, before that can happen, the employee must first file a complaint with the secretary of labor, who then refers it to the Occupational Safety and Health Administration to investigate the complaint. An administrative law judge of the Department of Labor hears the evidence resulting from the investigation and renders a decision. The decision can be appealed to the Administrative Review Board of the Department of Labor. Congress established a time limit of 180 days within which the secretary of labor should render a decision based on this process. If there is no decision in 180 days, then the employee can bring a civil suit.

The effectiveness of the protection from retaliation is tempered by the very short 90-day statute of limitations within which the initial claim for retaliation must be brought. It is also tempered by the limited damages available: reinstatement, back pay with interest, and litigation expenses including attorney's fees.

The antiretaliation provisions are fairly broad in application because they apply not only to publicly traded companies (i.e., any company that registers its securities or must file reports under the Securities Exchange Act) but also to contractors, subcontractors, and agents of those companies. This means, for example, that if an accountant for Arthur Anderson suffered retaliation for reporting fraud at Enron, the accountant could now file a SOX complaint. The law may also cover U.S. citizens working for a foreign publicly traded company overseas or for a private foreign subsidiary of a covered U.S. company, although a court has held that SOX did not cover noncitizens working for a foreign subsidiary of a U.S. parent corporation (*Carnero v. Boston Scientific Corp.*), a precedent followed by several administrative law judges. If U.S. law is applied to employees in Europe, it may run afoul of European whistle-blower and privacy laws (discussed below).

A significant change in whistle-blowing law implemented in SOX is the provision for criminal penalties for retaliation. Section 1107 imposes penalties on a company or individual who "knowingly, with intent to retaliate, takes any action harmful to any person" who gives truthful information about any federal offense to a law enforcement officer. Although criminal penalties are not unprecedented—a few U.S. (Miceli & Near, 1992) and Australian states (Callahan & Dworkin, 2000), for example, impose criminal penalties for retaliation—it is unique in federal whistle-blower legislation. If convicted, the intentional retaliator is subject to a fine and/or imprisonment of up to ten years.

Section 1107 covers retaliation against whistle-blowers who provide information about *any* federal offense to a law enforcement officer. There is great potential for broad application to whistle-blowing about nonsecurities issues. Also, it applies to any company including nonprofits, and individuals, not just the organization. It can also possibly apply to nonorganization members because the language includes retaliation against "any person." This section may become the most important of all the SOX provisions in terms of whistle-blowing, and could develop into a general whistle-blower protection statute.

State Laws Protecting Whistle-Blowers

The focus of whistle-blower protection shifted from federal law to the states in the 1980s. It occurred in the courts through judges giving employees the right to sue in tort for wrongful firing in violation of public policy. The wrongful firing theory, created as an exception to employment at will, allows employees to bring suit against any size employer. The tort cases can result in large awards because they often include punitive damages. Since punitive damages are based on the jury's estimate of what it would take to punish the company and prevent similar wrongdoing, the damages can be in the hundreds of thousands to millions of dollars.

All states have now also enacted some form of whistle-blower protection legislation. All protect the whistle-blower from retaliation.

This growth of whistle-blower protection laws has occurred despite the dearth of evidence that protection from retaliation encourages whistle-blowing or is very effective (Callahan & Dworkin, 2000). Although all protect from retaliation, there is great variance in other aspects, such as the type of whistle-blowing protected (the majority protect only public employees), the appropriate recipient of the report, the subject of protected whistle-blowing (generally, a violation of a law, rule, or regulation), the quality of evidence of wrongdoing required, and the remedies provided to the whistle-blower who suffers retaliation (Callahan & Dworkin, 2000; Miceli & Near, 1992). For example, although whistle-blower protection is most often justified with reference to societal interests, state laws are more likely to encompass protection for employee harms such as violation of OSHA-type laws, minimum wage violations, protection of health care workers, and violations of civil rights versus covering the environment or child welfare. The proliferation of legislation has created a conflict in some whistle-blower wrongful firing suits. When the employee suffering retaliation brings the suit, the employer claims that the suit is not allowed because it has been preempted by a state or federal whistle-blower law. These laws provide for smaller recoveries and are often more restricted in terms of coverage and procedural protections. Judicial decisions regarding whether the suit is allowed vary from state to state.

Lawsuits, seen as a way to encourage whistle-blowing as well as protecting the whistle-blower, are being threatened by another development. The ability of employees to sue for wrongful firing in violation of public policy has been seriously affected by the growing demand of employers that employees sign arbitration agreements. These agreements require them to arbitrate all workplace disputes. In general, recoveries in arbitration are much smaller than in tort cases, and the proceeding is private. To the extent that punitive damages and publicity about suits and large awards deter wrongdoing by the sued organization as well as others, arbitration defeats this. The Supreme Court, however, is a strong defender of arbitration agreements. There is some disagreement over the enforceability of the agreements between some state courts and the Supreme Court. The applicability of arbitration clauses in whistle-blowing cases is beginning to be challenged because it undermines whistle-blowing (see, for example, *Boss v. Solomon Smith Barney, Inc.*).

Recent Court Decisions Regarding Retaliation

As discussed previously, Congress was particularly concerned to protect against retaliation under SOX and other laws. Like the Congress, the courts have also been increasingly proactive in punishing retaliation. This extends to recent decisions of the U.S. Supreme Court.

Both the courts and Congress have recognized that retaliation, if left unpunished, can discourage whistle-blowing. The courts do not have a list of what activities equal retaliation. The Supreme Court (in a recent Title VII case), ruled that the whistle-blower must prove that the action(s) was (were) "materially adverse," or that it would dissuade a reasonable worker from pursuing rights under the law, or blowing the whistle (*Burlington Northern & Santa Fe Ry. v. White*). This reflects the usual state standard. Actions that courts have found sufficient to constitute retaliation include a lateral transfer with the same pay and responsibilities that increases commuting time or requires a second residence (*Keeton v. Flying J Inc.*), reassignment that effectively amounts to a demotion because of reduced job responsibilities or less distinguished title, or insisting that an employee spend more time on the arduous aspects of the job (*Burlington*). Adverse actions can take place in or outside the workplace.

In a similar vein, courts have recognized the right of employees to sue for retaliation even though they have quit. If the employee can prove that she was "constructively discharged," she may have a successful case of wrongful firing in violation of public policy. The public policy tort theory is recognized by most states, and is often a preferred venue for whistle-blowers who have suffered retaliation because it carries with it the likely recovery of punitive damages in addition to actual damages such as lost wages and benefits. Constructive firing has been recognized for over a decade in state wrongful firing tort cases and in discrimination suits. In these cases, the employer drives the employee away rather than firing her. The plaintiff has to prove that the employer's actions were sufficiently severe that a reasonable employee would have quit. Some states also require proof that the employer's actions were intended to drive out the employee.

In a 2005 decision the U.S. Supreme Court expanded whistle-blower protection against retaliation in a case involving a discrimination claim under Title IX of the Civil Rights Act of 1964 (*Jackson v. Board of Education*). In that case, the coach of a girl's high school basketball team complained about discriminatory practices against the team and lost his coaching job and the extra pay it earned him. It was argued that protection was not needed under the statute because Jackson could have taken his complaint to the Department of Education's Civil Rights Office. Justice Ginsburg asked how often the Office of Civil Rights investigated complaints brought in Birmingham where the school was located. The answer was twice in 20 years. This lack of enforcement probably played a role in the decision. The Court said that if it did not protect someone who did not suffer discrimination but who suffered retaliation because he complained about discrimination against others, "reporting incidents of discrimination (which) is integral to Title IX enforcement … would be discouraged" and the very purpose of the law would be undermined. This was true even though Title IX—which applies to discrimination in education—does not mention retaliation, unlike many other civil rights laws. Although this case involved a public sector employer, its rationale can be applied to all types of whistle-blowing cases. Thus, the decision could have a far-reaching impact. However, as noted previously, after the membership of the Court changed in 2006, the U.S. Supreme Court narrowed First Amendment speech protection against retaliation for federal workers in whistle-blowing cases.

Laws Aimed at Encouraging Whistle-Blowing through Incentives

Federal Laws and State Equivalents

The False Claims Act (FCA)   In the *Durand* case that opened this chapter, Durand received a large portion of the recovery under the False Claims Act (FCA) (U.S. Department of Justice, 2003). The False Claims Act is a federal law that provides incentives for whistle-blowing (False Claims Amendment Act of 1986). Enacted in 1863 in response to contractors' cheating the government, it was significantly revised in 1986 to make monetary recoveries for whistle-blowers easier and more generous, and thereby encourage more whistle-blowing regarding government contractor fraud. Under the FCA, the whistle-blower (called a relator) files a *qui tam* suit with the Department of Justice (DOJ) on behalf of the U.S. government. If the information is novel and the false claims are proved, the whistle-blower receives up to 30% of the judgment if the DOJ does not join in the prosecution of the suit, and up to 25% if it does.

Since fraud under government contracts tends to be significant—
$100 billion per year or more (Miceli & Near, 1992)—and individual
suits can involve multimillions of dollars, the law's recovery possibilities have proved to be the most significant piece of legislation in
terms of spurring whistle-blowing. During the first quarter of 2006,
nearly $1 billion was recovered; in 2002, $1.1 billion was recovered in
qui tam actions (U.S. Department of Justice, 2002). It is much more
effective than merely protecting the whistle-blower from retaliation or even giving the whistle-blower a private cause of action for
retaliation, which is the traditional approach of most state whistle-
blower legislation (Callahan & Dworkin, 1992, 2000). Pre-1986,
there were fewer than six FCA suits brought per year; now there
are hundreds. FCA settlements and judgments have totaled over
$17 billion and virtually all whistle-blowers have recovered a million
dollars or more—even though the majority of suits are settled: of the
$1.1 billion recovered in *qui tam* suits in 2002, $160 million went to
the whistle-blowers bringing the claim.

The FCA values information over motive, and blowing the whistle
to gain a large recovery is fine as long as the information is novel
and leads to successful prosecution. The first wave of suits tended
to involve defense contractors; the second wave, the health care
industry. In the past few years, the drug industry has been the largest
single sector charged with health care fraud. From 2002 to 2003, the
government recovered $1.98 billion; of that, $1.33 billion was from
the pharmaceutical sector (U.S. Law Week, 2006). The next wave
may involve fraud related to the Iraqi war and Hurricane Katrina.
New entities such as universities are also being sued under the law
(Selingo, 2006; Walters, 2006). A false claims legal bar that facilitates
FCA suits has developed (Callahan & Dworkin, 1992).

There are other federal laws that provide rewards for information
regarding violation of that law, but they have been much less successful in spurring whistle-blowing. Reasons for this include smaller
amounts awarded to the whistle-blower and inconsistency in giving
the award (Selingo, 2006; Walters, 2006). An example of this is the
Internal Revenue Service (IRS) reward program for information
about tax cheats. Recently, several revisions similar to those that
changed the False Claims Act were instituted to increase recoveries.
These include more certain and quicker payment of awards and,
possibly, larger rewards (Herman, 2006). This has resulted in larger
recoveries due to whistle-blowing (Herman, 2007).

State False Claims Acts   As of 2006, one-third of the states and the District of Columbia, seeing the size and success of recoveries under the federal FCA, and in light of shrinking funds and expanding budgets, have enacted false claims laws that are similar to, and in some respects broader than, the federal law (see appendix). California and Florida were the first to pass the false claims acts and, as with the federal law, their laws have resulted in significant recoveries. Some of the state laws apply only to Medicaid fraud, others are general false claims statutes (see appendix).

As in the federal law, all states have a range of recovery, with the judge determining how much the whistle-blower should receive. Illinois' distribution system is unique. The law specifies that one-sixth of the recovery go to the attorney general, one-sixth to the Department of State Police, and two-thirds to the *qui tam* plaintiff (Illinois Compiled Statutes, 2004). Nevada is the most generous; up to 50% of the recovery can go to the whistle-blower. Factors the courts consider in determining the amount include how substantially the relator contributed to the case, whether the case primarily depended on disclosures from other sources (in which case, the relator cannot recover more than 10% under the FCA), and whether the relator planned, initiated, or participated in the wrongdoing (U.S. Government Accountability Office, 2006). As noted earlier, all the statutes protect the whistle-blower from retaliation, and all require a reasonable belief, not accuracy, in order to be protected.

Corporate Sentencing Guidelines

Another federal approach that encourages whistle-blowing through incentives is the Corporate Sentencing Guidelines. Unlike the False Claims Acts, though, the incentives benefit the organization, not the individual whistle-blower. The guidelines encourage organizations to establish a code of ethics and a whistle-blowing procedure that is well-publicized, monitored, and under which complaints are acted on without retaliation to the whistle-blower. Failure to follow these procedures can result in increased sanctions such as large fines, corporate probation, and mandated negative publicity if the organization is convicted of federal crimes. Compliance can result in reduced penalties and fines. Hotlines were specifically mentioned as an appropriate whistle-blowing procedure, and many companies started using them as a result of this law.

Trends   The use of rewards to spur whistle-blowing is likely to grow. Recently passed federal legislation designed to get states to pass false claims legislation to help control medical costs will be an important incentive. The 2006 deficit reduction act contains a section designed to combat Medicaid fraud and recover federal funds through encouraging states to pass targeted false claims acts.Congress is particularly interested in encouraging whistle-blowing in this area because the federal government pays 60% of Medicaid, and fraud under it far outpaces other federal funds fraud. Health care fraud is the number-one drain on state and federal treasuries. It is the main target of current federal *qui tam* actions, comprising 46% of the 2,490 claims filed from 1987 to 2005 (compared to 33% for defense contractor fraud). Likewise, recoveries in medical fraud cases by relators have been much larger ($842 million versus $291 million in health care fraud) as have government recoveries ($5 billion versus $1.4 billion). In a recent case involving Swiss pharmaceutical company Serano, five whistle-blowers will split $51.8 million (Gibeaut, 2006).

The federal government expects to spend $192 billion on Medicaid for the 2006 fiscal year, so it is clear why detecting fraud is of such interest (Gibeaut, 2006). The states should be interested as well because, in addition to the usual FCA state recovery of their 40% of Medicaid funds plus fines, the states can recover an additional 10 percentage points if their law follows the federal model. Even though states can currently share in Medicaid recoveries, the state can get increases through triple damages, too, if they pass their own laws. The U.S. Department of Health and Human Services issued guidelines in August 2006 regarding state compliance with the federal law. Among other things, the state law must allow the case to go forward even if the state decides not to join, and it is recommended that the relator should get at least 15% of a recovery (Gibeaut, 2006).

Another trend may flow from the deficit reduction act. The act requires that health care providers give employees education programs on fraud and how to file false claims complaints. If an entity receives $5 million in annual payments under a state Medicaid plan, it must establish written policies for its employees, contractors, and agents about state and federal FCA laws, and the organization's procedures for detecting fraud, waste, and abuse. Further, it must include a "specific discussion" of the laws, including whistle-blower protections, in the employee handbook. It remains to be seen whether this will increase whistle-blowing or claims for retaliation, but it has been predicted that there "may soon be as many as 26 states that have FCAs" (U.S. Law Week, 2006).

Congress continues to try to stop retaliation and encourage whistle-blowing in other ways. In the 2002 Notification and Retaliation Act (No Fear Act, 2002) Congress requires federal agencies to create annual reports to it, the attorney general, and the Office of Personnel Management (OPM) on disciplinary actions taken for conduct by employees that is inconsistent with federal whistle-blower protections. The law also requires reporting about discrimination to the EEOC. The OPM recently ruled that "oral admonishments" unaccompanied by any other discipline of employees for conduct that may be in violation of federal whistle-blowing and discrimination laws does not need to be reported. Reports must include the number of federal court cases pending or resolved, the number of employees that were disciplined and the nature of the discipline, and how much it had to pay to the judgment fund for payment in connection with the cases. Additionally, it must report the number of employees disciplined for violations of whistle-blower statutes regardless of the existence of a lawsuit. OPM is supposed to conduct a "comprehensive study" in the executive branch to identify best practices for taking appropriate disciplinary actions for conduct that is inconsistent with federal whistle-blower protection laws and issue advisory guidelines for the agencies. The study will be based on agency reports. As the study has yet to be done, its impact on retaliation is unknown.

As the foregoing discussion illustrates, there is a growing and ever-widening array of whistle-blowing legislation. Although the United States may be the most active country in terms of enacting whistle-blowing legislation, it is not unique in its increasing focus on whistle-blowing as a means to combat wrongdoing. Many other countries and international organizations have enacted some form of whistle-blower legislation.

Whistle-Blowing Outside the United States

Legislatures in several countries have adopted whistle-blowing laws to encourage whistle-blowing, heighten transparency, and deter wrongdoing. The majority of these countries have a common law tradition or a legal system strongly influenced by that tradition. Many have been influenced by U.S. whistle-blowing legislation. Countries with legislation include the United Kingdom, New Zealand, Australia (state and territorial legislation), Canada, Ireland, Israel, South Korea, and Japan. In addition, multinational organizations such as the United Nations have adopted rules protecting whistle-blowers. Of these countries, the United States, the United Kingdom and Australia have probably most closely documented and discussed the effects of their laws. As a review of the whistle-blowing laws in every country is beyond the scope of this book, we have chosen to focus on these countries for an in-depth discussion.

As in all U.S. whistle-blowing statutes, these laws protect whistle-blowers from retaliation. As in U.S. state legislation, they also tend to encompass a broad array of wrongdoing. However, they vary in important ways in other aspects such as whether external reporting must be done to particular recipients, whether protection of the whistle-blower should depend on the motive behind the whistle-blowing, whether financial incentives are offered, whether the whistle-blower must first report the wrongdoing within the organization, and whether only reporting on public sector wrongdoing is protected. To make these points clearer, we take legislation from the United Kingdom and Australia as examples, and compare and contrast them with U.S. legislation. One key similarity is that whistle-blowing to the media is frowned on or not protected in any of these countries. No U.S. state identifies the media as a proper recipient, and the U.K. protects reporting to the media only when strict perquisites are met under limited circumstances (No Fear Act, 2002). In Australia, only the state of New South Wales authorizes a media report, and this only under limited circumstances (Protected Disclosure Act, 1994). This reluctance is likely the result of legislators' mistrust of media whistle-blowers' motives.

A second similarity is that, in all three, protection under the statute is denied for bad-faith whistle-blowing (Callahan et al., 2004). Virtually all U.S. jurisdictions require a reasonable belief that wrongdoing is occurring; most Australian statutes are similar. The United Kingdom similarly does not protect bad faith reporting but in addition also requires that the disclosure tend to show one or more of specified violations listed in the statute (Employment Rights Act, 1996). A third similarity is that public sector employees receive greater protection than those working in the private sector. Often private sector employees are not included in statutory protections.

In general, employer-employee confidentiality is more important in the United Kingdom than in the United States and Australia. This is reflected in the fact that the U.K. legislation requires internal reporting in most circumstances. Australian and the large majority of U.S. statutes favor external reports. In terms of the severity of the wrongdoing, the U.K. and U.S. statutes do not use normative terms regarding the wrongdoing, but several Australian statutes do (Callahan et al., 2004; Miceli & Near, 1992).

Probably the biggest difference between whistle-blowing laws in the United States and those in the United Kingdom and Australia is the reluctance or refusal of the last two to reward whistle-blowers as is done under the FCA and equivalent state statutes. Indeed, the U.K. legislation specifically denies protection to whistle-blowers who give information for gain. In the United States, motive for the reporting is less important than getting useful information.

Recommendations for Policy

SOX

There is growing evidence that the whistle-blower protections in SOX are not working. One study reports that through May 2006, of the 677 completed SOX complaints, 499 were dismissed and 95 were withdrawn. This demonstrates that, at the least, success at this level is an uphill battle (Solomon, 2004). Of the cases that went to an administrative law judge, only six (2%) of the 286 resulted in a decision for the employee; there were 30 settlements (Earle & Madek, 2007). Another study shows similar results (Moberly, 2007). Further, it reports that whistle-blowers won *none* of the 159 retaliation cases that OSHA resolved in 2006. The statutory scheme gives the illusion of protection without giving truly meaningful opportunities or remedies to achieve it. Some of the reasons for this lack of success include the procedural complexity in bringing a claim, the very short statute of limitations, and the inadequacy of remedies considering the risk and time it takes to negotiate a claim to conclusion. Additionally, OSHA decision makers and judges have given extremely restrictive interpretations to the statute, misinterpreted the burden of proof required to prove retaliation, and OSHA has received no additional funding to handle the claims (Dworkin, 2007b).

An example of these problems is shown by the well-publicized case of *Welch v. Cardinal Bankshares Corporation* (2006). Welch's situation was detailed in a front-page article in the *Wall Street Journal* (Solomon, 2004). Welch, the chief financial officer of Cardinal Bankshares, refused to certify the organization's financial statements because of company auditing practices and possible insider trading. He notified the CEO and the auditor about his concerns. He was fired in October 2002. Welch filed a claim with OSHA as SOX requires; the hearing officer found that the company had cause to fire him. Welch appealed that decision to the Administrative Law Judge (ALJ), who held in January 2004 that Welch had shown that he was fired because he had complied with his duty to disclose information, and he ordered Welch reinstated. Welch had trouble finding a job after his firing and was unemployed until April 2003. That new job was abolished in May 2004, and he has been unemployed since. The company appealed the ALJ decision to the Administrative Review Board (ARB), which dismissed it. In February 2005, the OSHA ALJ then issued a Supplemental Recommended Decision and Order. The company argued that Welch would have been fired anyway because of the enmity and distrust between Welch and the other employees, and because he was unfit. Further, it argued the remedy was inappropriate because another employee would have to be fired to reemploy Welch. These arguments were rejected and the judge ordered that Welch be made whole. Both parties appealed that decision. The ARB on March 31, 2006, decided that the reinstatement order of January 2004 was in effect. Cardinal was given leave to appeal to the ARB to stay the effect of the preliminary order. This is where the case stands as of this writing.

Both Welch and his family have had to pay a high price for his whistle-blowing and the subsequent claim. While waiting for the last decision in his favor, he had to sell his farm and he and his family moved to a smaller house. He and his wife drained their retirement accounts. And the issue is not yet settled (Solomon, 2004). The limited SOX remedies cannot make him whole.

If over two decades of several attempts to make protection effective for government employee whistle-blowers under the CSRA have been unsuccessful, especially given the existence of an official agency that is designed to act as advocate and protector for whistle-blowers, it is highly unlikely that mere adjustments to the current SOX scheme, as proposed by some scholars, are likely to be successful. A more radical change is needed in order to create effective protection. SOX should be reformed to implement a reward system similar to that in the False Claims Act. Observers of wrongdoing should be allowed to bring a sealed claim to court, and if the information is novel and leads to a successful case, the reporter should receive a significant reward, and the government should be allowed to intervene. One issue under such a scheme involves the source of the reward. There are several ways a significant reward fund could be created.

One source of a reward for SOX whistle-blowing, and the easiest, could be a "fee to play" imposed on all companies who list on the exchanges (Dworkin, 2007a). While it would not be significant for any one company, it could create a sufficient fund, especially if increased by a percentage of recovered fines to adequately reward whistle-blowers for the risks taken in providing the information. However, costs associated with SOX are already cited as one of the main problems with the law, so this fee may not garner adequate support.

Because the wrongdoing involves fraud or other falsifications, the reward could be based on a percentage of the fraud amount (trebled) plus fines similar to the formula used in the FCA. The FCA provides for a fine of up to $10,000 per false claim incident. The claim would be brought for the government and the individual bringing it, even if the government has not been injured by the fraud—a provision that might cause such a law to be subject to constitutional challenge (Bucy, 2002; Rapp, 2007). A potential problem with this plan is that it is subject to standing challenges because government funds are not usually involved, unlike FCA claims. (However, Sunstein, 1992, argues the government can choose to give bounties to help enforce any law.) Although it is not clear these challenges would be successful, the issue could be overcome if Congress passed incentive legislation encouraging the states to include securities fraud in their false claims statutes similar to the Deficit Reduction Act discussed above (Dworkin, 2007a). State entities commonly invest in securities through workers' compensation and pension funds, among other investments, so they would have standing. However, the state would have to argue that the fraudulently induced price for the stock is a claim encompassed by the law (Rapp, 2007).

Professor Geoffrey Rapp has proposed a different and innovative way to fund SOX whistle-blower awards. He suggests amending the Fair Fund provisions of SOX so that the whistle-blower is given adequate compensation through administrative channels, in order to make the whistle-blowing worth the psychological, emotional, and economic risk (Rapp, 2007). The SEC currently has limited power to give rewards but seldom does so and they are often small. This situation is similar to the IRS scheme which is being revised because of its failed incentives. In order to be most effective, a minimum percentage should be guaranteed to the whistle-blower bringing new and useful information.

At a minimum, the statute of limitations should be expanded to at least 180 days or one year—the time limitations of many whistleblower statutes (Dworkin, 2007a). OSHA employees and administrative law judges should receive training specific to SOX requirements, and Congress should make clear exactly what activity it intended to protect and which employees and employers are included within the law. Finally, if the above changes are not implemented, an effort should be made to inform employees that they cannot expect much protection from SOX if they blow the whistle.

The Foreign Reach of SOX

There is a potential drawback to any scheme that rewards whistleblowing. It would be inconsistent with most foreign whistle-blowing legislation. As discussed above, other countries do not approve of large monetary awards for whistle-blowing (Callahan et al., 2004). This can be cured by providing an exemption for companies operating in countries that have adequate whistle-blower schemes and employee protections. For example, the European Commission has proposed its own version of business ethical standards, the Action Plan, as a reaction to SOX. It is seen as a "more multi-dimensional approach," placing shareholder interests as one of a group of protected interests (Roberts et al., 2004). There are also International Financial Reporting Standards in place for virtually all listed European companies (Wardell et al., 2005). Exemptions already exist under security laws for foreign companies (17 CFR §§ 249.220f, 240.3a12-3(b), 239.31 to 34; Woo, n.d.) so such an exemption would not be novel. Additionally, U.S. courts seem to be moving to limit the international reach of SOX's whistle-blowing sections.

Although SOX was passed in response to domestic issues, it was written badly and in haste (Vagts, 2003; Roberts et al., 2004). The

ramifications of the economic and political effects of extraterritorial application lacked adequate consideration. This is true of Section
806, the primary whistle-blowing section. It is broadly written and
makes virtually no distinction between domestic and foreign companies that have securities registered or listed in the United States
and it has the potential to reach foreign companies and encompass
U.S. employees working abroad.

There have, of course, been important failures in countries other
than the United States. Examples include Parmalat in Italy and OneTel
in Australia. So far there are few judgments on the extraterritorial
reach of SOX, but in the first important appellate decision regarding
whistle-blowing and extraterritorial application of SOX, the first circuit found that SOX did not protect a foreign worker who reported
accounting irregularities at a foreign subsidiary of a U.S. corporation
(*Carnero v. Boston Scientific,* 2006). The first circuit found that the
worker's allegations fit within SOX's whistle-blower protection section
because he was an employee of a publicly traded company subject to
the act, and his allegations of wrongdoing were the kind covered by the
law. However, it also found that the law did not have extraterritorial
coverage under his circumstances. The decision was based on several
factors, the most important of which was a presumption against extraterritorial application of U.S. laws without clear congressional intent.
It stated that Congress is "primarily concerned with domestic conditions." This, of course, denies the reality that over 1,000 foreign companies list their securities in the United States and voluntarily subject
themselves to U.S. laws, and that Congress was assumedly aware of
this globalization of the securities market when it enacted SOX. The
court said that there was nothing in the legislative history of SOX that
indicated that Congress gave any consideration to either the possibility or the problems of overseas application. The court found unpersua-
sive the worker's argument that to exempt him from protection would
frustrate the basic purpose of SOX, which is to protect investors in U.S.
securities markets as well as the integrity of the markets. It remains
to be seen whether other courts will follow the first circuit's lead.
Although there are good policy arguments as well as sufficiently broad
language in SOX to encompass cases such as the employee in the case
just discussed, consistent application of the nonterritorial reach of the
section would help alleviate some of the fears of other countries, such
as Germany and France, which see the U.S. policy as being too broad

and—among other reasons for concern—reminiscent of Nazism and World War II (Gibeaut, 2006; Callahan et al., 2004).

These countries also feel that confidential transmission of information is preferable to anonymity, thereby providing a paper trail so that information can be followed up and rechecked, ultimately so that no one can be condemned nor have their reputation sullied without absolute certainty of the information. The conflict with U.S. federal laws' drive toward hotlines is obviously a concern. In 2005, French and German regulators refused to approve a whistle-blower mechanism that McDonald's Corporation and CEAC/Exide (in France) and Wal-Mart (in Germany) sought that would make their policies there coincide with U.S. SOX whistle-blower protections. Other European countries have joined the debate about these privacy concerns, and on February 1, 2006, an EU commission composed of privacy experts from the member states proposed a nonbinding resolution that U.S.-listed companies would have to negotiate such provisions separately with each country. This, of course, would create tremendous compliance headaches for companies.

Hotlines

There are several recommendations regarding how to make hotlines effective. In addition to properly collecting, recording, and disseminating information, they should provide multilingual services, 24-hour availability, a toll-free number, a mechanism to follow up with anonymous reporters, documentation of follow-up and resolution (EthicsLine, 2005), communication of complaints to the internal auditor in Section 404 SOX violations, response to the complaint in a timely manner, and adequate notice to the employees of the existence of the hotline (Daher, 2005; *Metropolitan Corporate Counsel*, 2006). Additionally, the hotlines should have trained interviewers, and there should be prearranged distribution of call reports based on subject, seriousness, and involvement of senior management (Bishop, 2006).

Hotlines and other types of whistle-blowing recipients find that a large percentage of the reports they receive involve human resources management issues (Sapino Jeffreys, 2005). Some of the reports may clearly involve wrongdoing and ethical considerations (e.g., perceived illegal discrimination), but others may not (e.g., a suggestion that benefit program coverage should be expanded). Of course, the same might be said about reports that do not involve human resources. Or, the company may have intended that only SOX violations go through the hotline. These points raise several questions. For example, should hotlines limit the types of reports processed, as some firms direct? Should all SOX reports be submitted to the audit committee of the board of directors, even if they involve human resources or other nonfinancial issues? Should they be filtered so that only the most important financial issues reach the audit committee? Traditionally, audit committees have focused on fraud and financial wrongdoing. Filtering out nonfinancial complaints or financial complaints judged less important raises the possibility that management might be able to block a matter that needed to be forwarded, or a seemingly minor complaint does not reach the committee, and it blows up into a full-scale problem. Unfortunately, we do not have sufficient empirical evidence to make recommendations regarding these questions. At the time of this writing, a plethora of Web sites (including many established by law firms offering services) propose advice concerning the involvement of human resources functions in hotlines established in response to SOX. In any event, it has been noted that employee concerns that do not appear to present traditional ethics issues or obvious SOX violations may still have ethical implications, if viewed broadly, and may be suitable for hotlines for that reason (Connors, 2007).

Role-Prescribed or Required Whistle-Blowing

One development that may be on the increase is required whistle-blowing. In many states those who work with children are required to report any evidence of abuse. Some states also require reporting of elder abuse by employees involved in elder care (Callahan & Dworkin, 2000). Additionally, as companies face increased liability under laws such as SOX, the organizations themselves may require reporting of wrongdoing (Heard & Miller, 2006b).

Summary

Whistle-blowing is increasingly recognized worldwide as important in ensuring the transparency and integrity of governments, global markets, and organizations. The contribution of insiders with

information about wrongdoing that would be hard to obtain otherwise is growing in importance as organizations become more complex and dispersed. Governments are recognizing this development
and enacting legislation to facilitate whistle-blowing and protect
whistle-blowers. The model that has worked the best in the United
States is the incentive model, and its use is likely to grow in the next
several years. SOX may be revised to include this model so that it is
more effective. We need to assess systematically what practices work
best in other countries. However, if information about wrongdoing
is the main goal of encouraging whistle-blowing, quality information should trump motive.

Appendix

State False Claims Acts

States	Who Can Bring the Suit	Covered Claims	Liability of the Defendant	Reward to *qui tam* Plaintiff if Government Takes Action	Reward to *qui tam* Plaintiff if Government Does Not Take Action
Arkansas 20-77-900	Attorney general or *qui tam* plaintiff(s)	False/fraudulent claims made knowingly			10%, $100,000 (max), no liability for expenses
California Government Code Sections 12650 to 12656	Attorney general or *qui tam* plaintiff(s)	Political subdivision funds State funds	Three times the damages, cost of the civil action, and possible civil penalty up to $10,000 per act	The *qui tam* plaintiff shall receive an amount the court finds reasonable for reasonable expenses	The *qui tam* plaintiff shall receive an amount the court finds reasonable for reasonable expenses
Delaware False Claims and Reporting Act Sections 1201 to 1209	Attorney general or *qui tam* plaintiff(s)	Knowingly defrauding the government	$5,500 to $11,000 per act plus three times the damages	15% to 25% of the action proceeds or settlement	25% to 30% of the proceeds and possibly reasonable amount decided by the court for civil penalties and damages
District of Columbia False Claims Act Chapter 2 Sections 308.03 and 308.13 to 21	Corporate counsel		$5,000 to $10,000 per act	10% to 20% of the action proceeds or settlement	25% to 40% of the action proceeds or settlement

State / Act	Enforcement	Description	Penalty	Reward (action)	Reward (intervention)
Florida False Claims Act Chapter 68 Sections .081 to .092	Department of Banking and Finance	Deters persons from knowingly causing or assisting in causing state government to pay claims that are false	$5,000 to $10,000 per act plus three times the damages	15% to 25% of the action proceeds or settlement	25% to 30% of the proceeds and possibly attorney's fees
Hawaii False Claims Act Part 2 Chapter 661 Sections 21 to 29 and Part 10 Chapter 46 Sections 171 to 179	Attorney general or *qui tam* plaintiff(s)	Knowingly making false claims	$5,000 to $10,000 per act plus three times the damages	15% to 25% of the action proceeds or settlement	25% to 30% of the proceeds and possibly attorney's fees
Illinois Reward and Protection Act Chapter 175 Sections 1 to 8	Attorney general or *qui tam* plaintiff(s)	Knowingly making a false claim to get money from state	$5,000 to $10,000 per act plus three times the damages	One-sixth of proceeds goes to the attorney general, one-sixth to the Department of State Police, and two-thirds to the *qui tam* plaintiff	One-sixth of proceeds goes to the attorney general, one-sixth to the Department of State Police, and two-thirds to the *qui tam* plaintiff
Indiana False Claims and Whistle-blowers Protection Act IC Chapter 5-11-5.5 Sections 1 to 18	Attorney general, inspector general, or *qui tam* plaintiff(s)	Presents, knowingly, a false claim to the state for payment or approval	No less than two times the damages	15% to 25% of the action proceeds or settlement	25% to 30% of the proceeds and possibly attorney's fees

continued

States	Who Can Bring the Suit	Covered Claims	Liability of the Defendant	Reward to *qui tam* Plaintiff if Government Takes Action	Reward to *qui tam* Plaintiff if Government Does Not Take Action
Massachusetts					
False Claims Act Chapter 159, Section 18, Sections 5a to 5o	Attorney general or *qui tam* plaintiff(s)	Presents, knowingly, a false claim to the state for payment or approval	$5,000 to $10,000 per act plus three times the damages	15% to 25% of the action proceeds or settlement	25% to 30% of the proceeds and possibly attorney's fees
Michigan					
MCL 400.611	Attorney general or *qui tam* plaintiff(s)			15% to 25%, plus costs, expenses reasonable attorney fees	25 to 30% of proceeds
Nevada					
Submission of False Claims to State or Local Government NRS Chapter 357 sections .010 to .250	Attorney general or *qui tam* plaintiff(s)	Knowingly presents or causes to be presented a false claim for payment or approval	$2,000 to $10,000 per act	15% or 33% of the action proceeds or settlement	25% to 50% of the proceeds from the action or settlement plus a reasonable amount for expenses
New Hampshire					
False Claims Act Chapter 167:61 Sections b to e	Attorney general or *qui tam* plaintiff(s)	Knowingly presents or causes to be presented a false claim for payment or approval	$5,000 to $10,000 per act	15% to 25% of the action proceeds or settlement	15% to 25% of the action proceeds or settlement

New Mexico	Attorney general or *qui tam* plaintiff(s)	Knowingly makes a false claim to get money from state	Liable to state for three times the amount of damages the state sustains	15% to 20% of the action proceeds, fees, costs	25% to 30% reasonable expenses, fees, and costs
Tennessee 7-1-5-182-71-5-186	Attorney general or *qui tam* plaintiff(s)	Knowingly presents or causes to be presented a claim for payment	$5,000 to $10,000 plus three times the amount of damages	10% to 15% proceeds, fees, and costs	25% to 30% reasonable fees and costs
Texas Texas Human Resource Code 36.001-132	Attorney general or *qui tam* plaintiff(s)	Knowingly presents or causes to be presented a false claim for payment of approval; presents a claim that contains info that the person knows to be false	$5,000 to $10,000 per violation plus administrative penalty	15% to 25% of proceeds and costs depending on the extent of their participation	*See previous column
Virginia Fraud Against Taxpayers Act Chapter 842 and Chapter 8.01-216 Sections 1 to 19	Attorney general or *qui tam* plaintiff(s)	Conspires to defraud, knowingly presents or causes to be presented a false or fraudulent claim for payment or approval	$5,000 to $10,000 per act	15% to 25% of the action proceeds or settlement	25% to 35% of the proceeds

7

Practical Implications of the Research and Legal Changes, and Conclusion

It is self-evident that whistle-blowing can be very beneficial for societies and their members, for example, when a hazardous product is taken off the market, or when stock options are properly reported as a result of whistle-blowing. Some observers may be concerned that whistle-blowing can also be costly to organizations (e.g., by undermining the authority structure, relationships, or trust in organizations). But increasingly, research shows whistle-blowing, and appropriate response to it, can also benefit the organizations in which wrongdoing is occurring (e.g., Glomb et al., 1997; Magley & Cortina, 2002; Miceli & Near, 1994a; Miceli et al., 2001b). Nowhere is this point better exemplified than in the comments of one of the world's leading investors:

> Warren E. Buffett, chairman of the board of Berkshire Hathaway, a global investment firm with 180,000 employees, praised the company's recently installed hotline in his 2005 chairman's letter. "Berkshire would be more valuable today if I had put in a whistleblowing (hot)line decades ago," he wrote. "The issues raised are usually not of a type discoverable by audit, but relate instead to personnel and business practices." (Slovin, 2006, p. 46)

Thus, managers who wisely and ethically do not allow the negative consequences of wrongdoing to play out, and do not want lawmakers or legal authorities to further intervene in their activities, can take steps to improve conditions for whistle-blowers. These steps may encourage whistle-blowers to limit their reports to internal channels, thus reducing the risks and costs associated with external disclosure, such as bad publicity. Thus, one key purpose of this chapter is to identify steps that such managers can take to avoid the negative effects of wrongdoing and whistle-blowing.

It is ironic that effective organizational response to whistle-blowing can produce many potential benefits, yet whistle-blowing still is an uncommon event. Unfortunately, this is not because organizational wrongdoing is also unusual, thus rendering whistle-blowing unnecessary. Instead, as discussed in previous chapters, research and media reports indicate (a) that most employees who perceive that wrongdoing is occurring do not act on it, primarily because they believe nothing will be done to correct the problems, and (b) that these beliefs are often well founded. These findings suggest, in many instances, that no advice we can offer in this chapter will make a difference. Our advice is predicated on the assumption that there is a sincere wish on the part of the top management team to encourage appropriate internal whistle-blowing, but this condition obviously is not present in certain situations. Presumably, legislators or others have more to say about encouraging reluctant wrongdoers to change or punishing those who refuse. We also offer advice to legislators, and to policy makers, potential or actual whistle-blowers, and other parties. But, because most of this book has been dedicated to reviewing management research, our focus is primarily on management and, in particular, on those managers who want to develop the important strategic strength of proactively avoiding wrongdoing and its aftermath.

Ideally, a chapter offering advice about whistle-blowing would be thoroughly grounded in a comprehensive body of controlled research, and this research would address costs relative to the benefits of practical options. Ideally, the advice might use—but would not rely greatly on—impressions, guesses, logical deduction, or personal experiences. What seems logical or reasonable—and perhaps true in one situation—may not be consistent with what is more generally found to be true. For example, it may seem "obvious" that threatening retaliation will reduce the incidence of whistle-blowing, because threats impose a cost and suggest high risk of more costs, for example, ruining one's career. But empirical evidence strongly suggests that threatening retaliation does not discourage many whistle-blowers, and indeed may encourage some to report wrongdoing to the media or other outsiders, as in the case of tobacco industry whistle-blower Dr. Jeffrey Wigand, discussed previously. And, advice based on personal experiences may be contradictory. For example, one advisor may suggest that organizational systems should become more formalized, to ensure greater procedural justice and reduce

TABLE 7.1   Some Questions Regarding Whistle-Blowing Hotlines

- Holding everything else constant, do hotlines produce more complaints than other methods, such as informally encouraging employees to report concerns to their supervisors?

- Are the hotline complaints valid and do they offer evidence of actual wrongdoing, or do they reflect petty concerns, efforts to embarrass someone, etc.?

- What is the "signal-to-noise" ratio of hotlines versus other methods? Must someone listen to and process 10 or more complaints in order to hear one valid complaint?

- What difference does it make to offer anonymous complaining as an option? Do more employees come forward, or is it harder to follow up when investigating such complaints?

- What are the characteristics of more successful hotlines versus other methods?

- Is it better and more cost effective NOT to encourage whistle-blowing, but instead to endeavor to avoid wrongdoing in the first place?

- Is there some way to quantify the benefits of correcting wrongdoing identified in hotline complaints with the cost of establishing and maintaining hotlines?

- Are there net advantages of outsourcing the hotline function (e.g., employees may feel freer from potential retaliation if reporting to a third party), and if so, do they outweigh the net advantages, if any, of in-house hotlines?

- Do industry, organizational, or employee characteristics make a difference? For example, if a hotline system has worked successfully in a relatively newer and smaller organization with highly educated, young employees, is there evidence it will be equally successful in a large, bureaucratic organization in which employee demographic (or job) characteristics vary widely?

the probability that issues will fall between the cracks, and to satisfy legal requirements (e.g., SOX). Another advisor may instead assert that such formalization undermines trust in the organization, that it may be perceived as "CYA" or "window dressing," and that formalization may not foster—and may even interfere with—building the kind of culture that truly rewards and sustains ethical and productive behavior. How can managers sort out such contradictions?

Further, general advice without comprehensive empirical evidence backing it may not be very useful. For example, one could recommend that an organization establish a hotline to encourage valid internal complaints. But before accepting this recommendation, managers might want to know the answers to specific questions, such as those shown in Table 7.1, pertaining to hotlines.

Alternative potential sources of answers to such questions exist. Fellow managers could offer responses by describing their own experiences with hotlines or based on what they believe could happen. Interviews with or surveys of managers could aggregate these experiences or opinions, to identify and report general trends or shared views. Academics could review existing research on what drives people to blow the whistle, for example, and use reason to develop advice about hotlines. But the best answers would come from controlled research that directly examined questions like those in Table 7.1.

Unfortunately, to our knowledge, such research is rare to nonexistent. For example, we know of no published studies that have (a) systematically varied (or even measured) employer actions, such as training or improved communications specifically designed to discourage retaliation or to correct problems identified by whistle-blowers, and (b) then measured the effects independently, for example, through before-and-after measures of complaint levels or employee perceptions. Obviously, access to data that would meet rigorous standards of experimental design is a major issue, but also, conducting this research is challenging because top academic journals demand a theoretical basis for predictions. Surveys of non-randomly-selected managers or complaint recipients about what they think would bring employees forward, or their experiences with different techniques, may be the best information that now is publicly available.

Therefore, we must rely on the other sources as described above. We caution readers about the limitations of the advice in this chapter, and urge organizations and researchers to undertake more rigorous research directly examining practical questions. In the discussion that follows, we attempt to specify the source or basis for particular recommendations.

Actions That Managers Can Take

There appear to be two ways to stop corruption and wrongdoing in organizations: (a) for external forces (e.g., government regulatory agencies or the free market) to exert influence over the organization to convince top management to terminate ongoing wrongdoing or avoid new wrongdoing; and (b) for internal forces within the organization to exert pressure on members not to engage in wrongdoing to start with—because dismantling an organization culture that normalizes wrongdoing, after the fact, is very difficult (Misangyi et al., in press). Cultures that normalize wrongdoing (Ashforth & Anand, 2003) provide a "logic of corruption" that may be best disrupted by "institutional entrepreneurs" who attempt to reframe the culture, through "legitimating accounts" that support symbolic identities and meanings that give forth to a new, "anticorrupt logic" (Misangyi et al., in press). It strikes us, to the extent that the term can be appropriately applied to employees below the level of top management, that whistle-blowers might be one of the most important types of institutional entrepreneurs to launch such a change in the culture of the organization that supports normalization of wrongdoing. The question then is how to encourage whistle-blowing. Managers who do so may avoid the obviously intrusive external forces that would otherwise exert pressure on them to avoid new wrongdoing or terminate existing wrongdoing.

Other than the works by Treviño, Weaver, and colleagues described previously in this book, we know of only one study involving interviews and surveys with managers focused specifically on identifying actions to encourage whistle-blowing. This study, which has been described in two preliminary reports (Heard & Miller, 2006a, 2006b), was conducted jointly by the International Business Ethics Institute, in partnership with others, including the Ethics and Compliance Officer Association. At the time of our writing, more specific information about methodology has not been published.

In general, the results of that study and of prior empirical research support the notion that top managers should create a culture for encouraging good performance that is ethical. Preventing behavior that undermines this goal and responding appropriately to irregularities, including perceived wrongdoing, obviously must be a part of such a culture, because these actions promote self-correction and reinforcement of ethical values and standards. In fact, Weaver noted that organizations have the opportunity to create the development of moral agency among their members, thereby leading to stronger moral identity among those members: "moral actions can reinforce moral identity, making it more central in one's overall self-concept" (Weaver, 2006, p. 351). He suggested that moral behavior is the wrong dependent variable; instead we should be concerned about developing moral identity among organization members, because only a strong sense of moral identity can lead an employee to develop a schema of moral agency that will allow that person to engage in moral behavior on a consistent basis. Organizations reinforce the development of moral identity through their actions, and moral behavior, engaged in by employees, reinforces the culture of moral identity among organization members as a group. But organizations "that foster moral muteness" provide less opportunity for the development of moral identity, likely leading to less moral behavior among members (Weaver, 2006, p. 352). Where moral identity is an essential intermediate variable in the whistle-blowing process is not a settled matter at this point and remains for future research. In any event, we believe that managers can best foster strong moral identity, and we hope—moral behavior—among members through creation of a positive organization culture.

The creation and maintenance of a positive culture is a long-term, comprehensive goal, and there are many systems that can support the development of that culture. These can be roughly categorized into (a) policies and human resource systems, for example, involving organizational entry, training and development, and employer financial incentives for whistle-blowers; and (b) systems to investigate and respond to concerns.

Policies and Human Resource Systems

According to a *Wall Street Journal* article (Lublin, 2006), experts on sexual harassment advise that employers should create a "tough" anti-retaliation policy that permits dismissing employees who retaliate. Similar policies may be appropriate for other types of wrongdoing as well, and policies to encourage whistle-blowing should go beyond protection from retaliation and punishing the whistle-blower, as has been detailed (e.g., Heard & Miller, 2006a). Policies can be incorporated into the materials given to employees during orientation and made available on company intranet systems. Below we discuss how organizations can support policies and "walk the walk" in action.

Organizational Entry To the extent that dispositions and other individual differences are important determinants of employee behavior, research suggests that the selection process is important. Employees can search for and select employees who possess attributes associated with observation of wrongdoing, and whistle-blowing.

As discussed in Chapter 2, preliminary research suggests that negative affectivity is associated with observation of wrongdoing, but not necessarily with whistle-blowing. Employees with high negative affectivity more *correctly* may recognize wrongdoing than do people with low negative affectivity scores; if so, they would be valuable employees. However, if they tend to be overly critical, perhaps training would help to clarify organizational definitions of wrongdoing.

If dispositions such as optimism contribute to whistle-blowing, then human resources managers could take steps to ensure that optimistic applicants are included in those selected. Of course, there is another side to this argument. As suggested in the research on negative affectivity and speculation on the effects of extreme optimism, highly positive people may distort reality, for example, by not seeing wrongdoing when it is occurring (Peterson, 2000). Perhaps a middle ground, or a commitment to diversity of personalities, will be shown to be ideal.

The limited research to date suggests that proactivity is associated with whistle-blowing by employees who have observed wrongdoing. There seems to be little downside risk regarding recruiting and hiring highly proactive people, because proactive personality is associated not only with whistle-blowing within the organization, but also with other positive outcomes such as sales success (e.g., Crant, 1995). These findings (Miceli et al., 2001b) provide even more reason for those critical of whistle-blowing to rethink their views. Proactive people can provide a very positive resource to the organization—in sales, in prosocial organizational behavior, in problem-solving—though some managers may feel threatened by them.

After newcomers join the organization, orientation materials can be helpful. In many larger organizations, employees are provided with employee handbooks at the time of orientation. Many companies include codes of ethics and antiretaliation policies in these handbooks (Lublin, 2006). For example, Michaels Stores Inc. recently added an antiretaliation policy to its corporate code of conduct, which middle and upper managers must sign annually. "Management primarily wanted to ensure a pleasant working environment free from all types of harassment," says a spokeswoman for the Irving, Texas, company. "The fact that it could potentially reduce legal exposure was a secondary focus" (Lublin, 2006, p. B4). Lawyers may encourage employers to have employees sign a form stating that they have read and understand the whistle-blowing policies (and other policies, such as those concerning sexual harassment and retaliation).

Advice concerning the specific content of materials pertaining to whistle-blowing has been offered; for example, code standards should show how seriously the organization takes employee concerns, tells employees what to expect when raising concerns (Heard & Miller, 2006a, 2006b), and, most importantly, where to take concerns. As described in Chapter 6, clear procedures, actively and effectively maintained, reduce not only harassment liability but also the likelihood of punitive damages. They can also help reduce fines and penalties under the Corporate Sentencing Guidelines (United States Sentencing Commission, 1991).

Training and Development   Organizations should provide training to reduce the incidence of wrongdoing (such as discrimination, including sexual harassment) and retaliation against those who complain (Lublin, 2006). For example, Cardinal Building Maintenance Inc., a commercial janitorial service, requires supervisors and managers to attend an annual five-hour class about workplace bias and harassment, and one-fourth of the course focuses on retaliation (Lublin, 2006, p. B4).

Similarly, Heard and Miller (2006a) recommended training, both for employees and for managers, dedicated exclusively to raising concerns, avoiding retaliation, and recognizing when retaliation is occurring. They provided specific suggestions on the content and process of such training. For example, trainers should discuss reasons to report concerns, show how concerns will be addressed, and emphasize that speaking up produces a positive impact (Heard & Miller, 2006a). Obviously, the vast body of research on training and development has identified many ways to enhance the value and transfer of training in general (e.g., Hatala & Fleming, 2007; Shapiro, King, & Quiñones, 2007), and it could be applied to whistle-blowing training as well. While all of this advice is reasonable, we know of no controlled research demonstrating the effectiveness of training regarding whistle-blowing and such research is sorely needed. Despite this dearth of research, the federal government has begun to require training about whistle-blowing, as mentioned in Chapter 6. This mirrors what many states have done in the area of sexual harassment.

Employer Financial Incentives for Whistle-blowers   Here we consider the question of whether the employer's voluntarily offering whistle-blowers financial incentives, such as a percentage of savings recovered as a result of whistle-blowing (e.g., where embezzlement is caught), a salary increase in a merit system, a one-time cash bonus (e.g., in a suggestion system), or some other financial reward for whistle-blowing, affects whistle-blowing. As for financial incentives offered by entities *other* than the employing organization, such as the federal and state governments in the case of fraud committed by contractors, we discuss these in the section of this chapter focusing on advice for policy makers.

As Phase 3 of the whistle-blowing model indicates, observers of wrongdoing consider the costs and benefits of acting, along with other factors. The simplest interpretation of motivation theory would suggest that valued employer rewards for internal whistle-blowing would lead to greater internal reporting, all other factors such as potential retaliation being equal or minimized. Consistent with the model, a KPMG survey showed that "workers said rewards or incentives for adhering to company standards would reinforce ethics programs" (Ridge, 2000, p. A1).

However, as we reported in our 1996 review, we know of no private sector U.S. organizations that provide direct financial incentives specifically to reward whistle-blowing, other than in the case of accountants and internal auditors, for example, at the consulting firm BDO Seidman (e.g., Rankin, 2004). Further, other than the work described in Chapter 6, the research literature generally has not examined whether financial incentives actually affected whistle-blowing. Because both financial incentives and whistle-blowers are exceedingly rare, the coexistence of low frequencies of both implies that it is possible that they do vary together, and the more financial incentives, the more whistle-blowing. Of course, without further evidence, this is simply an untested hypothesis.

One study (U. S. Merit Systems Protection Board, 1981) posed a hypothetical question on a survey: employees in general (not just observers of wrongdoing or whistle-blowers) were asked whether they would be more willing to blow the whistle if they received financial rewards for reporting wrongdoing. Somewhat surprisingly, a large majority said this would *not* affect their behavior. On the one hand, this is consistent with the fact most whistle-blowers to date have acted without clear financial incentives. Maybe they could see important nonfinancial benefits already in the situation, are extremely selfless, or process information in ways most people might consider "emotional" rather than a rational assessment of expected costs and benefits. On the other hand, most past whistle-blowers' experiences, and the survey result, do not necessarily demonstrate that the majority of employees really are uninfluenced by financial incentives, for at least four reasons.

First, in general, psychologists and others have long debated the extent to which people's descriptions of how they would act in a given situation (when presented with a hypothetical scenario by a researcher) reflect real behavior when actually in that situation. People may want to please the researcher or respond in ways that are consistent with the image they want to have of themselves. Of course, variables such as social desirability or self-monitoring (whether biases or dispositional tendencies) may also influence actual work-place behavior (in this case, actual whistle-blowing) as well (e.g., Hewlin, 2003; Premeaux & Bedeian, 2003; Smith & Ellingson, 2002; Turnley & Bolino, 2001). But the key point is that what people say they would do is not necessarily the same as what they would actually do, and what people say would influence their behavior is not necessarily what actually influences them. More specifically, a recent meta-analysis of whistle-blowing studies showed that the predictors of whistle-blowing intentions (such as those that may be measured with a hypothetical question on a survey) are not necessarily the same as the predictors of actual whistle-blowing (Mesmer-Magnus & Viswesvaran, 2005).

Second, some form of variable pay is widely used by private employers in the United States and the vast majority of these programs are individually based merit pay (salary increase) programs or bonus systems (Zall, 2001). If managers did not believe or find through experience that employees could be encouraged, via pay, to behave in ways that top management wanted, why would they operate these systems, which are costly and difficult to administer? And if an employer wanted valid whistle-blowing as well as good job performance, why could it not use similar systems to encourage either?

Third, in the United States at least, taboos and privacy concerns often discourage employee admissions that money is valued or influential on their effort. Even CEOs are expected to say that they live for the challenge of their work first and foremost. Millionaire athletes are not worthy of respect unless they play "for the love of the game." Yet, clearly the amounts and nature of compensation influence their behavior.

Fourth, respondents may have viewed this question as asking whether they must be bribed in order to behave in a morally correct or appropriate way. The vast majority of respondents had indicated in a previous question on the same survey that they approved of the reporting of wrongdoing. Because it may be unacceptable to most people to admit that cash incentives would be necessary to do the "right" thing, it may have been easier to simply say they would make no difference. For any of these reasons, then, survey responses relative to incentives may bear little relationship to what employees actually think and do, and more research is needed to determine whether and how compensation can be structured to encourage whistle-blowing.

Systems to Encourage, Investigate, and Respond to Expression of Concerns

When a concern is voiced, managers should be certain to focus on the wrongdoing alleged in the complaint and not engage in attacks on the complainant. A full and fair investigation should be undertaken and swift corrective action taken when the complaint is well-founded. To the extent confidentiality is not at issue, positive feedback indicating how the problem has been corrected should be shared with others as well, for example, "thanks to a report from one of our associates, we were alerted to this problem and took the following actions." Where complaints are unfounded, employees can be counseled on what is lacking; for example, is the evidence unclear? Below we discuss systems that can help facilitate this general advice.

Internal Communication Channels and Hotlines   According to a KPMG survey of private and public sector employees (e.g., Grimsley, 2000), more than four-fifths of respondents would choose their supervisor or another manager as the complaint channel, if they were to report concerns (Heard & Miller, 2006b). But the same survey showed that "'people are not reporting misconduct because they are not encouraged to do so,' says Richard Girgenti, a KPMG executive" (Ridge, 2000, p. A1). Thus, managers should "create a corporate culture where dialogue and feedback are regular practice—and this

should extend to every level of employee throughout the organization. Such a culture can build the foundation of an open problem-
solving environment, demonstrate to employees that it is safe to
raise concerns, and exhibit that the organization takes retaliation
seriously" (Heard & Miller, 2006a, p. 2).

Heard and Miller recommended anonymous surveys to assess
employee perceptions, as a first step in a two-way communication
process in which employees express their views. They offered specifics
about the content and analysis of the surveys, and recommended
follow-up focus groups. They also recommended that multiple,
effective communication channels be available, to enable employees
to select the person(s) with whom they are most comfortable sharing
sensitive information. Alternative channels are essential to avoiding
liability in sexual harassment cases so that the victim does not have
to report to the harasser; the same logic would apply here.

Consistent with this advice, researchers have found a positive
correlation between increased internal whistle-blowing and having
specific, identified routes for whistle-blowing, a particular person
identified to receive and follow-up the information, and a strong, non-
retaliatory policy encouraging whistle-blowing (Barnett, Cochran, &
Taylor, 1993; Miceli & Near, 1992). Open door policies do not meet
these requirements. They are also unlikely to result in compliance
under the Federal Sentencing Guidelines (United States Sentencing
Commission, 1991).

The Investigation Process and Correction of Wrongdoing   The
primary purpose of the investigation process is to determine
whether the complaint has merit, so that appropriate actions can
be taken. Organizations and their members are not well served by
ignoring real wrongdoing, such as discrimination or serious unsafe
working conditions. But they are also not well served by rewarding
the gadfly or chronic low performer seeking to distract attention, nor
by wasting time on frivolous complaints. As Perry noted, "although
the authenticity of a whistle-blower's complaint may be irrelevant for
the organization that chooses to ignore it or to retaliate against the
whistle-blower, it is clearly relevant to the organization that wishes
to respond appropriately. Responsive organizations are faced with
investigating the complaint to identify whether it is authentic or
inauthentic" (Perry, 1991, p. 12).

Determining merit or authenticity often is easier said than done. Obviously, some whistle-blowers can be mistaken, or may find objectionable certain types of behavior that are not widely defined as wrongdoing, but there have been many documented cases where valid concerns were ignored. Further, as documented in Chapter 1, many complaint recipients perceive that only a tiny minority of complaints are valid, but other data suggest that in reality many more have substance, at least under certain circumstances. Unfortunately, the validity of complaints, and predictors and consequences of validity, have rarely been studied systematically; so, findings must be considered preliminary. But they certainly raise a critical point: Obviously, employers who perceive that complaints are frivolous are unlikely to take corrective action, and if they refuse to act on a large proportion that are valid, then even employees with valid concerns will quickly conclude that nothing will happen if they complain. This creates a vicious circle in which employees rarely report real wrong-doing, so officials take few corrective actions, to which employees react by believing nothing would be done to correct wrongdoing if it were reported, and reports drop further. The extant information suggests that organizations should examine not only the numbers of complaints filed, but also what proportion of complaints is found to be meritorious. They should look for ways to improve investigations or take other steps—such as clarifying what wrongdoing is, what evidence employees should provide, etc.—where these numbers are low.

In their study of employers' advice and practices, Heard and Miller identified two key tendencies that should be avoided: (1) "shooting the messenger," in which focus is misdirected from resolving the wrong-doing and toward punishing the whistle-blower, and (2) eliminating the "bad apples" (punishing the wrongdoers) but failing to "identify a systemic cause or rectify the actual problem" (Heard & Miller, 2006a, p. 7). They offered steps for employer consideration, including:

- "Ensure responsibility for investigations is clearly delineated and effective processes are in place for conducing investigations;
- Ensure investigations can take place relatively quickly;
- Focus on the complaint, not the complainant (as we also noted at the opening of this section of the chapter);
- Ensure communication gaps are closed (i.e., lack of communication between HR and the Ethics Office can have serious implications, e.g., under SOX);

- Take reports of retaliation seriously and follow up on them;
- Discipline those that commit wrongdoing;
- Provide feedback to the individual that reported the wrongdoing" (Heard & Miller, 2006a, p. 7).

We would call particular attention to the advice on retaliation. Litigation regarding retaliation is the largest source of discrimination claims currently. As noted in a recent article appearing in *Business Week,* in 2005 and 2006, retaliation claims represented 30% of all charges individuals filed with the Equal Employment Opportunity Commission, an increase from about 20% 10 years ago. Further, a recent Supreme Court ruling clarified that excluding an employee from meetings, relocating his or her office, or other actions falling far short of firing could lead to liability (Orey, 2007).

Again, because of a dearth of controlled empirical research specifically examining the effects of implementing such recommendations, we cannot offer citations in support of them. However, all seem reasonable, based on the research on how and why whistle-blowing occurs and on the importance of effectiveness in the process.

Heard and Miller (2006a) emphasized that, if an anonymous survey or other assessment of employee perceptions reveals problems, it is important for organizations to rectify the problems. Once a specific incident of wrongdoing has occurred, it is not too late to realize benefits, if communications from management to employees are open. After a specific incident has been reported and wrongdoing remedied, companies can publish "scrubbed reports of actual cases to illustrate the action taken by the organization to rectify problems and punish wrongdoers" (Heard & Miller, 2006a, p. 7). Implementing this recommendation would likely help counteract employees' tendency—demonstrated in controlled research—to believe nothing could or would be done if wrongdoing were reported. Consistent with this advice, research (Miceli et al., 2001b) suggests that encouraging reporting and immediate correction about which employees are informed may also have desirable effects almost as good as those resulting from preventing wrongdoing in the first place. These benefits go *beyond* reducing tangible costs to the organization associated with wrongdoing itself (e.g., adverse publicity, damaged reputation, lawsuits); managers who prevent or correct wrongdoing may engender positive feelings and favorable consequences among employees.

Monitoring and Following Up Implementing programs and actions intended to encourage whistle-blowing is not sufficient; managers need to monitor the success of the programs and make changes where needed. For example, in the case of sexual harassment, the *Wall Street Journal* recommends that a thorough follow-up be conducted several months after the initial intervention to ensure that retaliation does not occur (Lublin, 2006). Similarly, Heard and Miller recommend steps for maintaining effective communication, for example, by reminding employees about the available channels (Heard & Miller, 2006a). Periodic republication also reduces legal liability and is required under certain federal laws.

Advice to Whistle-Blowers and Potential Whistle-Blowers

Prevailing legal arguments, both in U.S. law (Miceli & Near, 1992) and British law (Callahan et al., 2004; Vinten, 1994), suggest that "whistle-blowing is warranted if the whistle-blower believes, in good faith, that the wrongdoing has implications for public policy; that is, some portion of society is endangered by the organization's actions" (Near & Miceli, 1996, p. 508). Further, ethicists have indicated that one condition necessary for the justification of whistle-blowing is that "the whistle-blower has acted after a careful analysis of the danger: (a) how serious is the moral violation; (b) how immediate is the moral violation; (c) is the moral violation one that can be specified?" (Bowie, 1982, p. 143). Clearly, such prescriptions depend on the accuracy of the potential whistle-blower's observation of the facts surrounding the wrongdoing (Near & Miceli, 1996), and they imply that the nature of the wrongdoing is critical. They may also depend on the process used by the whistle-blower (e.g., taking steps to embarrass a perceived wrongdoer or interfere with legitimate work processes, rather than focusing on solving the problem) (Miceli & Near, 1997).

Therefore, it is not surprising that many experts who work with whistle-blowers (e.g., Devine, 1997) emphasize the importance of having sound evidence and following good process. This process should be informed by the relevant law (to enable the whistle-blower to retain the maximum protection available) and the literature on distributive, procedural, and interactional justice (e.g., Miceli & Near, 1997). For example, it is important for whistle-blowers to know that large rewards under the False Claims Act are not available unless the information is useful and novel, and leads to a conviction. Unfortunately, because there is little research on specific tactics and their relative effectiveness, we cannot be as specific here as we would like to be.

Advice to Policy Makers

In some sense, given the risks and costs, the perception on the part of many complaint recipients that few cases have merit, and the limited direct rewards for whistle-blowing, it is remarkable that anyone ever chooses to challenge organizational wrongdoing. As noted in Chapter 6, the legal protections for employees do not guarantee protection from retaliation. Further, research described earlier strongly suggests that legal changes focused on encouraging organizations to change the wrongdoing, and punishing organizations that ignore whistle-blowers, would have greater impact.

Preliminary research on corporate response to legal changes showed few changes, at least early on. A survey of human resource executives from Fortune 1000 firms (Near & Dworkin, 1998) asked whether their firms changed their whistle-blowing policies in response to changes in new state statutes (see also Dworkin, Near, & Callahan, 1995). The authors expected that firms might have created internal channels for whistle-blowing in response to the new legislation, but very few firms indicated that they had created their policies in responses to legal changes. For most, this meant reliance on an open door policy as their primary mechanism for internal whistle-blowing. Unfortunately, most employees do not see such policies as effective or protective, and they have not been used successfully to encourage internal reporting of wrongdoing (Keenan, 1990).

These studies, of course, predated passage of SOX. Moberly has charged that, prior to this event, legislative attempts designed to encourage whistle-blowing in order to reduce retaliation fit what he termed the "anti-retaliation model" and were largely unsuccessful because the laws focused only on discouraging retaliation against whistle-blowers and not on encouraging whistle-blowing behavior (Moberly, 2006). He argued instead for the structural model, exemplified by SOX, which both: (a) provides incentives for whistle-blowers by showing them clearly that whistle-blowing is not disloyal to the firm but supports it, and (b) provides clear, safe, and effective channels for whistle-blowing by providing that the complaint recipient should be an independent member of the audit committee of the board of directors. As he noted, prior to the most recent wave of scandals in the late 1990s, several legislative attempts in both the anti-retaliation model and the structural model were unsuccessful, because they were not implemented properly.

As discussed in Chapter 6, most companies have established hotlines as an intermediary recipient between the whistle-blower and the audit committee, and this may reduce the effectiveness of the model. Some commentators recommend that the organization have a designated recipient inside the company, such as an ombudsperson in addition to a hotline.

Success is possible only if the legislative models prohibit retaliation against whistle-blowers, provide sufficient incentive to persuade whistle-blowers that coming forward is in the best interests of society and the firm, and create effective channels for reporting the wrongdoing, anonymously or otherwise, to safe complaint recipients outside the chain of command in the firm and at the top of the firm (i.e., the audit committee). Once firms recognize the potential of SOX and other structural methods to root out wrongdoing early and provide channels for its internal reporting, so lawsuits may be avoided and problems rectified quickly, they will be better able to use these structures to improve their overall effectiveness and reduce costs.

Laws that require whistle-blowing procedures and encourage whistle-blowing may also have the effect of making whistle-blowing more acceptable and positive. There is some evidence that private employers have changed their policies over time, in part because employees and citizens demand it. For example, a survey by the Ethics Resource Center found that 79% of employers have a written ethics standard, up from 60% in 1994 (Grimsley, 2000). We believe that employers will be more likely to take such actions in the future, because of pressures from individual employees who are increasingly responding to legislative changes aimed directly at potential whistle-blowers. For example, SOX, governing public companies (e.g., those listed on exchanges), requires some additional actions focused on effectiveness in correcting wrongdoing rather than preventing retaliation, for example, requiring that corporate lawyers report misconduct to top management and, if there is no response, to the board

(Dwyer et al., 2002). Future research should examine whether this is sufficient incentive to organizations to take responsive action.

The literature on sexual harassment law can serve as an example for how whistle-blowing law and corporate practice (e.g., training) could be improved (e.g., Dwyer et al., 2002). Over the past 20 to 25 years, U. S. Supreme Court decisions have provided more incentives and penalties for employers, and surveys indicated that there is much greater awareness and disapproval of sexual harassment in varying forms than previously (e.g., Erdreich, Slavet, & Amador, 1995). Thus, one effect of oversight of employers seems to be that employees show greater awareness of wrongdoing and their legal rights in the workplace. In fact, as mentioned in Chapter 6, a new law applies to federal agencies and requires them to pay for settlements and judgments against them in discrimination and whistle-blower cases out of their agency budgets, and thus "will hit agencies in their pocketbooks" (Barr, 2002, p. B2). Further, agencies are required to file reports with Congress and the attorney general on data such as the number of complaints filed against them by employees, the disposition of these cases, the total monetary awards charged against the agency, and the number of agency employees disciplined for wrongdoing involving discrimination or harassment (Barr, 2002).

There are potential financial incentives for citizens who save the federal government money by informing it of fraud by contractors or other activity (e.g., Zingales, 2004). As noted previously, the False Claims Act, dating to the Civil War, allows whistle-blowers to collect up to 30% of the damages (Callahan & Dworkin, 1992; Seagull, 1995). In 1986, the False Claims Act was revised, such that whistle-blowers were more likely to receive a reward (Callahan & Dworkin, 1992). Prior to 1986, about six false claims for government funds had been reported per year by whistle-blowers. Since 1986, the number has jumped substantially, with more than 3,000 *qui tam* cases filed by 2004 (Phillips & Cohen, 2004). False Claims Act recoveries have exceeded $17 billion, with nearly $1 billion recovered in the first quarter of 2006 (Taxpayers Against Fraud Education Fund, 2006) and it has produced awards as high as $77 million (Haddad & Barrett, 2002). Also, as noted in Chapter 6, changes in the IRS reward structure have led to more reporting.

Recent studies indicate that SOX has not been effective in encouraging whistle-blowing; indeed, it has been reduced since the law's passage. Several commentators have urged that SOX be amended to include rewards in order to make it more effective and have discussed various ways to create a reward fund. Whether it is possible to encourage private sector employers to offer financial incentives has not been determined.

If potential whistle-blowers are motivated to act by financial rewards, then private employers may be more likely to protect themselves—as well as to help other members of society—by changing their policies and procedures to prevent wrongdoing in the first place and to terminate it when informed by their employees that wrongdoing is ongoing. We believe that these changes in the legal environment eventually will have an important impact on encouraging employees who observe wrongdoing to blow the whistle. As discussed in previous chapters, the type of wrongdoing (specifically wrongdoing that results in fraud against the federal government) will probably become an important predictor of whether employees who observe wrongdoing decide to blow the whistle.

Conclusion

Throughout this chapter, we have attempted to provide concrete suggestions to the parties involved in the whistle-blowing process. Unfortunately, research has not developed to the point where we can offer specific, unequivocal evidence in support of all of these suggestions. In the earlier chapters, we have identified research needs and challenges. We hope that this book will be useful to those interested in the whistle-blowing process.

References

Akabayashi, A. (2002). Euthanasia, assisted suicide, and cessation of life support: Japan's policy, law, and an analysis of whistle-blowing in two recent mercy killing cases. *Social Science and Medicine, 55*, 517–527.

Alford, C. F. (2001). *Whistleblowers: Broken lives and organizational power.* Ithaca, NY: Cornell University Press.

Alford, C. F. (2003). Women as whistleblowers. *Business and Professional Ethics Journal, 22*(1), 67–76.

Altemeyer, B. (1999). To thine own self be untrue: Self-awareness in authoritarians. *North American Journal of Psychology, 1*, 157–164.

Anand, V., Ashforth, B. E., & Joshi, M. (2004). Business as usual: The acceptance and perpetuation of corruption in organizations. *Academy of Management Executive, 18*(2), 39–53.

Anonymous. (1996, January 29). Somalia coverup? *Maclean's, 109*, 17.

Anonymous. (2002, January 12). Whistleblowing: Peep and weep. *The Economist,* 55–56.

Aquino, K., Tripp, T. M., & Bies, R. J. (2001). How employees respond to personal offense: The effects of blame, attribution, victim status and gender status on revenge and reconciliation in the workplace. *Journal of Applied Psychology, 86*, 52–59.

Armenakis, A. (2004). Making a difference by speaking out: Jeff Wigand says exactly what's on his mind. *Journal of Management Inquiry, 13*(4), 355.

Ashforth, B. E., & Anand, V. (2003). The normalization of corruption in organizations. In R. M. Kramer & B. M. Staw (Eds.), *Research in organizational behavior* (Vol. 25, pp. 1–52). Amsterdam: Elsevier.

Ashkanasy, N. M., Windsor, C. A., & Treviño, L. K. (2006). Bad apples in bad barrels revisited: Cognitive moral development, just world beliefs, rewards, and ethical decision-making. *Business Ethics Quarterly, 16*(4), 449.

Associated Press. (2002, April 29). Rep: Enron got whistleblower advice. Retrieved February 17, 2004, from http://www.lawsonline.com/soeken/marble/apr02.html

Associated Press. (2007, April 13). CBS fires Don Imus from radio show. Retrieved April 19, 2007, from http://www.msnbc.msn.com/id/18072804/

Banaji, M. R., Bazerman, M. H., & Chugh, D. (2003, December). How (un)ethical are you? *Harvard Business Review,* 56–64.

Bandura, A. (1989). Human agency in social cognitive theory. *American Psychologist, 44,* 1175–1184.

Barakat, M. (2004, May 6). Whistle-blower wins claim against Atlantic Coast Airlines. *Washington Post,* p. E04.

Barber, A. E., Rau, B. L., & Simmering, M. J. (1996, August). *Compensation policies as signals in organizational recruitment.* Paper presented at the annual meeting of the Academy of Management, Cincinnati.

Barnett, T., Cochran, D. S., & Taylor, G. S. (1993). The internal disclosure policies of private-sector employers: An initial look at their relationship to employee whistleblowing. *Journal of Business Ethics, 12,* 127–136.

Barr, S. (2002, May 16). Making agencies pay the price of discrimination, retaliation. *Washington Post,* p. B2.

Barr, S. (2007, February 15). Working, or not, with everyone's safety in mind. *Washington Post,* p. D4.

Bateman, T. S., & Crant, J. M. (1993). The proactive component of organizational behavior: A measure and correlates. *Journal of Organizational Behavior, 14,* 103–118.

Bates, S. (1999, January 11). Europe is out to get me. *The Guardian,* T8.

Baucus, M. S. (1994). Pressure, opportunity, and predisposition: A multivariate model of corporate illegality. *Journal of Management, 20*(4), 699–721.

Baucus, M. S., & Baucus, D. A. (1997). Paying the piper: An empirical examination of longer-term financial consequences of illegal corporate behavior. *Academy of Management Journal, 40,* 129–151.

Baucus, M. S., & Near, J. P. (1991). Can illegal corporate behavior be predicted? An event history analysis. *Academy of Management Journal, 34,* 9–36.

Bazerman, M. H., & Banaji, M. R. (2004). The social psychology of ordinary ethical failures. *Social Justice Research, 17*(2), 111–115.

Beattie, N. (2000). Whistle blowing. *New Zealand Management, 47*(4), 60.

Bergman, M. E., Langhout, R. D., Cortina, L. M., & Fitzgerald, L. F. (2002). The (un)reasonableness of reporting: Antecedents and consequences of reporting sexual harassment. *Journal of Applied Psychology, 87*(2), 230–242.

Bishop, T. J. F. (2006, March). Is your hotline AAAA-rated? *Business Crimes,* 3–7.

Bok, S. (1980). Whistle-blowing and professional responsibilities. In P. Callahan & S. Bok (Eds.), *Ethics teaching in higher education* (pp. 277–295). New York: Plenum Press.

Boss v. Solomon Smith Barney, Inc. 263 F. Supp. 2d 684 (S.D. NY 2003).

Bowes-Sperry, L., & O'Leary-Kelly, A. M. (2005). To act or not to act: The dilemma faced by sexual harassment observers. *Academy of Management Review, 30*(2), 288–306.

Bowie, N. (1982). *Business ethics.* Englewood Cliffs, NJ: Prentice-Hall.

Brewer, G. A. (1996). *Incidence of whistleblowing in the public and private sectors.* Athens, GA: Department of Political Science, The University of Georgia.

Brewer, G. A., & Selden, S. C. (1998). Whistle blowers in the federal civil service: New evidence of the public service ethic. *Journal of Public Administration Research and Theory, 8*(3), 413–439.

Brewer, H. (2006, May/June). Compliance does cost. *Business Law Today,* 6.

Brief, A. P., & Motowidlo, S. (1986). Prosocial organizational behaviors. *Academy of Management Review, 4,* 710–725.

Brief, A. P., Buttram, R. T., & Dukerich, J. M. (2001). Collective corruption in the corporate world: Toward a process model. In M. E. Turner (Ed.), *Groups at work: Theory and research* (pp. 471–499). Mahwah, NJ: Lawrence Erlbaum.

Brooks, L., & Perot, A. R. (1991). Reporting sexual harassment: Exploring a predictive model. *Psychology of Women Quarterly, 15*(1), 31–47.

Bucy, P. H. (2002). Private justice. *Southern California Law Review, 76,* 1.

Burlington Northern & Santa Fe Ry. v. White. 2006 U.S LEXIS 4895 (2006).

Burton, B. K., & Near, J. P. (1995). Estimating the incidence of wrongdoing and whistle-blowing: Results of a study using randomized response technique. *Journal of Business Ethics, 14,* 17–30.

Callahan, E. S., & Dworkin, T. M. (1992). Do good and get rich: Financial incentives for whistle-blowing and the False Claims Act. *Villanova Law Review, 37,* 273–336.

Callahan, E. S., & Dworkin, T. M. (2000). The state of state whistleblower protection. *American Business Law Journal, 38*(1), 99–175.

Callahan, E. S., Dworkin, T. M., & Lewis, D. (2004). Whistle-blowing: Australian, U.K., and U.S. approaches to disclosure in the public interest. *Virginia Journal of International Law, 44,* 879–912.

Camerer, L. (2001). *Protecting whistle blowers in South Africa: The Protected Disclosures Act, no. 26 of 2000* (Occasional Paper No. 47 - 2001). Cape Town, South Africa: Institute for Security Studies, Organised Crime and Corruption Programme.

Campbell, D. J. (2000). The proactive employee: Managing workplace initiative. *Academy of Management Executive, 14*(3), 52–66.

Campbell, D. T., & Stanley, J. (1966). *Experimental and quasi-experimental designs for research.* Chicago: Rand McNally.

Carli, L. L., & Eagly, A. H. (1999). Gender effects on social influence and emergent leadership. In G. N. Powell (Ed.), *Handbook of gender and work* (pp. 203–222). Thousand Oaks, CA: Sage.

Carnero v. Boston Scientific Corp. 2004 U.S. Dist. LEXIS 17205 (D. Mass. August 27, 2004).

Case, J. (2000). Employee theft: The profit killer. Retrieved April 20, 2007, from http://retailindustry.about.com/library/uc/uc_case1.htm

CFO Magazine (2006). USA: Employees increasingly comfortable blowing the whistle. Retrieved March 27, 2006, from http://bert.lib.indiana. edu:did=664613311&sid=1&Fmt=3&clientld=12010&RQT=309&VName= PQD

Chiu, R. K. (2003). Ethical judgment and whistleblowing intention: Examining the moderating role of locus of control. *Journal of Business Ethics, 43*(1/2), 65.

Chua, A. C. H. (1998). Whistleblowing, red chips, and the provisional legislature in Hong Kong. *Public Administration Review, 58*(1), 1–7.

Civil Rights Act of 1964. 42 *U.S. Code* 2000 e-4(a).

Civil Service Reform Act of 1978. 5 *U.S. Code* § 2302.

Clean Water Act of 1972. 33 *U.S. Code* § 1251.

Clegg, S., & Dunkerley, D. (1980). *Organization, class and control.* London: Routledge & Kegan Paul.

Clemetson, L. (2003, October 5). Adviser to Bush's father redefines himself as wary whistle-blower. *New York Times,* pp. 1, 22.

Clinard, M. B. (1979). *Illegal corporate behavior.* Washington, D.C.: National Institute of Law Enforcement and Criminal Justice.

Coles, F. S. (1986). Forced to quit: Sexual harassment complaints and agency response. *Sex Roles, 14,* 81–95.

Connors, T. (2007, March/April). SOX benefits: The cost of compliance may be balanced by improved efficiency and quality. *Corporate Responsibility Officer,* 42–44.

Cortina, L. M., & Magley, V. J. (2003). Raising voice, risking retaliation: Events following interpersonal mistreatment in the workplace. *Journal of Occupational Health Psychology, 8*(4), 247–265.

Cortina, L. M., Lonsway, K. A., Magley, V. J., Freeman, L. V., Collinsworth, L. L., Hunter, M. et al. (2002). What's gender got to do with it? Incivility in the federal courts. *Law & Social Inquiry, 27*(2), 235–270.

Costanzo, P. R., & Shaw, M. E. (1966). Conformity as a function of age level. *Child Development, 37,* 967–974.

Crant, J. M. (1995). The Proactive Personality Scale and objective job performance among real estate agents. *Journal of Applied Psychology, 80*(4), 532–537.

Crant, J. M., & Bateman, T. S. (2000). Charismatic leadership viewed from above: The impact of proactive personality. *Journal of Organizational Behavior, 21*(1), 63–75.

Cullen, J. B., Victor, B., & Bronson, J. W. (1993). The Ethical Climate Questionnaire: An assessment of its development and validity. *Psychological Reports, 73*, 667–675.

Daft, R. L. (1978). A dual-core model of organizational innovation. *Academy of Management Journal, 21*, 193–210.

Daher, D. L. (2005, September/October). How to implement a whistleblower hotline and get the most out of it. *Internal Auditor,* 10.

Day, S. H., Jr. (1996). Rotblat Nobel gives hope to "Free Vanunu" campaign. *Bulletin of the Atomic Scientists, 52*(1), 5–6.

De Maria, W. (1997). The British whistleblower protection bill: A shield too small? *Crime, Law, and Social Change, 27*(2), 139–163.

DeGeorge, R. T. (1986). *Business ethics* (2nd ed.). New York: Macmillan.

Devine, T. (1997). What to expect: Classic responses to whistle-blowing. In *Courage without martyrdom: The whistleblower's survival guide* (pp. 27–48). Washington, D.C.: Government Accountability Project and Fund for Constitutional Government.

Diener, E. (2000). Subjective well-being: The science of happiness and a proposal for a national index. *American Psychologist, 55*, 34–43.

Dobbin, F., & Kelly, E. L. (2007). How to stop harassment: Professional construction of legal compliance in organizations. *American Journal of Sociology, 112*(4), 1203.

Dobson, R. (1998, June 9). Sick to death of morals. *The Independent,* pp. S12–13.

Donaldson, T., & Dunfee, T. (1994). Toward a unified conception of business ethics: Integrative social contracts theory. *Academy of Management Review, 19*, 252–284.

Donaldson, T., & Dunfee, T. (1999). *The ties that bind* (Vol. 19). Boston: Harvard University Press.

Dougherty, T. W., Turban, D. B., Olson, D. E., Dwyer, P. D., & LaPrese, M. W. (1996). Factors affecting perceptions of workplace harassment. *Journal of Organizational Behavior, 17*, 489–501.

Dozier, J. B., & Miceli, M. P. (1985). Potential predictors of whistle-blowing: A prosocial behavior perspective. *Academy of Management Review, 10*, 823–836.

Drawbaugh, K. (2005). U. S. business counters some reforms. Retrieved February 20, 2005, from http://story.news.yahoo.com/news? tmpl= story&u=/nm/20050220/bs_nm/financial_corporate_reform_dc

Dutton, J. E., & Ashford, S. J. (1993). Selling issues to top management. *Academy of Management Review, 18*, 397–428.

Dutton, J. E., Ashford, S. J., O'Neill, R. M., Hayes, E., & Wierba, E. E. (1997). Reading the wind: How middle managers assess the context for selling issues to top managers. *Strategic Management Journal, 18*(5), 407–423.

Dutton, J. E., Ashford, S. J., O'Neill, R. M., & Lawrence, K. A. (2001). Moves that matter: Issue selling and organizational change. *Academy of Management Journal, 44*(4), 716.

Dworkin, T. M. (2007a). SOX and whistleblowing. *Michigan Law Review, 105*(8), 1757–1780.

Dworkin, T. M. (2007b, August 12). *It's time to change "your" SOX.* Paper presented at the annual conference, Academy of Legal Studies of Business.

Dworkin, T. M., & Baucus, M. S. (1998). Internal vs. external whistle-blowers: A comparison of whistle-blowing processes. *Journal of Business Ethics, 17*(12), 1281–1298.

Dworkin, T. M., & Callahan, E. S. (2002, April). *The mouth of truth.* Paper presented at the International Whistle-Blowing Conference, Indiana University, Bloomington, IN.

Dworkin, T. M., & Near, J. P. (1987). Whistle-blowing statutes: Are they working? *American Business Law Journal, 25*(2), 241–264.

Dworkin, T. M., & Near, J. P. (1997). A better statutory approach to whistle-blowing. *Business Ethics Quarterly, 7*(1), 1–16.

Dworkin, T. M., Near, J. P., & Callahan, E. S. (1995). *Governmental and social influences on corporate responsibility.* Paper presented at the International Association of Business and Society, Vienna, Austria.

Dwyer, P., Carney, D., Borrus, A., Woellert, L., & Palmeri, C. (2002, December 16). Year of the whistleblower: The personal costs are high, but a new law protects truth-tellers as never before. *Business Week,* 106.

Dyck, A., Morse, A., & Zingales, L. (2007, February). *Who blows the whistle on fraud?* Retrieved December 7, 2007 from www.nber.org/papers/w12882

Eagly, A. H. (1983). Gender and social influence: A social psychological analysis. *American Psychologist, 38,* 971–981.

Earle, B., & Madek, G. A. (2007). The mirage of whistleblower protection under Sarbanes-Oxley: A proposal for change. *American Business Law Journal, 44*(1), 1–54.

Eisenhardt, K. M. (1989). Agency theory: An assessment and review. *Academy of Management Review, 14,* 57–74.

Ellis, S., Barak, A., & Pinto, A. (1991). Moderating effects of personal cognitions on experienced and perceived sexual harassment of women at the workplace. *Journal of Applied Social Psychology, 21*(16), 1320–1337.

Emerson, R. E. (1962). Power-dependence relations. *American Sociological Review, 27,* 31–41.

Employment Rights Act (1996). ch. 18, § 43(B)(1) (United Kingdom).

England, P. (1979). Women and occupational prestige: A case of vacuous sex equality. *Signs, 5,* 252–265.

Erdreich, B. L., Slavet, B. S., & Amador, A. C. (1995). *Sexual harassment in the federal workplace: Trends, progress, continuing challenges* (Report of the Merit Systems Protection Board). Washington, D.C.: U.S. Government Printing Office.

ESPN Radio. (2007, April 13). "The Big Show with Dan and Keith" program concerning the firing of Don Imus [Radio]. US: Insider.ESPN.go.com

EthicsLine. (2005). *Special report.* Retrieved March 30, 2006, from www.ethicsline.com

Everton, W. J. (1996). *The effect of whistleblowing consequences and perceived similarity on peer perceptions of whistleblowers.* Unpublished doctoral dissertation, Ohio University, Athens.

Fain, T. C., & Anderton, D. L. (1987). Sexual harassment: Organizational context and diffuse status. *Sex Roles, 17,* 291–311.

Falbo, T., & Belk, S. S. (1985). A short scale to measure self-righteousness. *Journal of Personality Assessment, 49,* 172–177.

False Claims Amendment Act of 1986, 31 *U.S.Code* § 287.

Farrell, D., & Petersen, J. C. (1989, November 9). *The organizational impact of whistleblowing.* Paper presented at the annual meeting of the American Society of Criminology, Reno, NV.

Farrell, D., & Rusbult, C. (1990). *Impact of job satisfaction, investment size, and quality of alternatives on exit, voice, loyalty, and neglect responses to job dissatisfaction: A cross-lagged panel study.* Paper presented at the Best Paper Proceedings of the national Academy of Management meeting, San Francisco, CA.

Farrell, G. (2007, July 30). Sarbanes-Oxley has been a pretty clean sweep: Most agree it's a big success. *USA Today,* p. 6B.

Feldman, E. (2002, April 12–13). *The twins of silence: The dilemma of the good faith whistleblower.* Paper presented at the International Conference on Whistle-Blowing, Bloomington, IN.

Ferguson, L. J., & Near, J. P. (1987). *The whistle-blowing phenomenon: A look at social, situational, and personality influences.* Paper presented at the annual meeting of the Midwest Academy of Management.

Ferguson, L. J., & Near, J. P. (1989, November). *Whistle-blowing in the lab.* Paper presented at the annual meeting of the American Criminological Society, Reno, NV.

Figg, J. (2000). Whistleblowing. *The Internal Auditor, 57,* 30–37.

Fiske, A. P., & Tetlock, P. E. (1997). Taboo trade-offs: Reactions to transactions that transgress the spheres of justice. *Political Psychology 18,* 255–297.

Fitzgerald, L. F., Drasgow, F., Hulin, C. L., Gelfand, M. J., & Magley, V. J. (1997). The antecedents and consequences of sexual harassment in organizations: A test of an integrated model. *Journal of Applied Psychology, 82*(4), 578–589.

Fitzgerald, L. F., Drasgow, F., & Magley, V. J. (1999). Sexual harassment in the armed forces: A test of an integrated model. *Military Psychology, 11*(3), 329–343.

Fitzgerald, L. F., & Ormerod, A. J. (1991). Perceptions of sexual harassment: The influence of gender and academic context. *Psychology of Women Quarterly, 15*(2), 281–294.

Fitzgerald, L. F., Swan, S., & Magley, V. J. (1997). But was it really sexual harassment? Legal, behavioral, and psychological definitions of the workplace victimization of women. In W. O'Donohue (Ed.), *Sexual harassment: Theory, research, and treatment* (pp. 5–28). Needham Heights, MA: Allyn & Bacon.

French, J. R. P., Jr., & Raven, B. H. (1959). The bases of social power. In D. Cartwright (Ed.), *Studies in social power* (pp. 118–149). Ann Arbor, MI: University of Michigan Press.

French, W., & Weis, A. (2000). An ethics of care or an ethics of justice. *Journal of Business Ethics, 27*, 125–136.

Frey, J. (2002, January 25). The woman who saw red: Enron whistle-blower Sherron Watkins warned of the trouble to come. *Washington Post,* pp. C1, C8.

Fritz, N. R. (1989). Sexual harassment and the working woman. *Personnel, 66*, 4–8.

GAP (Government Accountability Project). (2006, June 23). *Government approves whistle-blower rights breakthrough.* Press release.

Garcetti v. Ceballos, 126 Sup. Ct. 1951 (2006).

Giacalone, R. A., Jurkiewicz, C. L., & Dunn, C. (2005). Foreword. In R. Giacalone, C. L. Jurkiewicz, & C. Dunn (Eds.), *Positive psychology in business ethics and corporate responsibility* (Vol. 1, pp. ix-x). Greenwich, CT: Information Age Publishing.

Gibeaut, J. (2006, May). *Culture Clash: Other Countries Don't Embrace Sarbanes or America's Reverence of Whistle-Blowers,* A.B.A. Journal, p. 10–11.

Gilligan, C. (1982). *In a different voice: Psychological theory and women's development* (Reissue edition 1993 ed.). Cambridge, MA: Harvard University Press.

Gino, F., & Bazerman, M. H. (2007). Slippery slopes and misconduct: The effect of gradual degradation on the failure to notice others' unethical behavior (2/18/2007 draft), Harvard Business School. Pittsburgh, PA: Carnegie Mellon Tepper School of Business.

Glazer, M. P., & Glazer, P. M. (1989). *The whistle-blowers: Exposing corruption in government and industry*. New York: Basic Books.

Glomb, T. M., Munson, L. J., Hulin, C. L., Bergman, M. E., & Drasgow, F. (1999). Structural equation models of sexual harassment: Longitudinal explorations and cross-sectional generalizations. *Journal of Applied Psychology, 84*(1), 14–28.

Glomb, T. M., Richman, W. L., Hulin, C. L., Drasgow, F., Schneider, K. T., & Fitzgerald, L. F. (1997). Ambient sexual harassment: An integrated model of antecedents and consequences. *Organizational Behavior and Human Decision Processes, 71*(3), 309–328.

Goffman, E. (1963). *Stigma: Notes on the management of spoiled identity*. Englewood Cliffs, NJ: Prentice-Hall.

Goldman, B. M. (2001). Toward an understanding of employment discrimination claiming: An integration of organizational justice and social information processing theories. *Personnel Psychology, 54*(2), 361–386.

Goodman, T. (2007, April 20). It's no news that MSNBC's Olbermann knows how to do news best. *San Francisco Chronicle*, p. E1.

Gordon, G. G. (1991). Industry determinants of organizational culture. *Academy of Management Review, 16*(2), 396–415.

Gouldner, A. W. (1960). The norm of reciprocity. *American Sociological Review, 25*, 161–178.

Graham, J. W. (1986). Principled organizational dissent: A theoretical essay. In L. L. Cummings & B. M. Staw (Eds.), *Research in organizational behavior* (Vol. 8, pp. 1–52). Greenwich, CT: JAI Press.

Graves, F., & Goo, S. K. (2006, April 17). Boeing parts and rules bent, whistle-blowers say. *Washington Post*, p. A01.

Green, M. (2004, January). How's my accounting? *Best's Review*, p. 66.

Grimsley, K. D. (2000, June 14). Office wrongdoing common. *Washington Post*, p. E02.

Gundlach, M. J., Douglas, S. C., & Martinko, M. J. (2003). The decision to blow the whistle: A social information processing framework. *Academy of Management Review, 28*(1), 107–123.

Gutek, B. A. (1985). *Sex and the workplace: The impact of sexual behavior and harassment on women, men, and organizations*. San Francisco, CA: Jossey-Bass.

Gutek, B. A., & Cohen, A. G. (1987). Sex ratios, sex-role spillover, and sex at work: A comparison of men's and women's experiences. *Human Relations, 40*, 97–115.

Gutek, B. A., & Dunwoody, V. (1987). Understanding sex in the workplace. In A. Stromberg, L. Larwood, & B. A. Gutek (Eds.), *Women and work: An annual review* (Vol. 2). Newbury Park, CA: Sage.

Gutek, B. A., Morasch, B., & Cohen, A. G. (1983). Interpreting social-sexual behavior in a work setting. *Journal of Vocational Behavior, 22,* 30–48.

Hacker, A. (2003). *Mismatch: The growing gulf between women and men.* New York: Scribner.

Haddad, C., & Barrett, A. (2002, June 24). A whistle-blower rocks an industry. *Business Week,* 126–130.

Hananel, S. (2002, September 1). Whistle-blower report cites abuses. *Washington Post,* http://www.whistleblowers.org/html/Whistle-Blower%20Report%20Cites%20Abuses.htm

Hatala, J.-P., & Fleming, P. R. (2007). Making transfer climate visible: Utilizing social network analysis to facilitate the transfer of training. *Human Resource Development Review, 6*(1), 33–63.

Heard, E., & Miller, W. (2006a, Summer). Creating an open and non-retaliatory workplace. *International Business Ethics Review,* pp. 1–7.

Heard, E., & Miller, W. (2006b, Summer). Effective code standards on raising concerns and retaliation. *International Business Ethics Review,* pp. 1–11.

Henik, E. (2007, June 26). Mad as hell or scared stiff? The effects of value conflict and emotions on potential whistle-blowers. *Journal of Business Ethics,* http://www.springerlink.com/content/k1rg728173771147/

Herman, T. (2006, June 22). IRS reworks its whistle-blower program. *Wall Street Journal,* p. D1.

Herman, T. (2007, May 16). Whistleblower law scores early success. *Wall Street Journal,* p. D3.

Hersh, S. M. (2004, May 17). Chain of command. *The New Yorker, 80,* 38.

Hesson-McInnis, M. S., & Fitzgerald, L. F. (1997). Sexual harassment: A preliminary test of an integrative model. *Journal of Applied Social Psychology, 27*(10), 877–901.

Hewlin, P. F. (2003). And the award for best actor goes to …: Facades of conformity in organizational settings. *Academy of Management Review, 28*(4), 633.

Hewlin, P. F., & Rosette, A. S. (2005, August). *Stigma avoidance: A precursor to workplace discrimination.* Paper presented at the annual national meeting of the Academy of Management, Honolulu, Hawaii.

Hirschman, A. O. (1970). *Exit, voice, and loyalty.* Cambridge, MA: Harvard University Press.

Hodson, R. (2002). Demography or respect? Work group demography versus organizational dynamics as determinants of meaning and satisfaction at work. *The British Journal of Sociology, 53*(2), 291.

Hofstede, G. (1980). *Culture's consequences: International differences in work-related values.* Beverly Hills, CA: Sage.

Hofstede, G. (1999). Problems remain, but theories will change: The universal and the specific in 21st-century global management. *Organizational Dynamics, 28*(1), 34–44.

Hofstede, G., Neuijen, B., Ohayv, D. D., & Sanders, G. (1990). Measuring organizational cultures: A qualitative and quantitative study across twenty cases. *Administrative Science Quarterly, 35,* 286–319.

Hopkins, N. (1999). MIT and gender bias: Following up on victory. Retrieved August 1, 2005, from http://chronicle.com/colloquy/99/genderbias/background.htm

Hulin, C. L., Fitzgerald, L. F., & Drasgow, F. (1996). Organizational influences on sexual harassment. In M. Stockdale & B. Gutek (Eds.), *Sexual harassment in the workplace: Perspectives, frontiers, and response strategies* (Vol. 5, pp. 127–150). Thousand Oaks, CA: Sage.

Hutchinson, S., Sowa, D., Eisenberger, R., & Huntington, R. (1986). Perceived organizational support. *Journal of Applied Psychology, 71*(3), 500–507.

Illinois Compiled Statutes, 175/1-/8 (2004).

Ip, G. (2007, April 27). Maybe U.S. markets are still supreme. *Wall Street Journal,* p. C11.

Jackson v. Board of Education (544 U.S. 167 2005).

Jensen, M. C., & Meckling, W. H. (1976). Theory of the firm: Managerial behavior, agency costs, and ownership structure. *Journal of Financial Economics, 3,* 305–360.

Jernberg, D. V. (2003, June 30). Whistle-blower hot lines carry own risks. *Business Insurance,* 10.

Johnson, R. A. (2002). *Whistleblowing: When it works—and why.* Boulder, CO: L. Rienner Publishers.

Jones, E. E., Farina, A., Hastorf, A., Markus, H., Miller, D. T., & Scott, R. A. (1984). *Social stigma: The psychology of marked relationships.* New York: Freeman.

Jones, T. M. (1991). Ethical decision making by individuals in organizations: An issue-contingent model. *Academy of Management Review, 16,* 366–395.

Jubb, P. B. (1999). Whistleblowing: A restrictive definition and interpretation. *Journal of Business Ethics, 21,* 77–94.

Judge, T. A., Heller, D., & Mount, M. K. (2002). Five-factor model of personality and job satisfaction: A meta-analysis. *Journal of Applied Psychology, 87*(3), 530–541.

Kalev, A., & Dobbin, F. (2006). Enforcement of civil rights law in private workplaces: The effects of compliance reviews and lawsuits over time. *Law & Social Inquiry, 31*(4), 855.

Kalev, A., Kelly, E., & Dobbin, F. (2006). Best practices or best guesses? Assessing the efficacy of corporate affirmative action and diversity policies. *American Sociological Review, 71*(4), 589.

Karr, A. R. (1998a, December 15). Employer retaliation is charged by more employees. *Wall Street Journal*, p. 1.

Karr, A. R. (1998b, December 15). New EEOC chairwoman Ida Castro's first meeting. *Wall Street Journal*, p. 1.

Keenan, J. P. (1990). Upper-level managers and whistleblowing: Determinants of perceptions of company encouragement and information about where to blow the whistle. *Journal of Business and Psychology, 5*, 223–235.

Keenan, J. P. (2002a). Comparing Indian and American managers on whistleblowing. *Employee Responsibilities and Rights Journal, 14*(2/3), 79–89.

Keenan, J. P. (2002b). Whistleblowing: A study of managerial differences. *Employee Responsibilities and Rights Journal, 14*(1), 17–32.

Keenan, J. P. (2007). Comparing Chinese and American managers on whistleblowing. *Employee Responsibilities and Rights Journal, 19*, 85–94.

Kelley, K. M., Sabin, E. J., & Wyrwich, K. (2005, April 15). *The impact of moral intensity on whistle-blowing intentions*. Paper presented at the Graduate Student Association Poster Symposium, St. Louis University, St. Louis, MO.

Keeton v. Flying J Inc. 1313 U.S.L.W. (BNA) 1313 (6th Cir. November 29, 2005).

Kerr, J., & Slocum, J. W., Jr. (2005). Managing corporate culture through reward systems. *Academy of Management Executive, 19*(4), 130.

Kidder, D., & Parks, J. M. (2001). The good soldier: Who is s(he)? *Journal of Organizational Behavior, 22*(8), 939.

Kim, S. H., Smith, R. H., & Brigham, N. L. (1998). Effects of power imbalance and the presence of third parties on reactions to harm: Upward and downward revenge. *Personality and Social Psychology Bulletin, 24*(4), 353–361.

King, G., III. (1994). *An interpersonal analysis of whistle-blowing.* Indiana University, Bloomington, IN.

King, G., III. (1997). The effects of interpersonal closeness and issue seriousness on blowing the whistle. *Journal of Business Communication, 34*(4), 419–436.

King, G., III. (2001). Perceptions of intentional wrongdoing and peer reporting behavior among registered nurses. *Journal of Business Ethics, 34*, 1–13.

Knapp, D. E., Faley, R. H., Ekeberg, S. E., & Dubois, C. L. Z. (1997). Determinants of target responses to sexual harassment: A conceptual framework. *Academy of Management Review, 22*(3), 687–729.

Knox, M. L. (1997, March-April). Ghosts of the Cold War. *Sierra, 82*, 24–25.

Kohlberg, L. (1969). Stage and sequence: The cognitive developmental approach to socialization. In D. A. Goslin (Ed.), *Handbook of socialization theory and research*. Chicago: Rand McNally.

Koss, M. P., Goodman, L. A., Browne, A., Fitzgerald, L. F., Keita, G. P., & Russo, N. F. (1994). *No safe haven: Male violence against women at home, at work, and in the community.* Washington, D.C.: American Psychological Association.

Krell, E. (2002, September). Corporate whistle-blowers: How to stop wrong-doing dead in its tracks. *Business Finance: Winning Strategies for CFOs,* 16–22. Retrieved December 7, 2007 from www.businessfinancemag.com/magazine/archives/article.html?articleID=13898&highlight=dead%20in%20its%20tracks

Lacayo, R., & Ripley, A. (2002, December 22). Persons of the Year 2002: Cynthia Cooper, Coleen Rowley and Sherron Watkins. *Time Magazine.* Retrieved April 9, 2007 from http://www.time.com/time/personoftheyear/2002/

LaFontain, E., & Tredeau, L. (1986). The frequency, sources, and correlates of sexual harassment among women in traditional male occupations. *Sex Roles, 15,* 433–442.

Lambert, S. J. (2000). Added benefits: The link between work-life benefits and organizational citizenship behavior. *Academy of Management Journal, 43*(5), 801–815.

Lane, C. (2006a, June 23). Court expands right to sue over retaliation on the job. *Washington Post,* p. A16.

Lane, C. (2006b, May 31). High court's free-speech ruling favors government: Public workers on duty not protected. *Washington Post,* p. A01.

Langer, E. (1983). *The psychology of control.* Beverly Hills, CA: Sage.

Latané, B. (1981). The psychology of social impact. *American Psychologist, 36,* 343–356.

Latané, B., & Darley, J. M. (1968). Group inhibition of bystander intervention. *Journal of Personality and Social Psychology, 10,* 215–221.

Latané, B., & Darley, J. M. (1970). *The unresponsive bystander: Why doesn't he help?* New York: Appleton-Century-Crofts.

Laver, R. (1996, February 19). A snitch in time. *Maclean's, 109,* 36.

Lee, J.-Y., Heilmann, S. G., & Near, J. P. (2004). Blowing the whistle on sexual harassment: Test of a model of predictors and outcomes. *Human Relations, 57*(3), 297–322.

Leonnig, C. (2007). Judge dismisses Plame lawsuit. *Washingtonpost.com.* Retrieved July 19, from http://www.washingtonpost.com/wp-dyn/content/article/2007/07/19/AR2007071901395.html?referrer=email

Lewis, D. (2002). *The contents of whistleblowing procedures in the UK: Some empirical research.* Paper presented at the International Conference on Whistle-Blowing, Indiana University, Bloomington, IN.

Loe, T. W., Ferrell, L., & Mansfield, P. (2000). A review of empirical studies assessing ethical decision-making in business. *Journal of Business Ethics,* no. 25, 185–204.

Lublin, J. S. (2006, April 17). Theory and practice: Retaliation over harass-
    ment claims takes focus. *Wall Street Journal,* p. B4.

Lublin, J. S. & Scannell, K. (2007, July 30). Critics see some good from
    Sarbanes-Oxley. *Wall Street Journal,* p. B1.

Luthans, F. (2002). Positive organizational behavior: Developing and
    managing psychological strengths. *Academy of Management Executive,*
    16(1), 57–72.

Magley, V. J. (2002). Coping with sexual harassment: Reconceptualizing
    women's resistance. *Journal of Personality and Social Psychology,*
    83(4), 930–946.

Magley, V. J., & Cortina, L. M. (2002, April). *Retaliation against military
    personnel who blow the whistle on sexual harassment.* Paper presented
    at the annual meeting of the Society for Industrial and Organizational
    Psychology, Toronto, Ontario, Canada.

Maleng, N. (2004, September 9). Fraud prevention information. Retrieved April
    20, 2007, from http://www.metrokc.gov/proatty/fraud/employee.htm

Martin, J. (2000). Hidden gendered assumptions in mainstream organizational
    theory and research. *Journal of Management Inquiry, 9*(2), 207–216.

Martin, J. (2004, June 27). Let's hear it for the rats. *Washington Post,* p. D6.

Martin, S. E. (1984). Sexual harassment: The link between gender stratifi-
    cation, sexuality, and women's economic status. In J. Freeman (Ed.),
    Women: A feminist perspective (pp. 54–69). Palo Alto, CA: Mayfield
    Publishing Company.

McCutcheon, L. E. (2000). Is there a "whistle-blower" personality? *Psychology:
    A Journal of Human Behavior, 37*(2), 2–9.

McNeely, B. L., & Meglino, B. M. (1994). The role of dispositional and situ-
    ational antecedents in prosocial organizational behavior: An exami-
    nation of the intended beneficiaries of prosocial behavior. *Journal of
    Applied Psychology, 79*(6), 836–844.

Merton, R. K. (1957). *Social theory and social structure* (2nd ed.). Glencoe,
    IL: Free Press.

Mesmer-Magnus, J. R., & Viswesvaran, C. (2005). Whistleblowing in orga-
    nizations: An examination of correlates of whistleblowing intentions,
    actions, and retaliation. *Journal of Business Ethics, 62,* 277–297.

Metropolitan Corporate Counsel (2006). Project corporate counsel—legal
    service providers: Successful implementation of an ethics and compli-
    ance training system: Some key considerations. Retrieved March 29,
    2006, from http://web.lexis-nexis.com/universe/printdoc

Miceli, M. P., Dozier, J. B., & Near, J. P. (1991). Blowing the whistle on
    data-fudging: A controlled field experiment. *Journal of Applied Social
    Psychology, 21*(4), 271–295.

Miceli, M. P., & Near, J. P. (1984). The relationships among beliefs, organizational position, and whistle-blowing status: A discriminant analysis. *Academy of Management Journal, 27,* 687–705.

Miceli, M. P., & Near, J. P. (1985). Characteristics of organizational climate and perceived wrongdoing associated with whistle-blowing decisions. *Personnel Psychology, 38,* 525–544.

Miceli, M. P., & Near, J. P. (1988). Individual and situational correlates of whistle-blowing. *Personnel Psychology, 41,* 267–282.

Miceli, M. P., & Near, J. P. (1992). *Blowing the whistle: The organizational and legal implications for companies and employees.* New York: Lexington.

Miceli, M. P., & Near, J. P. (1994a). Listening to your whistle-blowers can be profitable! *Academy of Management Executive Journal, 8*(3), 65–72.

Miceli, M. P., & Near, J. P. (1994b). Relationships among value congruence, perceived victimization, and retaliation against whistle-blowers: The case of internal auditors. *Journal of Management, 20,* 773–794.

Miceli, M. P., & Near, J. P. (1997). Whistle-blowing as antisocial behavior. In R. Giacalone & J. Greenberg (Eds.), *Antisocial behavior in organizations* (pp. 130–149). Thousand Oaks, CA: Sage Publications.

Miceli, M. P., & Near, J. P. (2002). What makes whistle-blowers effective? Three field studies. *Human Relations, 55*(4), 455–479.

Miceli, M. P., & Near, J. P. (2005a). Standing up or standing by: What predicts blowing the whistle on organizational wrongdoing? In J. Martocchio (Ed.), *Research in personnel and human resources management* (Vol. 24, pp. 95–136). Greenwich, CT: JAI/Elsevier Press.

Miceli, M. P., & Near, J. P. (2005b). Whistle-blowing and positive psychology. In R. Giacalone, C. L. Jurkiewicz, & C. Dunn (Eds.), *Positive psychology in business ethics and corporate responsibility* (Vol. 1, pp. 85–102). Greenwich, CT: Information Age Publishing.

Miceli, M. P., & Near, J. P. (2006). How can one person make a difference? Understanding whistle-blowing effectiveness. In M. J. Epstein & K. O. Hanson (Eds.), *The accountable corporation* (Vol. 4, pp. 201–221). Westport, CT: Praeger Publishers.

Miceli, M. P., & Near, J. P. (2007). Stopping organizational wrongdoing: What price do whistle-blowers pay? In S. W. Gilliland, D. D. Steiner, & D. P. Skarlicki (Eds.), *Managing social and ethical issues in organizations* (Vol. 5, pp. 295–324). Greenwich, CT: Information Age Publishing.

Miceli, M. P., Near, J. P., & Schwenk, C. P. (1991). Who blows the whistle and why? *Industrial and Labor Relations Review, 45,* 113–130.

Miceli, M. P., Rehg, M., Near, J. P., & Ryan, K. (1999). Can laws protect whistle-blowers? Results of a naturally occurring field experiment. *Work and Occupations, 26*(1), 129–151.

Miceli, M. P., Van Scotter, J., Near, J. P., & Rehg, M. (2001a). Responses to perceived organizational wrongdoing: Do perceiver characteristics matter? In J. M. Darley, D. M. Messick, & T. R. Tyler (Eds.), *Social influences on ethical behavior* (pp. 119–135). Mahwah, NJ: Lawrence Erlbaum.

Miceli, M. P., Van Scotter, J. R., Near, J. P., & Rehg, M. T. (2001b). *Individual differences and whistle-blowing.* Paper presented at the 61st Annual Meeting of the Academy of Management, Best Paper Proceedings, Washington, D.C.

Miethe, T. D. (1999). *Whistle-blowing at work: Tough choices in exposing fraud, waste and abuse on the job* (2nd ed.). Boulder, CO: Westview Press.

Misangyi, V. F., Weaver, G. R., & Elms, H. (in press). Ending corruption: The interplay between institutional logics, resources, and institutional entrepreneurs. *Academy of Management Review.*

Moberly, R. E. (2006). Sarbanes-Oxley's structural model to encourage corporate whistleblowers. *Brigham Young University Law Review, 2006*(5), 1107–1180.

Moberly, R. E. (2007). Unfulfilled expectations: An empirical analysis of why Sarbanes-Oxley whistleblowers rarely win. *William & Mary Law Review, 49*(1), 65–155. (Available at http://ssrn.com/abstract=977802)

Moore, J. E. (2000). Why is this happening? A causal attribution approach to work exhaustion consequences. *Academy of Management Review, 25*(2), 335–348.

Morrison, E. W., & Milliken, F. J. (2000). Organizational silence: A barrier to change and development in a pluralistic world. *Academy of Management Review, 25*(4), 706–725.

Morrison, E. W., & Milliken, F. J. (2003). Guest editors' introduction: Speaking up, remaining silent: The dynamics of voice and silence in organizations. *Journal of Management Studies, 40*, 1353–1358.

Morrison, E. W., & Phelps, C. C. (1999). Taking charge at work: Extrarole efforts to initiate workplace change. *Academy of Management Journal, 42*(4), 403–419.

Moscovici, S. (1976). *Social influence and social change.* London: Academic Press.

National Labor Relations Act of 1935. 29 *U.S. Code* § 158(a)(4) (1994).

Near, J. P., & Dworkin, T. M. (1998). Responses to legislative changes: Corporate whistleblowing policies. *Journal of Business Ethics, 17*, 1551–1561.

Near, J. P., Dworkin, T. M., & Miceli, M. P. (1993). Explaining the whistle-blowing process: Suggestions from power theory and justice theory. *Organization Science, 4*, 393–411.

Near, J. P., & Jensen, T. C. (1983). The whistle-blowing process: Retaliation and perceived effectiveness. *Work and Occupations, 10*, 3–28.

Near, J. P., & Miceli, M. P. (1985). Organizational dissidence: The case of whistle-blowing. *Journal of Business Ethics, 4*, 1–16.

Near, J. P., & Miceli, M. P. (1987). Whistle-blowers in organizations: Dissidents or reformers? In B. M. Staw & L. L. Cummings (Eds.), *Research in organizational behavior* (Vol. 9, pp. 321–368). Greenwich, CT: JAI Press.

Near, J. P., & Miceli, M. P. (1988). *The internal auditor's ultimate responsibility: The reporting of sensitive issues*. Altamonte Springs, FL: The Institute of Internal Auditors Research Foundation.

Near, J. P., & Miceli, M. P. (1995). Effective whistle-blowing. *Academy of Management Review, 20*, 679–708.

Near, J. P., & Miceli, M. P. (1996). Whistle-blowing: Myth and reality. *Journal of Management, 22*(3), 507–526.

Near, J. P., Van Scotter, J. R., Rehg, M. T., & Miceli, M. P. (2004). Does type of wrongdoing affect the whistle-blowing process? *Business Ethics Quarterly, 14*(2), 219–242.

Nemeth, C. (1979). The role of an active minority in intergroup relations. In W. A. S. Worchel (Ed.), *The social psychology of intergroup relations* (Ch. 14). Belmont, CA: Brooks/Cole.

Nesmith, J. (2004, Sunday, December 5). FDA fights charge of lax drug safety. *The Atlanta Journal-Constitution*, A3.

Nevius, C. W. (2006, November 12). Olbermann taps a well of discontent as the anti-O'Reilly. *San Francisco Chronicle*, http://www.sfgate.com/cgi-bin/article.cgi?f=/c/a/2006/11/12/MNGV9MB4681.DTL

Noelle-Neumann, E. (1974). The spiral of silence: A theory of public opinion. *Journal of Communication, 24*(2), 42–51.

Noelle-Neumann, E. (1991). The theory of public opinion: The concept of the spiral of silence. In J. A. Anderson (Ed.), *Communication yearbook* (pp. 256–287). Newbury Park, CA: Sage.

Noelle-Neumann, E. (1993). *The spiral of silence: Public opinion—our social skin* (2nd ed.). Chicago: University of Chicago Press.

No Fear Act of 2002. Pub. L. No. 107–174, 116 Stat. 566 (2002).

Orey, M. (2007, April 23). Fear firing: How the threat of litigation is making companies skittish about axing problem workers. *Business Week*, 52. Retrieved December 7, 2007 from http://proquest.umi.com/pqdweb?did=1256941411&Fmt=3&clientid=5604&RQT=309&VName=PQD

Ostroff, C., & Harrison, D. A. (1999). Meta-analysis, level of analysis, and best estimates of population correlations: Cautions for interpreting meta-analytic results in organizational behavior. *Journal of Applied Psychology, 84*(2), 260–270.

Park, H., Rehg, M. T., & Lee, D. (2005). The influence of Confucian ethics and collectivism on whistleblowing intentions: A study of Korean public employees. *Journal of Business Ethics, 58*(4), 387–403.

Parkes, K. R. (1990). Coping, negative affectivity, and the work environment: Additive and interactive predictors of mental health. *Journal of Applied Psychology, 75*, 399–409.

Parmerlee, M. A., Near, J. P., & Jensen, T. C. (1982). Correlates of whistleblowers' perceptions of organizational retaliation. *Administrative Science Quarterly, 27*, 17–34.

Pearlstein, S. (2004, June 23). Fed approval of bank merger ignores record. *Washington Post*, p. E1.

Pearlstein, S. (2005, March 30). Chamber misses moral of Enron story. *Washington Post*, p. E1.

Perry, J. L. (1991). *The organizational consequences of whistleblowing.* Unpublished manuscript, Bloomington, IN.

Perry, J. L. (1992, August). *The consequences of speaking out: Processes of hostility and issue resolution involving federal whistleblowers.* Paper presented at the Academy of Management, Las Vegas.

Perry, J. L. (1993). Whistleblowing, organizational performance, and organizational control. In H. G. Frederickson (Ed.), *Ethics and public administration* (pp. 79–99). Armonk, NY: M. E. Sharpe.

Perry, J. L., & Wise, L. R. (1990). The motivational bases of public service. *Public Administration Review, 50*, 367–373.

Peterson, C. (2000). The future of optimism. *American Psychologist, 55*, 44–55.

Pfeffer, J. (1981). *Power in organizations.* Marshfield, MA: Pitman.

Pfeffer, J. (1994). The costs of legalization: The hidden dangers of increasingly formalized control. In S. B. Sitkin & R. J. Bies (Eds.), *The legalistic organization.* Thousand Oaks, CA: Sage Publications.

Pfeffer, J., & Salancik, G. R. (1978). *The external control of organizations.* New York: Harper & Row.

Phillips, J. R., & Cohen, M. L. (2004). False Claims Act: History of the law. Retrieved March 24, 2006 from http://www.phillipsandcohen.com/CM/FalseClaimsAct/hist_f.asp

Pomeroy, A. (2007). Beware the "boiling frog syndrome." *HRMagazine, 52.* Retrieved December 7, 2007 from http://www.shrm.org/hrmagazine/articles/0507/0507executive.asp

Premeaux, S. F., & Bedeian, A. G. (2003). Breaking the silence: The moderating effects of self-monitoring in predicting speaking up in the workplace. *Journal of Management Studies, 40*(6), 1537.

Pressler, M. W. (2003, July 12). Coke says accounting is under U.S. probe. *Washington Post*, p. E1.

Protected Disclosure Act (1994). § 19 (New South Wales Acts).

Quinn, S. (2006, September 22). Ex-Halliburton worker calls for probe. *Business Week*, http://www.businessweek.com/ap/financialnews/D8KA482G480.htm

Rankin, K. (2004, November 22). P.C.A.O.B. wants auditors to blow the whistle. *WebCPA.com*. Retrieved March 29, 2007 from http://www.webcpa.com/article.cfm?articleid=8921

Rapp, G. C. (2007). Beyond protection: Invigorating incentives for Sarbanes-Oxley corporate and securities fraud whistleblowers. *Boston University Law Review, 87*(91), 92–156.

Ravishankar, L. (2004). Encouraging internal whistleblowing in organizations. Retrieved October 1, 2004, from http://www.scu.edu/ethics/publications/submitted/whistleblowing.html

Rehg, M. T. (1998). *An examination of the retaliation process against whistleblowers: A study of federal government employees.* Unpublished doctoral dissertation, Indiana University, Bloomington.

Rehg, M. T., Miceli, M. P., Near, J. P., & Van Scotter, J. R. (in press). Predictors and outcomes of retaliation against whistle-blowers: Gender differences and power relationships. *Organization Science.*

Rehg, M. T., Near, J. P., Miceli, M. P., & Van Scotter, J. R. (2004). *Predictors of retaliation against whistle-blowers: Outcomes of power relationships within organizations.* Best Paper Proceedings of the 64th Annual Meeting of the Academy of Management, New Orleans, E1–E6.

Rehg, M. T., & Parkhe, A. (2002, April 12–13). *Whistle-blowing as a global construct: Cultural influences on reporting wrongdoing at work.* Paper presented at the International Conference on Whistle-Blowing, Bloomington, IN.

Reilly, T., Carpenter, S., Dull, V., & Bartlett, K. (1982). The factorial survey technique: An approach to defining sexual harassment on campus. *Journal of Social Issues, 38,* 99–110.

Rest, J. (1979). *Development in judging moral issues.* Minneapolis: University of Minnesota Press.

Ridge, P. S. (2000, May 11). Ethics programs aren't stemming employee misconduct, a study indicates. *Wall Street Journal,* p. A1.

Roberts, R. V. et al. (2004, June). Spilt milk: Parmalat and Sarbanes-Oxley internal controls reporting. *International Journal of Disclosure and Governance, 215.* Retrieved July 7, 2006, from http://proquest.umi.com

Robinson, S. L., & Kraatz, M. S. (1998). Constructing the reality of normative behavior: The use of neutralization strategies by organizational deviants. In R. W. Griffin, A. O'Leary-Kelly, & J. M. Collins (Eds.), *Dysfunctional behavior in organizations* (Vol. 1, pp. 203–220). Stamford, CT: JAI Press.

Romano, L. (2005, Sunday, December 4). Cunningham friends baffled by his blunder into bribery. *Washington Post,* p. A6.

Rothschild, J., & Miethe, T. D. (1999). Whistle-blower disclosures and management retaliation: The battle to control information about organizational corruption. *Work and Occupations, 26*(1), 107–128.

Rothwell, G. R., & Baldwin, J. N. (2006). Ethical climates and contextual predictors of whistle-blowing. *Review of Public Personnel Administration, 26*(3), 216–244.

Rothwell, G. R., & Baldwin, J. N. (2007). Ethical climate theory, whistle-blowing, and the code of silence in police agencies in the state of Georgia. *Journal of Business Ethics, 70*, 341–361.

Rowley, C. (2004). Personal communication to J. P. Near, Bloomington, IN.

Rynes, S. L., & Barber, A. E. (1990). Applicant attraction strategies: An organizational perspective. *Academy of Management Review, 15*, 286–310.

Salancik, G., & Pfeffer, J. (1978). A social information processing approach to job attitudes and task design. *Administrative Science Quarterly, 23*, 224–253.

Salancik, G. R., & Pfeffer, J. (1977). Who gets power and how they hold on to it: A strategic-contingency model of power. *Organizational Dynamics, 5*(3), 3–21.

Sapino Jeffreys, B. (2005, February 7). Handling the nuts and bolts of SOX compliance. *Texas Lawyer*, 9.

Sarbanes-Oxley Act (Corporate and Auditing Accountability, Responsibility, and Transparency Act of 2002), PL 107–204, 116 Stat 745 (2002).

Scandura, T. A., & Williams, E. A. (2000). Research methodology in management: Current practices, trends, and implications for future research. *Academy of Management Journal, 43*(6), 1248–1264.

Scannell, K. (2007, May 16). Costs fall again for firms to comply with Sarbanes. *Wall Street Journal*, p. C7.

Schneider, B. E. (1982). Consciousness about sexual harassment among heterosexual and lesbian women workers. *Journal of Social Issues, 38*, 75–98.

Scott, W. R. (1987). The adolescence of institutional theory. *Administrative Science Quarterly, 32*(4), 493.

Scott, W. R. (2001). *Institutions and organizations.* Thousand Oaks, CA: Sage.

Seagull, L. M. (1995). Whistleblowing and corruption control: The GE case. *Crime, Law, and Social Change, 22*(4), 381–390.

Seibert, S., Kraimer, M. L., & Crant, J. M. (2001). What do proactive people do? A longitudinal model linking proactive personality and career success. *Personnel Psychology, 54*(4), 845–874.

Seibert, S. E., Crant, J. M., & Kraimer, M. L. (1999). Proactive personality and career success. *Journal of Applied Psychology, 84*(3), 416–427.

Seifert, D. L. (2006). *The influence of organizational justice on the perceived likelihood of whistle-blowing.* Unpublished Ph.D. dissertation, Washington State University, Pullman, Washington.

Seligman, M. E. P., & Csikszentmihalyi, M. (2000). Positive psychology: An introduction. *American Psychologist, 55*, 5–14.

Selingo, J. (2006, June 28). Expansion of reasons for whistle-blower lawsuits should worry colleges, lawyers' group is told. *Chronicle of Higher Education*, http://chronicle.com/daily/2006/06/2006062801n.htm

Shapiro, J. R., King, E. B., & Quiñones, M. A. (2007). Expectations of obese trainees: How stigmatized trainee characteristics influence training effectiveness. *Journal of Applied Psychology, 92*(1), 239.

Sims, R. L., & Keenan, J. P. (1998). Predictors of external whistleblowing: Organizational and intrapersonal variables. *Journal of Business Ethics, 17*, 411–421.

Sims, R. L., & Keenan, J. P. (1999). A cross-cultural comparison of managers' whistleblowing tendencies. *International Journal of Value-Based Management, 12*(2), 137–151.

Sivakumar, K., & Nakata, C. (2001). The stampede toward Hofstede's framework: Avoiding the sample design pit in cross-cultural research. *Journal of International Business Studies, 32*(3), 555–574.

Skarlicki, D. P., & Folger, R. (1997). Retaliation in the workplace: The roles of distributive, procedural, and interactional justice. *Journal of Applied Psychology, 82*(3), 434–443.

Skarlicki, D. P., Folger, R., & Tesluk, P. (1999). Personality as a moderator in the relationship between fairness and retaliation. *Academy of Management Journal, 42*(1), 100–108.

Sloan, M. (2007). The Joseph and Valerie Wilson legal support trust. Retrieved July 19, August 1, 2007, from http://www.wilsonsupport.org/

Slovin, D. (2006, June). Blowing the whistle. *Internal Auditor*, 45–49.

Smith, D. B., & Ellingson, J. E. (2002). Substance versus style: A new look at social desirability in motivating contexts. *Journal of Applied Psychology, 87*(2), 211–209.

Society for Human Resource Management. (2007, July 27). Urge your representative to VOTE NO on the Ledbetter Fair Pay Act to membership.

Solomon, D. (2004, October 4). For financial whistleblowers, new shields in an imperfect one. *Wall Street Journal*, p. 1.

Somers, M. J., & Casal, J. C. (1994). Organizational commitment and whistle-blowing: A test of the reformer and the organization man hypothesis. *Group and Organization Management, 19*(3), 270–284.

Spreitzer, G. M., & Sonenshein, S. (2004). Toward the construct definition of positive deviance. *American Behavioral Scientist, 47*(6), 828–847.

Starkey, P. L. (1998). *Whistleblowing behavior: The impact of situational and personality variables.* Unpublished doctoral dissertation, University of Mississippi, Oxford.

Staub, E. (1978). *Positive social behavior and morality: Social and personal influences* (Vol. 1). New York: Academic Press.

Staw, B. M., Sandelands, L. E., & Dutton, J. (1981). Threat-rigidity effects in organizational behavior: A multilevel analysis. *Administrative Science Quarterly, 26*, 501–524.

Story, L. (2007, April 11). NBC drops Imus show from its cable network. *New York Times*, Retrieved April 11, 2007 from http://www.nytimes.com/2007/04/11/business/media/11cnd-imus.html?ex=1177300800&en=e14ccace3197ac34&ei=5070

Sunstein, C. (1992). What's standing after Lujan? Of citizen suits, "injuries," and Article III. *Michigan Law Review, 91*, 163, 230.

Sutherland, E. H. (1949). *White collar crime*. New York: Holt, Rinehart, & Winston.

Swartz, M., with Watkins, S. (2003). *Power failure: The inside story of the collapse of Enron*. New York: Doubleday.

Tangri, S. S., Burt, M. R., & Johnson, E. B. (1982). Sexual harassment at work: Three explanatory models. *Journal of Social Issues, 38*(4), 33–54.

Tavakoli, A. A., Keenan, J. P., & Crnjak-Karanovic, B. (2003). Culture and whistleblowing: An empirical study of Croatian and United States managers utilizing Hofstede's cultural dimensions. *Journal of Business Ethics, 43*, 49–64.

Taxpayers Against Fraud Education Fund. (2006). False Claims Act recoveries top $17 billion since 1986, $1 billion in first 3 months of FY 2006. Retrieved January 24, 2007, from http://66.98.181.12/whistle77.htm

Thiessen, C. D. (1998). *Whistleblowing in the private and public sectors: Should Canada adopt a modified form of the American whistleblowing legislation?* Unpublished MPA thesis, The University of Manitoba.

Thompson, J. D. (1967). *Organizations in action*. New York: McGraw-Hill.

Timmerman, G., & Bajema, C. (2000). The impact of organizational culture on perceptions and experiences of sexual harassment. *Journal of Vocational Behavior, 57*, 188–205.

Treviño, L. K., & Weaver, G. R. (2001). Organizational justice and ethics program "follow-through": Influences on employees' harmful and helpful behavior. *Business Ethics Quarterly, 11*(4), 651–671.

Treviño, L. K., Weaver, G. R., & Reynolds, S. J. (2006). Behavioral ethics in organizations: A review. *Journal of Management, 32*(6), 951–990.

Treviño, L. K., & Youngblood, S. A. (1990). Bad apples in bad barrels: A causal analysis of ethical decision-making behavior. *Journal of Applied Psychology, 75*, 378–385.

Treviño, L. K., Weaver, G. R., Gibson, D. G., & Toffler, B. L. (1999). Managing ethics and legal compliance: What works and what hurts. *California Management Review, 41*(2), 131–151.

Turnley, W. H., & Bolino, M. C. (2001). Achieving desired images while avoiding undesired images: Exploring the role of self-monitoring in impression management. *Journal of Applied Psychology, 86*(2), 351.

Union of Concerned Scientists. (2006, July 20). FDA scientists pressured to exclude, alter findings; scientists fear retaliation for voicing safety concerns. Retrieved April 16, 2007, from http://www.ucsusa.org/news/press_release/fda-scientists-pressured.html

United States Sentencing Commission. *Sentencing Guidelines*. Chapter 8 (1991).

USA Today. (2006, July 19). Lawmaker alleges FDA, Merck collaborated. *USA Today*, online.

U.S. Department of Justice (2002, December 16). Justice department recovers over $1 billion in FY 2002. Press release. http://www.taf.org/statistics.html

U.S. Department of Justice. (2003). Astrazeneca Pharmaceuticals LP pleads guilty to healthcare crime; company agrees to pay $355 million to settle charges. Retrieved June 20, 2006, from http://www.usdoj.gov/opa/pr/2003/June/03_civ_371.htm

U.S. Government Accountability Office. (2006). *Information on False Claims Act litigation. Briefing for congressional requesters*. Retrieved January 31, 2006, from http://www.gao.gov.new.items/d06320r.pdf

U.S. Law Week (2006, February 7). Drug firms face whistle-blower worries, increased fraud recoveries, attorneys say. 74 U.S. Law Week 2461. Arlington, VA: Bureau of National Affairs.

U.S. Law Week (2006, November 7). Fraud education provision could spur more whistleblower lawsuits, attorney says. 75 U.S. Law Week 2264–2265. Arlington, VA: Bureau of National Affairs.

U.S. Merit Systems Protection Board. (1981). *Whistle-blowing and the federal employee*. Washington, D.C.: U.S. Government Printing Office.

U.S. Merit Systems Protection Board. (1988). *Sexual harassment in the federal government: An update*. Washington, D.C.: U.S. Government Printing Office.

Vagts, D. F. (2003). Extraterritoriality and the Corporate Governance Law. *American Journal of International Law, 97*, 289.

Van Dyne, L., Cummings, L. L., & McLean Parks, J. (1995). Extra-role behaviors: In pursuit of construct and definitional clarity (a bridge over muddied waters). In L. L. Cummings & B. M. Staw (Eds.), *Research in organizational behavior* (Vol. 17, pp. 215–285). Greenwich, CT: JAI Press.

Van Scotter, J. R., Miceli, M. P., Near, J. P., & Rehg, M. T. (2005). What difference can one person make? Organizational dependence relations as predictors of whistle-blowing effectiveness. *International Journal of Knowledge, Culture and Change Management, 4*. Retrieved from http://ijm.cgpublisher.com/product/pub.28/prod.65

Vinten, G. (1994). Whistleblowing—fact and fiction: An introductory discussion. In G. Vinten (Ed.), *Whistleblowing: Subversion or corporate citizenship* (pp. 1–20). New York: St. Martin's Press.

Walsh, F. (2006, August 2). Product recall costs Cadbury £20m. Retrieved April 20, 2007, from http://business.guardian.co.uk/story/0,,1835455,00.html

Walters, A. K. (2006, April 28). U.S. Supreme Court lets stand ruling that could increase colleges' exposure to whistle-blower suits. *Chronicle of Higher Education*, http://chronicle.com/weekly/v52/i34/34a03301.htm

Wanberg, C. R., & Kammeyer-Mueller, J. D. (2000). Predictors and outcomes of proactivity in the socialization process. *Journal of Applied Psychology, 85*(3), 373–385.

Wardell, T. et al. (2005, September/October). The convergence of governance. *World Financial Magazine.* Retrieved July 3, 2006, from www.mckennalong.com/assets/atachments/298.pdf

Warren, D. E. (2003). Constructive and destructive deviance in organizations. *Academy of Management Review, 28*(4), 622+.

Watson, D., & Clark, L. A. (1984). Negative affectivity: The disposition to experience aversive emotional states. *Psychological Bulletin, 96*, 465–490.

Watson, D., & Walker, L. M. (1996). The long-term stability and predictive validity of trait measures of affect. *Journal of Personality and Social Psychology, 70*(3), 567–577.

Weaver, G. R. (2001). Ethics programs in global businesses: Culture's role in managing ethics. *Journal of Business Ethics, 30*(1), 3.

Weaver, G. R. (2006). Virtue in organizations: Moral identity as a foundation for moral agency. *Organization Studies, 27*, 341–368.

Weaver, G. R., & Agle, B. R. (2002). Religiosity and ethical behavior in organizations: A symbolic interactionist perspective. *Academy of Management Review, 27*(1), 77–97.

Weaver, G. R., & Treviño, L. K. (1999). Compliance and values oriented ethics programs: Influences on employees' attitudes and behavior. *Business Ethics Quarterly, 9*(2), 315–335.

Weaver, G. R., Treviño, L. K., & Cochran, P. L. (1999a). Corporate ethics practices in the mid-1990s: An empirical study of the Fortune 1000. *Journal of Business Ethics, 18*, 283–294.

Weaver, G. R., Treviño, L. K., & Cochran, P. L. (1999b). Corporate ethics programs as control systems: Influences of executive commitment and environmental factors. *Academy of Management Journal, 42*, 41–57.

Weaver, G. R., Treviño, L. K., & Cochran, P. L. (1999c). Integrated and decoupled corporate social performance: Management commitments, external pressures, and corporate ethics practices. *Academy of Management Journal, 42*, 539–552.

Weber, M. (1947). *The theory of social and economic organization.* New York: Free Press.

Weinstein, D. (1979). *Bureaucratic opposition*. New York: Pergamon Press.

Weiss, E. M., & Lane, C. (2006, July 14). Vice president sued by Plame and husband. *Washington Post*, p. A03.

Welch v. Cardinal Bankshares Corporation. 454 F. Supp. 552 (W.D. Va. 2006).

Whittington, O. R., Pany, K., Meigs, W. B., & Meigs, R. F. (1992). *Principles of auditing* (10th ed.). Homewood, IL: Irwin.

Williams, J. H., Fitzgerald, L. F., & Drasgow, F. (1999). The effects of organizational practices on sexual harassment and individual outcomes in the military. *Military Psychology, 11*(3), 303–328.

Wise, T. (1995). *An analysis of factors proposed to affect the decision to blow the whistle on unethical acts*. Unpublished doctoral dissertation, Louisiana Technical University, Ruston.

Woo, C. (n.d.). The effects of the Sarbanes-Oxley Act on foreign private issuers. Unpublished paper.

World Bank. (2004). The costs of corruption. Retrieved April 8, from http://web.worldbank.org/WBSITE/EXTERNAL/NEWS/0,,contentMDK: 20190187~menu PK:34457~page PK:34370~pi PK:34424~theSite PK: 4607,00.html

Yoo, B., & Donthu, N. (2002). Review of "Culture's consequences: Comparing values, behaviors, institutions and organizations across nations," by Hofstede. *Journal of Marketing Research, 39*(3), 388–389.

Yoshida, S. (2001). *Business ethics*. Tokyo, Japan: Jichousha.

Zall, M. (2001). Pluses and minuses of variable pay. Retrieved January 12, 2007, from http://pubs.acs.org/subscribe/journals/tcaw/10/i09/html/ 09work.html

Zellner, W. (2002, December 16). Was Sherron Watkins really so selfless? *Business Week,* 110.

Zingales, L. (2004, January 18). Want to stop corporate fraud? Pay off those whistle-blowers. *Washington Post,* p. B02.

Author Index

Eisenhardt, K.M., 138
Ellis, S., 89, 90
Emerson, R.E., 137
Employment Rights Act, 168
England, P., 62
Erdreich, B.L., 200
ESPN Radio, 131, 134, 144
EthicsLine, 174
Everton, W.J., 26, 46, 50, 128

F

Fain, T.C., 46, 49, 89, 90
Falbo, T., 57
Farrell, D., 8, 34, 157
Feldman, E., 72
Ferguson, L.J., 27
Figg, J., 21
Fiske, A.P., 68
Fitzgerald, L.F., 41, 69, 70, 71, 89, 90
French, J.R.P., Jr., 73, 103, 111
Frey, J., 1, 33, 147
Fritz, N.R., 89, 90

G

Giacalone, R.A., 65
Gibeaut, J., 166, 174
Gilligan, C., 74
Gino, F., 95
Glazer, M.P., 24
Glomb, T.M., 34, 37, 41, 51, 183
Goffman, E., 128
Goldman, B.M., 54, 61, 77, 84
Gordon, G.G., 85
Gouldner, A.W., 65
Government Accountability Project, 156
Graham, J.W., 6
Graves, F., 1, 67
Green, M., 158
Grimsley, K.D., 18, 19, 91, 193, 199
Gundlach, M.J., 43, 91, 92
Gutek, B.A., 69, 70, 89, 90, 108

H

Haddad, C., 36, 153
Hananel, S., 25
Hatala, J.-P., 190
Heard, E., 175, 187, 188, 190, 193, 194, 195, 196
Henik, E., 68

Herman, T., 164
Hersh, S.M., 2, 142, 152
Hesson-McInnis, M.S., 46, 49
Hewlin, P.F., 128, 129, 192
Hirschman, A.O., 34, 61
Hodson, R., 63
Hofstede, G., 73, 87, 88, 123, 125
Hopkins, N., 132
Hulin, C.L., 69
Hutchinson, S., 51

J

Jensen, M.C., 138, 148
Jernberg, D.V., 158
Johnson, R.A., 8, 86, 87
Jones, E.E., 128
Judge, T.A., 63

K

Kalev, A., 121
Karr, A.R., 12, 21, 23
Keenan, J.P., 6, 14, 27, 45, 62, 69, 72, 73, 77, 82, 88, 123, 135, 198
Kelley, K.M., 77, 83
Kerr, J., 118
Kidder, D., 109
Kim, S.H., 12
King, G., 6, 10, 27, 77, 78
Knapp, D.E., 40, 47, 51
Knox, M.L., 72
Koss, M.P., 89, 90
Krell, E., 117

L

Lacayo, R., 8, 56, 60
LaFontain, E., 46, 59, 90
Lambert, S.J., 39
Lane, C., 12, 101
Langer, E., 42, 55
Latané, B., 35
Laver, R., 72
Lee, J.-Y., 15, 22, 50, 54, 60, 63, 69, 70, 77, 78, 80, 109, 112
Leonnig, C., 13
Lewis, D., 72
Loe, T.W., 58
Lublin, J.S., 23, 101, 157, 188, 189, 197
Luthans, F., 64

Subject Index

360-degree appraisal system, 122

A

Abu Ghraib prison, 2, 142
Accountability, and SOX, 157
Acquaintance-rated intent, 58
Altruism
    and moral development, 74
    as motivation for prosocial behavior, 36, 37
Ambient demoralizing effects, 41, 51
Ambiguity, tolerance for, 53
American Bar Association, 87
Anonymity
    drawbacks to, 158
    in experimental design, 29–30
    in submission of complaints, 158
    in surveys, 194
    vs. confidentiality, 174
Anxiety, among whistle-blowers, 127
Arbitration agreements, 161
Arthur Andersen, 34
Attribution of wrongdoing, 91–92
Australia
    differences from U.S. whistle-blower laws, 160, 169
    favoring of external reports, 169
Authoritarianism, as predictor of whistle-blowing, 57–58
Authority structure, and retaliation, 118

B

Bad-faith whistle-blowing, lack of protection for, 168
Bell-ringers, 86
Between-subject scenario designs, 27, 84
Big Five factors, 55

Blame, 15
Blowing the Whistle, 153
Boeing case study, 67, 81
Boiling frog syndrome, 95
Boss v. Solomon Smith Barney, Inc., 161
Bottom-up change, and retaliation, 120
Bridgestone/Firestone, 34
Bureaucratic organization, and retaliation, 118
Burlington Northern & Santa Fe Ry v. White, 162
Bystander intervention, 35–37, 36

C

Capital markets, improving through whistle-blowing effectiveness, 134
Carnero v. Boston Scientific Corp., 159
Case studies, in-depth, 28
Change
    in bureaucratic organizations, 118–119
    and material wrongdoing, 148
    top-down *vs.* bottom-up, 119–120
Child abuse provisions, 175
Chinese managers, and organizational propensity to whistle-blowing, 88
Civil Rights Act of 1964, 154, 162
Civil Service Reform Act, 155–156
Clean Water Act, 154
Closure, 16
Co-optation, and collective corruption, 96
Coercion, and collective corruption, 96
Cognitive decision-making, 42
Cognitive moral development (CMD), 58, 59
Collective corruption, 95, 96
Collectivist cultures
    attitudes toward whistle-blowing, 88
    complexity of loyalties in, 124
    and retaliation, 123

233